THE RESOLUTE LEADER
A Handbook on Leadership Development

The Jethro Mandate

Warren Crank

CHI–Books
PO Box 6462
Upper Mt Gravatt Brisbane
QLD 4122
Australia

www.chibooks.org
publisher@chibooks.org

The Resolute Leader
A Handbook on Leadership Development

Copyright © 2014 by Warren Crank

Print ISBN: 978-0-9875608-2-7
eBook ISBN: 978-0-9875608-3-4

Under International Copyright Law, all rights reserved. No part of this eBook may be reproduced, stored in a retrieval system, or transmitted in any form, including by any means electronic, mechanical, photocopying or otherwise in whole or in part without permission in writing from the publisher, except in the case of sermon preparation, reviews or articles and brief quotations embodied in critical articles. The use of occasional page copying for personal or group study is permitted and encouraged. Permission will be granted upon request.

Unless otherwise indicated, Scripture is taken from the HOLY BIBLE, NEW INTERNATIONAL VERSION®. NIV®. Copyright © 1973, 1978, 1984 by International Bible Society. Used by permission of Zondervan. All rights reserved.

Printed in Australia, United Kingdom and the United States of America.

Distributed globally via a range of outlets like: Ingram Book Group, Amazon USA, UK and Canada, Book Depository Ltd UK and others. Also in the USA via Spring Arbor – Christian Alliance nationwide and Barnes & Nobel. Also in the UK and Europe through Wesley Owen / Koorong UK. Available in Canada through outlets like Chapters, and also in Australia via Koorong Books.

Global eBook distribution through: Amazon Kindle, Apple iBookstore, Koorong.com, Wesley Owen (UK), Barnes & Nobel NOOK, Sony eReader, KOBO and others.

Editorial assistance: Geoff Holdway
Cover design: Dave Stone
Layout: Jonathan Gould

WHAT OTHER LEADERS ARE SAYING ABOUT THIS BOOK…

In *The Resolute Leader*, Warren Crank builds a helpful paradigm for leadership that is both practical and biblical. As a thoughtful practitioner, he's crafted a helpful handbook on leadership development that you should read with your leadership team.

Ed Stetzer
President of LifeWay Research, Nashville, USA

Leadership, mission, structure, alignment, organization are words that leaders constantly hear and often use. Yet, how these terms are implemented in order to develop strategic effective ministries is often difficult because the "how to's" are often assumed or in some cases ignored. *The Resolute Leader* meets the crucial need of explaining how the abstract intersects with the concrete enabling leaders to become highly effective in leading well. For those who can't figure it out and for those who think they have but aren't sure, it is a must read.

Dr Paul D. Borden
Author: Make or Break Your Church in 365 Days, USA

Every church planter should read *The Resolute Leader.* These leadership principles should be part of the core DNA of every church plant. It is essential to have a good mix of gifts and the right 'chemistry' in your leadership but without good structure growth will be limited. This book gives a simple clear strategy that will be just as effective when gathering and training the initial planting team as it will be when the church grows to any size in the future.

James Baker
Leader of the Mission to Queensland Church Planting Movement, QLD, Australia

I have watched and admired the way Warren Crank took leadership of a suburban congregation and, in a short space of time, transformed it into a dynamic, fast-growing church with national influence. In *The Resolute Leader,* Warren shares time-honored principles that are still working today; his own life and leadership are proof of it. I highly recommend.

James Macpherson
Senior Pastor Calvary Christian Church, QLD, Australia

Warren Crank is a brilliant practitioner but also an incredible strategist – *The Resolute Leader* has not only ideas to use but also philosophies to be considered.

Barry Mc Murtrie
Churches of Christ Pastor, Former Senior Pastor of Crossroads Church Corona, California, USA

Life was tough for Moses, but along came Jethro, his father-in-law. A new era was about to dawn. Not all his problems were solved but life became much more manageable. Ministry life and leadership is still tough, but along comes Warren Crank – shoulder to shoulder with Jethro. *The Resolute Leader* won't solve all ministry problems, but it will make it far more manageable! Warren writes out of a depth of experience of ministering in significant churches at critical times in their history. Not only has he has walked the journey with them he walks close with God and learns from Him and the lessons He taught Moses through Jethro. You can join him in applying these leadership principles for greater efficiency and effectiveness for the Kingdom of God!

Rev. Dr David Loder
General Superintendent Queensland Baptists Churches, QLD, Australia

As captain of a national sporting team, it's my job to take different egos, abilities, nationalities and agendas, and lead them to success. Warren does the same. He says in the book, that leadership isn't a competitive sport and he's exactly right. Being a leader is about getting the best out of people, and Warren has an amazing ability to make people better. His ministry has taught me about being a leader on the court, in my family, and in my religious beliefs. With him as my "captain" for the past 5 years I have been able to take the journey into faith and every day it is better than the last with God as my ultimate leader. Opportunities for leadership are everywhere in life and *The Resolute Leader* not only helps you understand how important it is to be a good leader, but teaches you how to be one.

Russell Hinder
Captain of the Townsville McDonalds Crocodiles National Basketball League Team, Australia, and Commonwealth Games gold medalist

CONTENTS

Dedication

Foreword   7

INTRODUCTION   9

CHAPTER 1 — THE JETHRO MODEL   13

CHAPTER 2 — MISSION RESOLUTION – PART 1   27

CHAPTER 3 — MISSION RESOLUTION – PART 2   45

CHAPTER 4 — ROLES   57

CHAPTER 5 — RECRUITING   75

CHAPTER 6 — RELATIONSHIPS   97

CHAPTER 7 — REWARDING   113

CHAPTER 8 — RESOURCING   127

CHAPTER 9 — REVIEWING   141

CHAPTER 10 — IMPLEMENTATION – TEAM LEADER   161

CHAPTER 11 — IMPLEMENTATION – CHURCH LEADER   167

Postscript   187

Appendix 1   189
Example of a Difficult Leadership Issue Going to Moses

Appendix 2   191
The Contemporary Relevance of The Jethro Model

Appendix 3   195
Mock up Role Description for a Small-group Teacher in Children's Church

Appendix 4   197
Suggested Template for a Meeting between the Senior Pastor and Team Leader

DEDICATION

For Michael, who knew I had a book in me.

For Andrew, who knew it was this one.

For Ellie: I've always admired your leadership qualities.
I love the passion you have for God and people.
I married up!
You are my lover and friend.
We lead together.

FOREWORD

Murder on the front steps of the church! What a dramatic event to cause a pastor to re-evaluate his life and ministry. Yet that's just what happened to Warren Crank. And what he now does with us is to take us into his world challenging us to journey with him, from the tentativeness of the struggling new pastor, who knew he wasn't succeeding, to where he is today – senior pastor of a growing multi staffed church impacting northern Australia. In his spare time he holds the top non-staff position for his denomination in the state of Queensland. If that wasn't enough he is also the chaplain of a national football team.

The best thing about this book *The Resolute Leader,* is it's not another well crafted manuscript written by someone who had time to research, attend lots of seminars, harvest great ideas from other famous practitioners and then cushioned by a hefty healthy publisher's advance, churn out words and ideas to inspire the rest of us. There are already too many other theoretical experts strutting their stuff for Warren to jostle onto that crowded platform.

Warren is a working pastor. He started from the bottom, learning by trial and error, mostly from his mistakes. He was wise enough not to make the same mistakes twice. He was also unafraid to do what most of us are too afraid to do – to engage repeatedly in rigorous self-evaluation.

He doesn't even dignify this work by calling it a "book". He refers to it as "a leadership handbook". How wise!

In other words it's not something to speed read and then to be balanced on a bookshelf as the latest addition to all the notes from previous seminars or must read books, to collect dust or provide a shelter for spiders. It's meant to be dipped into again and again, to be read and reread. One should not move to the next chapter until the end of the chapter summary of steps to be taken has been fully implemented.

As you will discover, the "3500 year old leadership classic" of "The Jethro Model" is all about the concept of Team. Many pastors and other leaders specialize in doing things themselves, rather than specializing in getting things done by others. They fall victim to the need to be needed. They tell themselves that delegation doesn't work because:

> I can do a better job myself
>
> Delegation takes too much time
>
> Others are already too busy
>
> No one will want to do this.

All this self-talk overlooks the fact that the primary purpose of team building and the necessity of delegation, is about the development of people, which is what is supposed to happen in every church.

There's no way that Nehemiah could have achieved his amazing feat of rebuilding the walls of Jerusalem in a record-breaking 52 days, if he hadn't first selected a team and deliberately delegated specialized tasks to various participants, most of whom outranked him in their area of expertise. It's amazing what a team can achieve when no one cares who gets the credit.

A famous anthropologist of the previous generation, Margaret Mead, once said, "Never doubt that a small group of thoughtful committed people can change the world; indeed it is the only thing that ever has".

Jesus supremely exemplified the concept by working through his team – the Apostles. Before and after that time there were, Moses and Aaron, Caleb and Joshua, Esther and Mordecai, Ezra and Nehemiah, Paul and Timothy, Barnabas and Mark.

Teamwork is the ability to work together toward a common vision, to direct individual accomplishment toward common objectives. It is the fuel that fires ordinary people to achieve extraordinary results. As a team moves forward together success takes care of itself. Winning might not be everything but it surely beats anything that comes in second. That is what *The Resolute Leader* is all about!

Teambuilding and delegation shifts pastors and leaders from being directors to becoming coaches of others in the work of the ministry, which is precisely what the Bible says we are to be (Eph. 4:11-14).

If you're struggling in leadership and ministry or you're just starting the journey and hoping to succeed, you have a breakout choice. You can wait for murder on the steps of your church or you can read and implement what's in this book.

Rev. Dr Stuart Robinson
Founding Pastor Crossway Baptist Church, Melbourne, Australia

INTRODUCTION

Do you need a leadership overhaul?

Moses' father-in-law replied,

'What you are doing is not good…'

(Exodus 18:17)

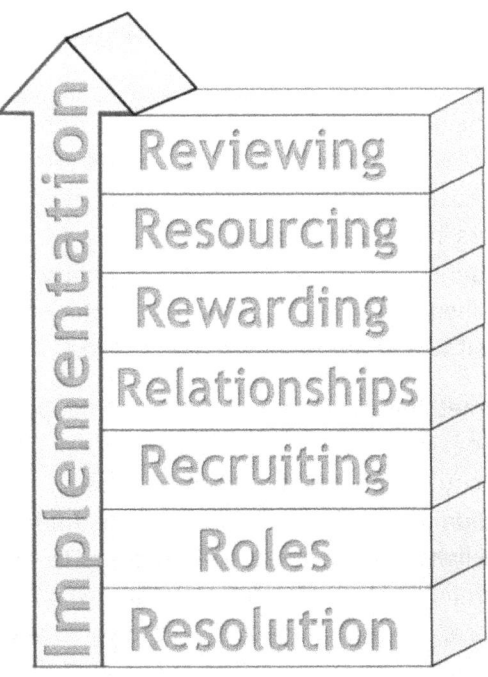

THE BURNING BUSH

There was a murder on the steps of our Church. I didn't do it. Honestly! I *wasn't* there. I have an alibi. It was Easter and I was away camping with my young family. I remember it was pouring down cold, hard rain at the campground. We were trying to set up our tent while most of the other campers were wisely packing up and leaving. I found out about the murder, not through a phone call from someone from my church, but through the gift of kindling. You see, the people packing up next to us gave us their dry, leftover campfire resources; some wood and some newspaper. We were wet and cold and grateful. I desperately wanted to get a warming fire going, so I grabbed the newspaper, knelt down beside the fireplace, and froze as I saw our church building on the front page. The murder was the headline story. I could hardly believe my freezing eyes. There, where the 12 church steps went down to meet the street, police-tape cordoned off a crime scene. You could see the congealed blood on the footpath. I sat down with that newspaper while the rain drenched our half-erected tent. The fire would have to wait.

That Easter-of-the-murder, I'd been a lead Pastor for a grand total of 1 year. It was my rookie year in the big league. The church that God called me to was a very traditional church in a struggling part of the city. It was demanding and exhausting. I felt like I was trying to do it all by myself. I knew I wasn't doing a good job. I didn't know how to lead my team. I didn't know how to lead a whole church. I felt like Moses who, in the early days of his leadership of Israel, was trying to do it all alone (Ex. 18:13-14). I was sinking into depression. My family was suffering. If Jethro, Moses' father-in-law, had critiqued my leadership strategy he would have concluded, "What you are doing is not good" (Ex. 18:17).

Now, I was supposed to be on a vacation and getting away from it all. I was trying to forget my failure. Instead, there I was reading that headline in the rain. Maybe, I should have just ignored it. The victim, whose blood was framed in a circle of police tape, was unknown to me so I didn't feel the loss in a close and personal way. In a way, it had nothing to do with me apart from the proximity of the felony to our church's entry. No one ever contacted me about it then or since. When I returned from our holiday the tape had been removed and the blood washed away. It was as if nothing had happened.

But something *did* happen. Something happened in me. As I stood on that spot I knew that I needed to do more to help the people in that part of our city. I knew that the church's mission was to reach more people. I just didn't know how to do it. I needed a leadership spark. I needed God to light the path. God did just that. He led me back to Moses and the burning bush. He led me to Jethro, who imparted some timely and enduring leadership advice. The front page of that newspaper was intended to start a fire. And, in a way, it did. It kindled something in me and ignited the basic idea for this book. That moment when I stood at the scene of the murder turned out to be a kind of "burning bush" experience for me. I sensed that God was saying something to me. He was calling me to resolve to rise up and lead! And, perhaps more importantly, I knew that I would help others to do the same. It became a defining moment in my life. Here, in this handbook, is what I've learned. Many Christian books and sermons include brief references to Jethro's leadership advice. However in this book we will mine more deeply into this rich vein of leadership wisdom. As we dig deeper, we'll unearth lasting principles that will help you create and develop a team in order to accomplish a God-given mission. You will discover that The Jethro Model:

- helps leaders thrive;
- is a team-building revelation;
- will enable you to help more people;
- is logical and easy to understand;
- is practical in application;
- will provide common leadership concepts and a shared leadership language that will help unify your team and church;
- is versatile and can cover a variety of leadership contexts.

This book will draw many insights from the leadership life of Moses, which is fitting because he was one of the outstanding Old Testament leaders. This book will also place special emphasis on the leadership mandate he received from his father-in-law, Jethro. These God-inspired instructions and time-honored principles are recorded in Exodus 18:13-26 and summarized in Deuteronomy 1:9-18. I've called it The Jethro Mandate.

THE RESOLUTE LEADER IS A 'HOW TO' HANDBOOK FOR TEAM LEADERS

The main substance of this book is written for emerging team leaders. If that's you, I will explain in *The Resolute Leader* how The Jethro Mandate and leadership model [The Jethro Model] will help you create and develop a team in order to accomplish a God-glorifying mission. If you implement the principles taught here, you will become a very effective leader.

More experienced leaders of already-existing teams will also find *The Resolute Leader* very useful. As Dr. Paul D. Borden wrote in commendation of this book; "Leadership, mission, structure and organization are words that leaders constantly hear and often use. Yet, how these terms are implemented in order to develop strategic effective ministries is often difficult because the "how to's" are often assumed or in some cases ignored. *The Resolute Leader* meets the crucial need of explaining how the abstract intersects with the concrete enabling leaders to become highly effective in leading well. For those who can't figure it out and for those who think they have but aren't sure, it is a must read." Implementing The Jethro Model, described in *The Resolute Leader*, will make you a better leader.

THIS IS A 'HOW TO' HANDBOOK FOR CHURCH LEADERS

The Resolute Leader also has special application for senior church leaders. Chapter 11 is devoted to the implementation of The Jethro Mandate from a church leader's perspective. I will demonstrate how The Jethro Model will help you organize and mobilize more leaders and teams in order that your church accomplishes a God-glorifying mission.

The task of leading a whole church is an onerous one. Like the Apostle Paul, we wonder "who is equal to such a task" (2 Cor. 2:16)? Truth be told, many church leaders know they are not leading well. Their church has no forward momentum. Too few are doing too much. There's an oversupply of problems and a shortage of solutions. What they are doing is simply *not* working! A church consultant would surely conclude, "What you are doing is not good." The question is, 'Do you need a leadership overhaul?'

When Jethro observed Moses' early attempts to lead Israel, he concluded that what Moses was doing was not good either (Ex. 18:17). Moses was taking on way too much. The mission to reach the Promised Land was in danger of stalling. It wasn't working. Moses desperately needed some 'how to' advice. And Jethro provided it. He gave Moses an inspired leadership model and mandate by which he organized and mobilized tiers of capable leaders. These leaders were to care for around two million people *while* they moved forward to claim the Promised Land. Do you share those twin aims: to care for people *while* your church moves forward? If the principles that Jethro passed on were good enough for Moses then they'll be good enough for you! *The Resolute Leader* will help you train up more and better leaders who will create and develop more and better teams. These teams will lead and care for people as your whole church moves forward together. You *will* gain ground! Let God give you a leadership overhaul through *The Resolute Leader*.

Moses' challenge was to implement Jethro's structure across the nation. For this to happen, he first had to explain everything about it in detail (Deut. 1:18). People needed to understand *what* the structure would look like and *why* The Jethro Model would be beneficial for everyone. The goal of this teaching process was that everyone would see how good it was and wholeheartedly adopt it. And they did (Deut. 1:14)! What was true back then remains true today. People need to understand *before* they will adopt. This book will explain to readers and leaders *how* and *why* The Jethro Model is so beneficial. *The Resolute Leader* doubles as a training handbook that is designed for wide distribution.

Chapter 1 THE JETHRO MODEL

Listen now to me and I will give you some advice,

and may God be with you.

(Exodus 18:19)

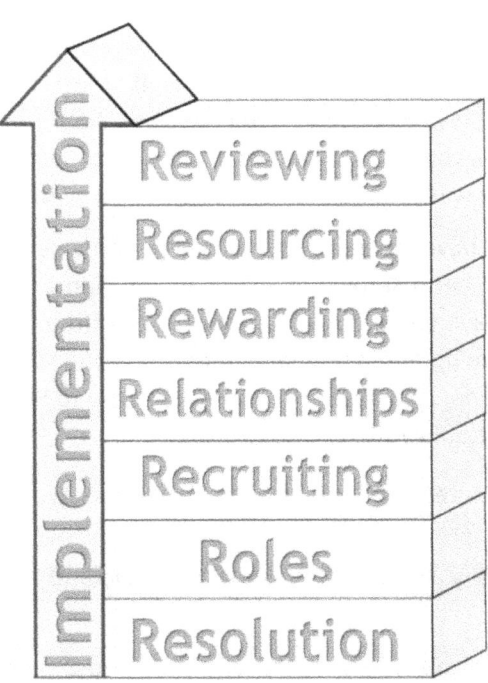

THE BACKDROP OF THE BURNING BUSH

The encounter between God and Moses at the burning bush is one of the most vivid and memorable stories in the Bible. For Moses, it was his defining moment. We read about it in the third chapter of the Book of Exodus. Moses was tending the flock of sheep belonging to his father-in-law Jethro, when he noticed a bush that was on fire but didn't burn up (Ex. 3:2). Curious about this mysterious phenomenon, he cautiously approached the strange shrub. But things were about to get stranger! More surprising than what could be *seen*, was what Moses *heard*. God spoke to him through the burning bush (Ex. 3:4). God said something to him through that fiery encounter that would change the course of Moses' life. God told Moses that he had to rise up and lead. Here's the account as recorded in Exodus 3:

> "Now Moses was tending the flock of Jethro his father-in-law, the priest of Midian, and he led the flock to the far side of the desert and came to Horeb, the mountain of God. There, the angel of the LORD appeared to him in flames of fire from within a bush. Moses saw that though the bush was on fire it did not burn up. So Moses thought, "I will go over and see this strange sight – why the bush does not burn up."
>
> When the LORD saw that he had gone over to look, God called him from within the bush, "Moses, Moses!"
>
> And Moses said, "Here I am."
>
> "Do not come any closer," God said. "Take off your sandals, for the place where you are standing is holy ground." Then he said, "I am the God of your father, the God of Abraham, the God of Isaac and the God of Jacob." At this, Moses hid his face, because he was afraid to look at God.
>
> The Lord said, "I have indeed seen the misery of my people in Egypt. I have heard them crying out because of their slave drivers, and I am concerned about their suffering. So I have come down to rescue them from the hand of the Egyptians and to bring them up out of that land into a good and spacious land, a land flowing with milk and honey...So now, go. I am sending you to Pharaoh to bring my people the Israelites out of Egypt" (Ex. 3:1-10).

When we consider the content of God's revelation to Moses, we realize that two important themes converge:

    1) God was acutely aware of the needs of people and had resolved to meet their needs.

    2) He sent Moses on a mission to meet those needs.

The needs of the people and the mission of God are directly and divinely connected.

Need to be met ⇨ 🔥 ⇦ Mission to meet that need

This was not an isolated case. This kind of convergence happens all the time. Down through history there have been countless *other* moments like this. They may not have been as dramatic. They may not have been as emphatic. But I know from my own experience that God continues to connect needs to be met with missions to meet them. He continues to raise up leaders who will resolve, under God, to lead all kinds of missions.

When I returned from my Easter holiday and stood on that spot where the blood had been, it seemed like a burning bush moment to me. That piece of pavement, where the church steps and the street met, became *another* symbolic place where the desperate needs of people and the dynamic mission of God seemed to converge. It seemed like holy ground. God was saying something to me. I had to rise up and lead, in order to meet that need.

Perhaps you can recall a moment when you felt God calling you to lead a mission of some kind in response to a perceived need. What was the need? Did you know? It might have been to help some people in a difficult or desperate situation. It might have been to help some people follow Jesus. It might have been to lead a church in God-glorifying worship. It could have been anything. Maybe that sense of God's call is very recent and very fresh for you. Could it be that *right now* you're trying to work out exactly what it all means? No leadership journey is exactly the same as another. Every burning bush experience is unique. The thing is that you feel compelled by God to rise up and lead. You know you're called to lead a team or even a church. Maybe you've tried to do that already but something went wrong. You might even feel like you've failed. The truth is that most of us make huge mistakes in the early days of our leadership development. I can't imagine, however, that any of your errors would be as grave as that of Moses.

MOSES' EARLY LEAD — WHAT WENT WRONG?

Moses grew up in the influential household of Pharaoh. He was a Prince of Egypt. He would have been accustomed to a certain level of power and it is apparent that he was willing to forcefully exert his influence. The Bible contains the following account of an early leadership misadventure:

> "One day, after Moses had grown up, he went out to where his own people were and watched them in their hard labor. He saw an Egyptian beating a Hebrew, one of his own people. Glancing this way and that and seeing no one, he killed the Egyptian and hid him in the sand. The next day he went out and saw two Hebrews fighting. He asked the one in the wrong, "Why are you hitting your fellow Hebrew?" The man said, "Who made you ruler and judge over us? Are you thinking of killing me as you killed the Egyptian?" Then Moses was afraid and thought, "What I did

must have become known." When Pharaoh heard of this, he tried to kill Moses, but Moses fled from Pharaoh and went to live in Midian..." (Ex. 2:11-15).

> **There was no guiding mission and no sense of where all this was heading.**

This reaction appears to have been impulsive and misguided. Moses was motivated by a white hot sense of injustice which is understandable. But it is also evident that he didn't have a plan. There was no guiding mission and no sense of where this was all heading. This wasn't a mission that God had given.[1] Perhaps he thought his gallantry would give him hero-leader status among his people; that he would be welcomed as their savior and hailed as their leader. But it didn't generate automatic allegiance. Not at all! The Hebrew people, in fact, did not think him worth following. It was a major anti-climax.

Being a leader isn't easy. This remains true even when it is God himself who has called you. It's hard to lead well. I learned that early. I didn't have a plan. I only had half-baked ideas and vague impressions about what I was to do. My actions were therefore often impulsive rather than guided by a goal. I was firing off arrows in many directions and not really hitting any strategic targets. I didn't inspire people's confidence. Consequently, I wasn't able to raise up effective leaders or teams. I didn't really know how to. It was a bad experience all round. I remember there were many times that I sat alone in my office wondering if I should just get out of the way and let someone else take over the lead.

Perhaps, you feel the same way sometimes. You know you have a leadership calling and even some leadership gifting, but you don't know what to do. Perhaps you worry sometimes that you're wasting time. Or, worse! Maybe you're suspicious that your half-baked leadership ideas and your scatter-gun leadership approaches are doing more damage than good. If that describes you, though it may be of cold comfort, you are certainly in good company. Moses didn't have a great early leadership experience either. When you really think about it Moses failed to meet the two most basic leadership criteria. To be a good leader:

1) you need to know *where* you're leading people;

2) you need to know *how* to lead people in such a way that they will willingly follow.

Maybe you haven't got one or both of those things going yet. You feel called to be a leader, but you're aware of your deficiencies. In my rookie year as a senior leader, I failed these tests too. But I resolved that, with God's help, I would discover the answers to those two questions. This book is written in response to the two burning questions that fired me up back then:

1) *Where* was I to lead people?

2) *How* was I to lead people?

For Moses, the answers to those questions came some forty years after that early leadership misfire (Acts 7:30). At the burning bush, God told Moses *where* he was to lead the people. It was Jethro, Moses' father-in-law, who showed him *how*. Fortunately, most of us won't have to wait that long. The Jethro Model will help you discover *where* God wants you to go and *how* to skillfully lead people there.

JETHRO, THE INSPIRED AND EXPERIENCED LEADER

Following his sensational leadership misadventure, Moses fled far away from Egypt and ran into the arms of Jethro and his family in distant Midian (Ex. 2:15-22). This proved to be a providential move. Jethro would play a decisive role in Moses' development as a leader. He was a wise spiritual mentor and an excellent leadership coach. The Bible introduces Jethro to us as "a priest of Midian". In every place that he is mentioned he is regarded as an esteemed and experienced spiritual leader.[2] It is worth noting that, on one occasion, Jethro was even given prominence over Aaron (Ex. 18:12). This was not only recognition of Jethro's genuine priestly ministry, it also authenticated Jethro's ministry as genuinely on God's behalf. This is underscored by the fact that the leadership advice that Jethro later gave to Moses was accepted as divinely approved and perhaps even commanded.[3] This book is based on that inspired mandate.

So, Jethro was an experienced campaigner and Moses was the emerging champion. God brings them together through remarkable circumstances (Ex. 2:16-20). God, in His infinite wisdom, teams up the rookie with a veteran. This proves to be a winning play!

BACK TO THE BURNING BUSH

The Bible tells us that Moses married one of Jethro's daughters and then tended Jethro's sheep for a "long period" in remote desert regions (Ex. 2:23). It was forty years in the wilderness (Acts 7:30). That would have afforded a lot of time to think about things. I can imagine that Moses reflected on the leadership aspirations of his early life in Egypt; on his current situation as an inconsequential nomad-shepherd; and on the fact that he couldn't really speak eloquently (Ex. 4:10). He was a no-one in the middle of nowhere. Sometimes, that's the place from which great leaders start. Some of God's best leaders seem to come out of nowhere.

You know the story by now. Moses saw that burning bush. God spoke to him personally. God gave Moses a mission. He was to lead that mission. God said, "So now, go. I am sending you to Pharaoh to bring my people out of Egypt" (Ex. 3:10). It would a high-risk, high-stakes, high-profile venture. And Moses feels like he's no one from nowhere. Yet, the divine origin of the mission could hardly have been clearer. God was commissioning him, giving him his holy marching orders at the scene of the burning bush. And Moses resolved to accomplish that mission.

THE EXODUS

Following his burning bush encounter, Moses returned to his father-in-law's home. There, he related his experience to his family and sought Jethro's blessing to return to Egypt and embark on the first phase of the mission (Ex. 4:18). Having received that blessing, Moses returns to Egypt. Over the ensuing months, the devastating events recorded in the Book of Exodus were played out (Ex. 4-13). In those chapters, the Bible records intense spiritual confrontations, nine miraculous plague-events and the Passover. The climax of all this was that, sometime on the night of the Passover, two million Israelites exited Egypt. Two million people on the move. That estimate is extrapolated from the number of Israelite men who participated in the exodus – an estimated six hundred thousand "men on foot" (Ex. 12:37). If you add to that number, women, children and older people, the estimated figure of two million seems reasonable.

Imagine leading and caring for an estimated two million people. Moses oversaw this mass migration from Egypt all the way to the Promised Land. What a challenge. Yet, things began well enough. He had his calling from God and he had a mission from God. God was doing great things (Ex. 18:8). So far, so good! When Jethro and family reunited with Moses somewhere near the mountain of God, Moses was able to bring a good report of God's amazing provision for his people.

LEADERSHIP PROBLEMS

That good report notwithstanding, some serious problems were beginning to emerge. Moses, perhaps on account of inexperience, was slow to perceive them. After all, it was only his rookie year in the major league. There were so many things still to learn. In fact it was Jethro, the veteran leader, who saw the problems and raised the alarm. Sure, Moses had the calling and Moses was leading the mission with all his might. But these things were not enough. What we soon discover is that he didn't have the necessary skills or the appropriate structure in order to lead people. He was trying to do everything by himself. Everyone came to Moses with their problems.

This is actually not an unusual scenario. I can certainly identify with it myself. In my early leadership years I was guilty of trying to do it all by myself. This is often the case when a leader has a genuine calling and is actually leading without the required skills and structures. There's no doubting that he is doing his best. But, sometimes just bringing your personal best isn't enough. It's so much bigger than you and there's so much more at stake. It's going to take a *team* of people, a *team* of leaders, to fulfill that God-given mission. You're super-efforts alone won't be satisfactory in the long run. You will wear yourself out and jeopardize the whole mission! These potential disasters were forecast by Jethro. He knew that if something didn't change, meltdown was inevitable. The following is a record of Jethro's disturbing observations and the leadership mandate that he gave to Moses.

> "The next day Moses took his seat to serve as judge for the people, and they stood around him from morning till evening. When his father-in-law saw all that Moses was doing for the people, he said, "What is this you are doing for the people? Why do you alone sit as judge, while all these people stand around you from morning till evening?" Moses answered him, "Because the people come to me to seek God's will. Whenever they have a dispute, it is brought to me, and I decide between the parties and inform them of God's decrees and laws." Moses' father-in-law replied, "What you are doing is not good. You and these people who come to you will only wear yourselves out. The work is too heavy for you; you cannot handle it alone. Listen now to me and I will give you some advice, and may God be with you. You must be the people's representative before God and bring their disputes to him. Teach them the decrees and laws, and show them the way to live and the duties they are to perform. But select capable men from all the people – men who fear God, trustworthy men who hate dishonest gain – and appoint them as officials over thousands, hundreds, fifties and tens. Have them serve as judges for the people at all times, but have them bring every difficult case to you; the simple cases they can decide themselves. That will make your load lighter, because they will share it with you. If you do this and God so commands, you will be able to stand the strain, and all these people will go home satisfied. Moses listened to his father-in-law and did everything he said. He chose capable men from all Israel and made them leaders of the people, officials over thousands, hundreds, fifties and tens. They served as judges for the people at all times. The difficult cases they brought to Moses, but the simple ones they decided themselves. Then Moses sent his father-in-law on his way, and Jethro returned to his own country" (Ex. 18:13-27).

THE JETHRO STRUCTURE - HOW IT WORKS

The basic structure outlined by Jethro is easy to see. Many leaders were to be appointed in various capacities and perhaps with different roles.[4] They were to care for people and lead the mission. Some leaders would care for ten, others fifty, a smaller number led hundreds and fewer still led thousands. The senior leaders entrusted with the care of hundreds and even thousands would obviously have had a significant, supervisory, leadership role. These numbers do not need to be taken literally but provided a useful guide to the distribution of the leadership burden. The intended outcome of creating these tiers of leaders is clearly stated in Exodus 18:23; to "satisfy" the needs of people in a way that wouldn't cause leader-burnout. That's what God wanted. He wanted the

> **The intended outcome of creating these tiers of leaders is clearly stated in Exodus 18:23; to "satisfy" the needs of people in a way that wouldn't cause leader-burnout.**

leadership structure of Israel to be organized, so that leaders were be mobilized to lead and care for people at every level. They helped to resolve conflicts, fix problems and alleviate burdens. If a problem proved too difficult for the leader of ten, then the case moved "up" the line to the leader of fifty. This principle applies right up through the leadership tiers. A very difficult issue would be passed on to a leader of hundreds. The extreme crisis was handed up to a leader of thousands. The higher the level of leadership, the greater the capacity required to bring godly resolutions to complex problems. This means that people leading hundreds and thousands need to be very competent when dealing with people's problems! Moses, of course, was serving at the uppermost level of leadership structure. That's why Jethro said, "have them bring every difficult case to you." In accordance with The Jethro Model, senior leaders get "every difficult case". If you want to read of such a case that Moses was asked to address see APPENDIX 1.

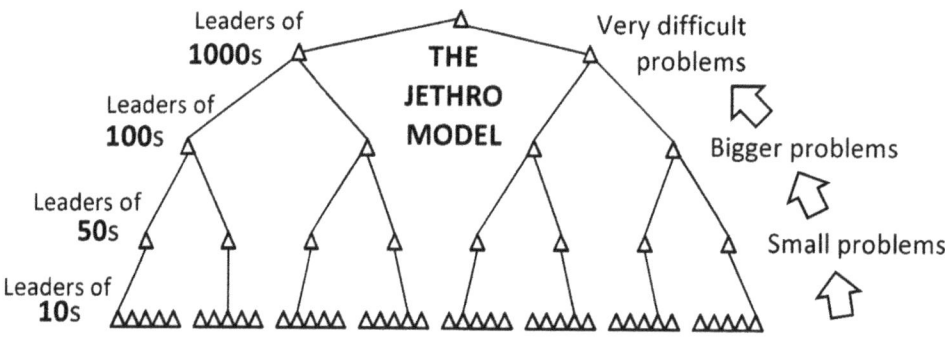

Now your team or church may not yet require leaders of hundreds or thousands. The structure, nevertheless, *can* support a mega-church for that, in a sense, was what Moses led. But the usefulness of The Jethro Model will become apparent to any leader who leads a team or church of even ten to fifty people. The principles apply regardless of the number of people or the nature of the mission. With this structure no one need be isolated in, or unnecessarily overwhelmed by, the challenges of caring for people and accomplishing God's mission. The leadership load is shared. There's always somewhere to go with a problem and someone you can to talk with or refer to. This ensures maximum effectiveness in fulfilling the mission. That's the beauty of the Jethro structure. This time-honored leadership framework is as helpful now as it was 3500 years ago! The inspired structure, and the principles that support it, are enduring and adaptable. They can equally be applied by a mega-church Pastor and a leader of a small team or church. The Jethro Model has wide application. *The Resolute Leader* will demonstrate that.

> **The usefulness of The Jethro Model will become apparent to any leader who leads a team or church of even ten to fifty people. The principles apply regardless of the number of people or the nature of the mission.**

Nevertheless, it may be that some readers have reservations about the applicability of The Jethro Model today. Perhaps, you are asking questions like, "Wasn't it just a provisional arrangement for forty or so years?", "Wasn't it only a logistical tool designed to get God's people from A to B?", "Wasn't Jethro's structure just an elaborate judicial system?" and "What about New Testament leadership 'models'?" These questions are addressed in APPENDIX 2.

A STRUCTURE THAT CARRIES YOUR CULTURE

What has God called you to *do*? What has God called you to *be*? These are important questions. Your answers will establish the leadership culture of your team and church. Your answers will inform not only *what* is done but also *how* it is done. God wants you to do the right thing the right way. Is there a sense that God is taking you somewhere? Have you got a clear and compelling mission? People will pick up on that. If the answer is 'no', then you will produce a culture of aimlessness and/or conflicting agendas. If your answer is 'yes', then there can be a shared resolve and contributing energies. Is there a shared and healthy understanding of how people are valued and cared for? If the answer is 'no', then leaders will be demoralized and people disenfranchised. If the answer is 'yes', then leaders will be supported and people will be served. You not only need to have the right goals, you also need to have the right values. When your goals and values are good and clear you are on your way to establishing a healthy leadership culture. In *The Resolute Leader,* I share how The Jethro Model is a structure that can carry your culture.

> **When your goals and values are good and clear you are on your way to establishing a healthy leadership culture.**

Think about it: the structure is meant to carry your culture. The goal of organizing is not to create a flow chart for your wall but to help ensure that your caring culture flows through everything and everyone. The structure is designed to help you *do* and *be* all that God wants you to *do* and *be*. That's what matters. That's why Moses was instructed to get organized. What were God's values that found expression in The Jethro Model? What kind of culture did God create and the structure support? Here is a list compiled from the passages above. These represent God's values.

1) They were to be God's people. God was to be honored as Savior and Guide.

2) A mission was to be accomplished. They were on the move.

3) Leaders mattered. They needed to be carefully chosen and allowed to lead.

4) Leaders were meant to thrive. To this end, the leadership load was to be shared.

5) People mattered; every single one. Their disputes, problems and burdens needed to be addressed and alleviated.

6) Organization was absolutely necessary to help ensure that individuals were cared for.

It's an impressive list, isn't it? Doesn't this represent the kind of culture that you want to establish in your team and church? Perhaps you feel called to create a culture of excellence, outreach and/or discipleship. It could be any God-honoring thing. But one thing's for certain – you will need a structure that will support your culture. *The Resolute Leader* can help you build into *everything* and *everyone* those things that God wants you to do and be.

Andrew's Story

I remember, some years ago now, attending my very first church leadership retreat. I was a very junior and inexperienced Deacon rubbing shoulders with some wise and long-serving spiritual warriors. During the 'get to know each other' session we were asked to learn a little about the person sitting opposite us. The idea was that we would share with the group something of what we learned. Our Pastoral Care Pastor was sitting across from me. I remember how he looked haggard and worn out. I began talking to him and learning about what was happening in his life. He was trying to do so much by himself. It was like the weight of the world was on his sagging shoulders. My heart began to break for those working for God's glory. The strain of leading can be unbearable.

From then on I became keenly aware that people in team-leader and church leadership roles were regularly being hurt and burnt out. I could do very little about it at that time because I had no idea what to do. I just saw leaders dropping out for all sorts of reasons and this greatly troubled me. This was not what I imagined ministry to be all about. I was ready for hard work but this was plainly and simply wrong.

Over the next few years the leadership group tried to address these issues. We would have a new idea and start off enthusiastically only to slowly drift back to where we were before. Another year would come around and we would all go through the same process again, almost repeating ourselves. We weren't going anywhere. We seemed to be pulling in many different directions with many different agendas. Our church was not growing and we simply didn't have the structure to sustain growth anyway. I was near to the point of exhaustion and ready to give up.

Warren's arrival at our church was a very special time for me. When we spoke about The Jethro Model concepts I became energized again. I could see how our church could grow and become more effective in a way that valued and protected leaders. Since then, we've been building on the hard work done by those who served before us. Now we have an overarching Mission Resolution which has provided our church family with clarity of purpose and has galvanized resolve. The Jethro Model has provided a simple shape and architecture to the church. Leaders are connected. People lead and serve at whatever level they are willing and able to. Everyone can now know why they are doing what they are doing and how it fits with the church's overall direction. All these things are now part of our leadership culture.

From my perspective, it has been interesting to compare those that adopted The Jethro Model early in comparison to those who are less advanced in its implementation. The early-adopters have faster-growing and more effective teams. From out of these teams, we are sending leaders to populate our church plants. These are the leaders who will shape the future for generations to come. When I look back at the impact of The Jethro Model in our church there is compelling evidence that these principles work powerfully! The challenge for us as a leadership group is to keep on teaching, training and making the necessary changes to ensure that The Jethro Model continues to be implemented right across the church family. This has become our mandate.

ANTICIPATING WHAT'S AHEAD

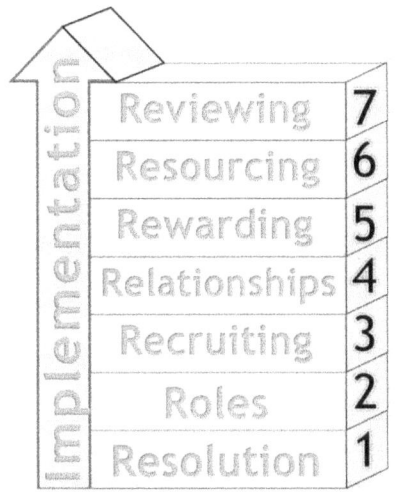

Seven levels with an elevator

What will be set out in the chapters that follow is my extrapolation of Jethro's structure. Not every concept in this book will exactly correspond to what we read from Exodus 18. But it's pretty close and I think the connections and correlations will be apparent. I'll start to teach the model in Chapter 2, beginning with the importance of articulating your Mission Resolution. The model is constructed in a logical order; level upon level. There are seven levels in all. You might think of it as a multistory building. You've got to start at the ground floor and work your way up. Down at Ground Level is your 'Resolution'. You will need to start there. Each new chapter will build on the one that preceded it. 'Reviewing' provides the view at the top. But to get there, *to take the elevator to the top*, you need to 'Implement' The Jethro Model. Implementation will raise your leadership altitude. That's why I like to say that the construction of The Jethro Model involves 'seven levels with an elevator'. You will have a new view of leadership.

At the end of each chapter there will be an 'Implementation Elevators' section designed to help you implement The Jethro Model. These will include exercises to help you create and develop your team as well as questions to guide reflection, exploration and discussion around key concepts. They are designed to be easy to use and will help you consider and apply the content of that chapter as it pertains to your situation. If you ascend the stories, chapter by chapter, and use the Implementation Elevators you will discover a better way to lead your team. The Jethro Model will help strengthen your resolve. It will help you organize and mobilize people in order to accomplish a God-glorifying mission. So, here's a quick overview of the chapters in *The Resolute Leader*.

Chapter 2 – Mission Resolution - Part 1

Moses was given a mission by God and he resolved to do it. You need to know precisely what it is that God wants you to do. You need to state your Mission Resolution. A Mission Resolution is an aspirational statement, requiring action steps with achievable outcomes. To help you articulate your God-given mission, we will look at five meanings of the word 'resolution'. These nuances concern story, vision, science, politics and music. We will approach the task of writing your Mission Resolution from each of these different angles.

Chapter 3 – Mission Resolution - Part 2

Stating your Mission Resolution is an important first step. Now it's time to resolve, under God, to get it done. In order to achieve your stated resolution you will need to embody two further meanings of the word 'resolution': these concern character and action. We will consider the importance of the character quality of being resolute. I will also demonstrate the necessity of planning and taking actions steps towards the achievement of your goals.

Chapter 4 – Roles

Once you know where you've got to go, you need to think about the types of gifts and skills that will be required to get you there. If your mission is big then you are going to need a lot of people with diverse gifts and roles to help you achieve the goals. So, you will need to ask and answer questions like:

- What needs to be done?
- What Roles are required?
- What mix of passions and gifts will need to be assembled to form a Dream Team?

In Chapter 4, you will be encouraged to design a Dream Team that will help you accomplish the God-given mission. I will make the case for creating Role Descriptions for your Dream Team *before* you even begin recruiting. This is because, ideally, you want to get the mix of roles right from the start. Good team design will ensure you have both breadth and balance in your team.

Chapter 5 – Recruiting

So, you know *where* you're going and *what* roles are required in order to get there. Now, you need the right people. *Who* do you recruit? This is a challenging level in the process. You've got to get this right! You can't just take anyone and put them anywhere. Jethro instructed Moses to only choose the right people for the role, to appoint the right people to lead the mission. These people were to be Moses' leadership team. He wisely chose people who feared God and were trustworthy, capable people (Ex. 18:21). Moses also developed leaders for future roles. We will explore ways that help us think about how we should choose the right leaders.

Chapter 6 – Relationships

The heart of a team is the strength of the team. The way people care for each other plays a big part in determining a team's cohesiveness, effectiveness and longevity. The team leader is responsible for the relational quality of the team. Some leaders aren't great at relationships. They might be visionaries but they don't relate well to people. This will end up being a limiting factor. We need to grow our capacity to care for the people that we lead. How can we relate and communicate to our teams better? I will give you some basic tips and some tools that will help. I promise you, if you apply the simple action plan provided you'll be on your way to becoming a great leader that people love to follow!

Chapter 7 – Rewarding

Moses celebrated the victories and honored contributing leaders. When a mission was accomplished the people partied! Following God was rewarding in so many ways. It still is. People are motivated by rewards. In the New Testament, Jesus promised rewards in heaven for a faithful and fruitful life on earth. Heaven knows how to party! This chapter teaches the value of celebrating the wins and encouraging the contributors. It will show you what to look for and make some suggestions as to how to make being on your team a rewarding experience.

Chapter 8 – Resourcing

Many missions fail because resources dry up. Conversely, many missions succeed because resources came in at the right time. How can you generate enough resources to achieve the mission God gave you? God can supply our needs in ways we cannot imagine. If it's *his* mission, we can count on *his* provision. Nevertheless, a little imagination and planning on our part could be part of that provision. Moses needed miracles, for sure! But he also needed to manage the resources available. Moses was a resourceful leader and you need to be as well. And it's not just about money. Your *team* is a God-given resource. The chapter on resources will inspire your faith and fuel your imagination so that you can position your team to receive God's provision for the mission.

Chapter 9 – Reviewing

A great leader can't afford to get complacent at this point. You have to care enough to evaluate everything and everyone associated with the mission that God commissioned for you. A great team leader needs to systematically and honestly review all aspects of the mission. And this includes the performance of the people on your team. Conducting reviews well requires some skill. This chapter on reviewing will encourage you to implement a review process, teach you some skills and provide you with some simple tools to make the task of reviewing achievable.

Chapter 10 — Implementation - Team Leader

By Chapter 10, it's time to decide to implement or not to implement The Jethro Model. To assist in the decision making process, I answer some of the common questions that team leaders ask before they commit. I take the opportunity to list detrimental implications of *not* implementing The Jethro Model before cataloguing the benefits if you do. Having decided to proceed, the task of implementation involves building The Jethro Model level by level; one to seven. Implementation will elevate you to new leadership heights. Will you make this *your* leadership mandate?

Chapter 11 — Implementation - Church Leader

The final chapter of *The Resolute Leader* will focus on the implementation of The Jethro Model from a Pastor's or church leader's perspective. Structure isn't the only thing that supports a great church. Powerful preaching and praying are among a short list of common traits of effective churches. The Jethro Model will enable you to do these things better. So, should you build The Jethro Model into everything? What things do you need to consider? I will set out the seven beneficial challenges associated with implementing The Jethro Model throughout your church.

Chapter 2 MISSION RESOLUTION – PART 1

So now, go. I am sending you...

(Exodus 3:10)

The torrential rain was followed by the summer's burning heat. Bodies lay half-buried around the hamlet of Gettysburg. The Union army had defeated the Confederates in the three day battle. The victory, however, had come at an enormous cost. Twenty-three thousand Union soldiers were dead, wounded or missing. Something had to be done to honor the fallen. For this solemn purpose, seventeen acres of land at the battle site was purchased to serve as a cemetery. November 19, 1863 was the chosen to be the occasion of the service of dedication. The Reverend Edward Everett, a great orator, was to give the much anticipated main address. A speaker's platform had been erected. A crowd of fifteen to twenty-two thousand had gathered.

Abraham Lincoln was not the main speaker. The President had been invited to attend only at the last moment. Upon acceptance he indicated that he would like to say a few words. He hurriedly travelled to Gettysburg by train arriving on the eve of the ceremony.

At 10 o'clock the next morning, Lincoln joined the procession to the cemetery just outside the township. Reverent Everett spoke for two hours about the war and the purpose for fighting it. His speech was well received. The President then rose to his feet and gave an address that lasted less than two minutes. There are a number of minor variations of Lincoln's speech captured by reporters present at the dedication. The following is the version authorized by the President himself:

> *"Four score and seven years ago our fathers brought forth on this continent, a new nation, conceived in liberty, and dedicated to the proposition that all men are created equal.*
>
> *Now we are engaged in a great civil war, testing whether that nation, or any nation so conceived and so dedicated, can long endure. We are met on a great battlefield of that war. We have come to dedicate a portion of that field, as a final resting place for those who here gave their lives that that nation might live. It is altogether fitting and proper that we should do this.*
>
> *But, in a larger sense, we cannot dedicate – we cannot consecrate – we cannot hallow – this ground. The brave men, living and dead, who struggled here, have consecrated it, far above our poor power to add or detract. The world will little note, nor long remember, what we say here, but it can never forget what they did here. It is for us the living, rather, to be dedicated here to the unfinished work which they who fought here have thus far so nobly advanced. It is rather for us to be here dedicated to the great task remaining before us—that from these honored dead we take increased devotion to that cause for which they gave the last full measure of devotion—that we here highly resolve that these dead shall not have died in vain—that this nation, under God, shall have a new birth of freedom—and that government of the people, by the people, for the people, shall not perish from the earth."* [5]

The short speech was a huge success and has come to be regarded as one of the best speeches in American history. Why? The answer has to do with *clarity*. Everett himself wrote (to the President), "I should be glad if I could flatter myself that I came as near to the central idea of the occasion, in two hours, as you did in two minutes." Lincoln got to the central idea. The answer has also to do with memorable *brevity*. John Hay, an eyewitness to the occasion, recalled the President's "half dozen words of consecration".[6] Interestingly, there are no known photographs of Lincoln giving his speech. The official cameraman was totally unprepared for such a short, sharp statement. Imagine his dismay as he looked up and saw the President returning to his seat! Its success also lay in its power to galvanize the *resolve* of the architects of a new nation: *that this nation, under God, shall have a new birth of freedom—and that government of the people, by the people, for the people, shall not perish from the earth.* Lincoln's mission was to establish a truly democratic nation. And his speech enunciated the Union's resolution to accomplish that mission.

This powerful story illustrates a founding principle of The Jethro Model. Lincoln articulated the Union's mission in a way that was clear, brief and resolute. He got to the 'central idea' of what was to be done and why. And people rallied behind him to see that mission accomplished. Leaders need to be able to state exactly what it is that they are resolving to do. They need to have a Mission Resolution.

THE CONTEXT OF GOD'S MISSION (AND YOURS)

What is *your* God-given Mission? What is it that *you* are, under God, resolving to do? If you are reading this book then you must have a sense that there's a big mission for you to accomplish. You have a determination to do something that will make a difference. Followers of Jesus are meant to be God's agents of positive change. Why is change so desperately needed? The answer is simple: life on earth is not as God originally intended it to be. Far from it! Ours is a fallen, frustrated world (Rom. 8:20-21). We are a fallen race (Gen. 3). We are all sin-biased (Rom. 3:10). The Bible makes the true and troubling observation that everything tends to slide downwards, a trajectory determined by humanity's inclination toward evil (Rom. 3:9-18). This leads to all kinds of problems, burdens and disputes – as Moses knew all too well (Deut. 1:12). It explains the prevalence of broken people, families, communities and nations.

> **These diabolical causes and consequences now form the backdrop for God's enduring mission and your mission too.**

And we're not unaided in our descent. The Bible says that, "the devil has been sinning from the beginning" (1 Jn. 3:8). His deception of Eve and Adam was the catalyst for the original sin (Gen. 3:1-4). This Satanic victory caused a seismic rift between the Creator and his creatures (Rom. 3:23). This rift is only bridged by Jesus and his reconciling work on the cross (Col. 1:21-22). The original sin also conceded to Satan spiritual authority which he exercises in the world today (2 Cor. 4:4). Consequently, and catastrophically, Satan's will is so often done on earth. He roams around menacingly, seeking opportunities to devour the weak and the vulnerable (1 Pet. 5:8). This is his diabolical mission. This is his dark resolve. So, the Bible reveals that the human race is inclined towards evil and this inclination is exaggerated by Satan's operations.

> "The reason the Son of God appeared was to destroy the devil's work" (1 Jn. 3:8).

The above causes and consequences now form the backdrop for God's mission and your mission too. There remains 'unfinished work'. God has resolved to rescue the world. His mission is to reconcile and restore (2 Cor. 5:19). He sent Jesus to accomplish this mission. The Bible says, "The reason the Son of God appeared was to destroy the devil's work" (1 Jn. 3:8). The decisive victory was won at the cross (Col. 2:13-15). And this victory is magnified as his kingdom advances and his church prevails. We are called to join God on mission; *to be dedicated here to the unfinished work*. Will you resolve to do this? Will you resolve to find out exactly what your contribution is to be? Will you, like Lincoln, resolve to get to 'the central idea'? And will you further resolve to create and develop a team in order to accomplish that God-glorifying mission? My prayer is that you will!

MOST PEOPLE DON'T KNOW WHAT THEY ARE MEANT TO DO

Sadly most people don't know what it is that they are supposed to do. They have no idea. Keith Abraham, an Australian performance coach, wrote:

> It is often said that for every 100 randomly chosen people, each would most likely fit into one of the following 4 areas...
>
> 3% of these have firm written goals with action plans to achieve them. These are the people who make things happen.
>
> 10% of these have firm goals that are not written down. These people think or expect things to happen.
>
> 60% of these people have vague or limited goals. They spend more time planning to go on their next holiday. These people are the ones who watch things happen.
>
> 27% of these people go through life with no goals at all. These people are the people who don't know what happened!!! They ask "Where did life go?"[7]

To be a great leader you need to be a '3%er'. You need to be one of those few people who have *written down* what you are resolving to achieve. But this isn't always an easy thing to do. Christian leaders are often confronted with an overwhelming number of possibilities and opportunities when it comes to discovering their mission. There's always more to do than can be done. It's hard to know where things begin and end. Consequently, a lot of leaders end up either 'unresolved and under-utilized' or 'over-committed and overwhelmed'. Let me explain.

Imagine all the things that you *could* do were piled like spaghetti into a pot. You have in front of you an enormous, crowd-feeding bowl of spaghetti. Everything contained in that huge bowl just seems twisted and tangled together into one big of pile of pasta. And you don't know where to start. But there is obviously way too much for you and your team in there! A lot of what is in there is for others to finish off. It's for other teams or another time.

When you are asked to *define* your mission, to get to the central idea, it can be hard to narrow it down into something actionable and achievable. But that is what you need to get to. You want something that you can break down into 'bite-sized' pieces. A decision has to be made. But some people *won't* decide. They just can't bring themselves to making a choice and making a start. It *all* seems so good. They just stare into the big bowl, frozen by indecision. Instead of being able to determine a direction and then *do* something productive, they end up not doing anything! Their lack of resolve means wasted time, talent and opportunities.

Some people respond in an opposite kind of way – they try to take on too much. They just dig their fork way in and wind on everything they possibly can. They take it all on. They over-commit. And too often what begins with frantic chewing ends with a fatal *choking*. They end up being overwhelmed. People like this become burnt out. Moses might have been numbered among them if it wasn't for Jethro's mandate. It was like Moses had stuck his fork right in the middle of that enormous mission, with millions of needs, and tried to spin up the whole lot! As a result, he was choking on more than he could chew (Ex. 18:17). It wasn't all for him. God had served up for him a small but significant portion of the overall work. He needed to resolve to do just that. This was a key to his leadership success. This is why it's critical that you discover exactly what mission God is asking you to lead and resolve to do just that. You need a Mission Resolution. You can't do it all but you will do that. Once you know what 'that' is, you need to accept that there will always be 'leftovers' for other teams or another time.

MISSION RESOLUTION

A Mission Resolution is an aspirational statement, requiring action steps with achievable outcomes. It's *aspirational* because it will forecast a better future. It's *actionable* because it will inform and inspire planning and doing. It's achievable because the changes it effects will be observable and measurable in space and time. The Jethro Model is built upon knowing your Mission Resolution. A Mission Resolution is the firm foundation upon which you can build an effective team. When you have one, you and your team will know precisely what it is that God is calling you to get done.

Moses resolved to embark on a number of God-given missions that were aspirational, actionable and achievable (only with God's help!). Let's look at one of them in the light of the above definition of a Mission Resolution. The first mission that God gave Moses

> **A Mission Resolution is an aspirational statement, requiring action steps with achievable outcomes.**

was communicated at Horeb, the mountain of God (Ex. 3:1). God said to Moses: "So now, go, I am sending you to Pharaoh to bring my people the Israelites out of Egypt" (Ex. 3:10). So, God stated the mission clearly. It was *aspirational*. Obviously *not* being slaves in Egypt meant a better future. This God-given mission required *action steps* in order to be achieved. Moses resolved to do what was required. The first major step was to return to Egypt in order to confront Pharaoh. The second major step was to bring God's people out of Egypt. With God's help it was *achieved* in time and space. According to Rabbinical Judaism, in 1313 BCE the Israelites left Egypt and entered the wide-open spaces of the Sinai Peninsula. The mission that God gave Moses incorporated the three basic elements of a mission according to the above definition – an aspiration statement, with action steps and achievable outcomes. These three elements can (and should) be developed in more detail, nevertheless they are basic to the nature of any given mission.

BIBLICAL EXAMPLES OF MISSION RESOLUTIONS

Some Christian leaders don't think knowing, pursuing and achieving their mission is important, or at least they undervalue these things. Perhaps they don't see the point of stating what you are resolved to do or don't think there's a Biblical precedent for this sort of thing. Maybe the idea of having an articulated Mission Resolution sounds too much like the language that belongs to the corporate world and doesn't seem spiritual enough. They fail to realize that God is definitely on a mission. God has made personal Mission Resolutions and they are set out in the Bible. Often, God is recorded as saying something like "I will" do this or that. God is setting out what he has resolved to do – what his mission is. For example, God's mission through Abraham is that, "all peoples on earth will be blessed" (Gen. 12:3). Here's the Mission Resolution in full:

> "The LORD had said to Abram, "Leave your country, your people and your father's household and go to the land I will show you. "I will make you into a great nation and I will bless you; I will make your name great, and you will be a blessing. I will bless those who bless you, and whoever curses you I will curse; and all peoples on earth will be blessed through you" (Gen. 12:1-3).

Let's consider this Mission Resolution with reference to the elements contained in our definition. Was there something to *aspire* to? Yes. God was on a mission to:

- show Abram the land God intended to give him;
- to make Abraham great;
- create a great nation;
- bless all the peoples of the earth.

They are four aspirational elements in God's Mission Resolution. In order to accomplish the mission, the following *action steps* were required:

- Abram was "to leave" his country, his compatriots and his father's house;
- Abram was to "go" to a land God would show him. He would be asked to "walk the length and breadth of it", *step by step* (Gen. 13:17).

The outcomes of this mission would be:

- a land for Israel to call 'home' that is still theirs today;
- a great reputation for Abraham (that is consistent across three major world religions);
- the creation of the enduring nation of Israel (it is remarkable that the nation still exists after thousands of years and despite repeated attempts to eradicate it);
- the blessing of all peoples through Jesus of Nazareth, the Light of the World!

All these were *achieved*. God's missions never fail. It may have taken centuries, and Abraham certainly didn't see it in his lifetime (Heb. 11:8-9, 13), "but it is the LORD's purpose that prevails" (Prov. 19:21). There's a lot of encouragement in that. The mission that God gave Abraham includes the elements that are essential to our definition of a Mission Resolution.

Jesus had his own, personal Mission Resolution. It was publicly articulated by Jesus as recorded in the Gospel of Luke:

> "The Spirit of the Lord is on me,
> because he has anointed me to preach good news to the poor.
> He has sent me to proclaim freedom for the prisoners,
> and recovery of sight for the blind,
> to release the oppressed,
> to proclaim the Year of the Lord's favor" (Lk. 4:18-19).

That is an *aspirational* statement. There would be favorable outcomes. People would be freed and released, their needs would be met. It required *action steps* – Jesus determined to reach out to people who were poor, imprisoned, blind and oppressed. He resolved to do this step by step and town by town (Mk. 1:38). The mission would be progressively *achieved* as more and more people heard the proclamation, received freedom, sight, release and experienced God's favor. Jesus consciously adopted this God-given Mission Resolution.

What about the Church? Let's consider one of Jesus' enduring Mission Resolutions for his Church:

> "...go and make disciples of all nations, baptizing them in the name of the Father and of the Son and of the Holy Spirit, and teaching them to obey everything that I have commanded you" (Mat. 28:19-20).

> **Everything flows out of knowing your mission and resolving to accomplish it.**

Here, again, are the essential elements for a Mission Resolution. The Great Commission is *aspirational* – it promises a better future for the people of all nations as the Kingdom of God expands. The mission requires *action* involving a number of *steps* – going, making, baptizing and teaching. The *outcome* of all this is *achieved* as more disciples from all the nations are reached, made, baptized, taught and, in turn, resolve to 'go' and make disciples. This particular Mission Resolution has been considered of such importance that it has been called the Great Com*mission*. Mission matters!

Sadly, too many churches remain *un*resolved when it comes to fulfilling the Great Commission. This resolve-deficit is evidenced by a *lack of* all the associated *actions;* there's not much going or making or baptizing. As a result, there is a *lack of outcomes* – it's rare that anyone is saved and made a true disciple who, in turn, reaches others. Churches like these are like islands surrounded by a sea of need. They become resorts where the Christians rest rather than bases from which people are deployed on missions. They are in maintenance mode rather than in mission mode. Unfortunately, not many pastors and leaders have a clear sense of what is to be done and they languish in uncertainty and ineffectiveness. Hopefully by now you can see that everything flows out of knowing your mission and resolving to accomplish it. Your Mission Resolution will maximize your efforts and galvanize your team. It will help you organize your diary and make the right strategic decisions. And, perhaps best of all, you will enjoy a sense of accomplishment when you see God's work get done. So, how can you discover your God-given Mission Resolution?

DISCOVERING YOUR MISSION RESOLUTION

What we are aiming for here is a clear, concise and compelling statement of what you are resolving to accomplish. Getting to that point is often a process. It can take time. There is a legend that Lincoln wrote his Gettysburg speech on the back of an envelope as he rode on the train to the ceremony. It is strictly a legend. It was a carefully composed speech. Lincoln's favorite reporter, Noah Brooks, stated that in the days leading up to the speech the President remarked that the speech was "written, but not finished".[8] In fact, Lincoln continued to revise it after the ceremony. This working and reworking illustrates that getting to the central idea can be a time-consuming process. Nevertheless, progression towards precision is important. That's the point.

THE POINT OF PRECISION

I'm not an archer. I'm not a bow hunter. I don't know much about the sport. But I do know this: you can't shoot an arrow straight and make it stick if the arrowhead is blunt. If you only have a vague impression of the target you are trying to reach, if you don't have something definite to aim at, your mission is sure to be frustrated and fail. You need to progress towards a point of precision. Unfortunately, too many leaders go off ill-prepared for missions that are ill-defined. It's like shooting a blunt arrow at a vague target. It's no wonder they waver and find it hard to make anything 'stick'. The good news is that you can sharpen your aim. You *can* reach a point of precision with your Mission Resolution. In the remainder of this chapter we will explore ways to reach a point of resolution with regard to your mission.

To guide you towards our goal, I will draw on five nuances of the word 'resolution'.[9] Each sense of the word relates to a different facet of life and experience. Each distinct meaning of the word 'resolution' can contribute to clarifying your Mission Resolution. These variations can help you progress from an impression to precision. This will require some careful reflection on your part. The Implementation Elevators at the end of the chapter will encourage this. Here are five of the meanings in the order that they will appear in the chapter:

1) *Story* – the part of a literary work in which the complications of the plot are resolved or simplified;

2) *Vision* – fineness of detail that can be distinguished in an image;

3) *Science* – the act or process of separating or reducing something into its constituent parts;

4) *Politics* – the formal statement of a decision;

5) *Music* – the progression of a dissonant tone or chord to a consonant tone or chord.

While what follows is written for leaders who are just beginning, these ideas will be useful for the development of established leaders and teams. The exercise of revisiting, reviewing, refreshing and recommitting to your Mission Resolution will help ensure a firm foundation for efficient and effective team ministry.

So how can you determine what your Mission Resolution is? We'll begin with your story.

STORY

We love stories. We are voracious watchers of movies and readers of novels. We are fascinated by colorful storylines. The most satisfying storytellers are skilful weavers of a complex plot. They describe life as we know it in its many and varied hues. Some of the colors clash. Some of the colors are subtle and seemingly insignificant. But all are necessary and no color inconsequential to the master storyteller. They can gather all the threads – complications, confusions, conflicts and chaos – and knit them together in a way that makes sense. Tensions resolve. Scenes line up. Random events are surprisingly connected. Suddenly, they show how we can make some sense of it all. There *is* a unifying theme. There *is* an underlying purpose. The story, seen from a certain perspective, was leading to a definite conclusion. Your storyline will help lead you to your Mission Resolution. God has been writing your story from the beginning (Ps. 139:13-16). He was getting you ready for the things he has made you to do (Eph. 2:10). You have been divinely prepared. These 'Divine Preparations' are experiences and events that God has used to equip you for your role in his mission. Many of these things were out of your control. They happened *to* you. You might feel good or bad about them. Like the type of family you were born into. Or the injustices you've witnessed as a child. Or the education you received. 'Divine Preparations' are often circumstances that God arranged or allowed in your life in which you had no say. They have, nevertheless, influenced you considerably and have helped shape you for your Mission Resolution.

Joseph's Mission Resolution was to store up food during seven good years in order to feed the world during the following seven years of drought.

There are a number of colorful examples of divine preparation in the Bible examples. One of them is Joseph. Joseph was born into a blended and somewhat dysfunctional family. There was great rivalry between the parents and children. Joseph was favored by his father and given a woven coat of many colors that highlighted his preferential treatment. He was hated by his jealous brothers. They sold him to slave traders who on-sold him in Egypt. All these circumstances were out of his control. Many providential things happened to Joseph in Egypt, things over which he exercised no influence. But God was in control. The many and varied threads of Joseph's life were being woven together by the Master Storyteller. Joseph miraculously rose to the second highest office in the land and then discovered his God-given mission in the grand scheme of things. As second-in-charge in Egypt, he had the opportunity to lead a massive relief effort. He oversaw a food-relief program that fed people who were starving because of a severe drought. When his brothers who sold him out came to him for food-relief, this is what he said:

> "You intended to harm me, but God intended it for good to accomplish what is now being done, the saving of many lives" (Gen. 50:20).

At the end of the Book of Genesis, Joseph's story resolves. We discover that there *is* a unifying theme. There *is* an underlying purpose to it all. The story, seen from a certain perspective, was always leading to a definite conclusion. Joseph's Mission Resolution was to store up food during seven good years in order to feed the world during the following seven years of drought. To this great task he brought his talents and his resolve. It's a great story!

There are times in our lives when it seems like everything merges together. Your story resolves. Scenes surprisingly line up. Random events are apparently connected. Your storyline has been leading you to a precise point. Suddenly, things that seemed disconnected – past experiences, present opportunities, gifts and passions – come together in such a way that your Mission Resolution is now breathtakingly obvious. God has been setting things up all along. You have been divinely prepared for this. You now see your life-story from a new perspective. You can say with conviction, "I was made for this!" When you trace the colorful threads of your life-story they can lead you right to your Mission Resolution.

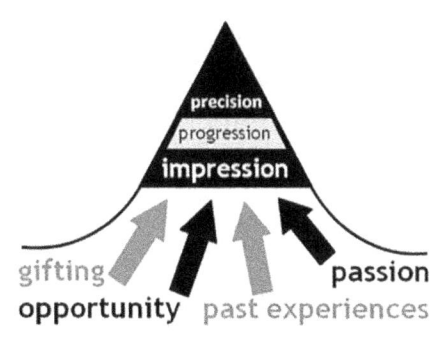

Michael's Story

Michael grew up in a home in which both parents struggled with mental health problems. Life was very chaotic and often traumatic. It was a tough upbringing. God was with Michael, nonetheless, and he became a follower of Jesus when he was fourteen. During his twenties Michael attended a large church but was continually frustrated by the lack of opportunities to serve in the area of his passion. He went to Bible College for four years but the doors remained closed for mission. He had the will but there didn't seem to be a way. These years were marked by discouragement and a growing disillusionment. It didn't seem to make sense. The threads of his story seemed to be completely disconnected.

When Michael married Ruth the story took a surprising turn. Ruth was a social worker specializing in homelessness. Together they shared the passion to practically help marginalized and disadvantaged people. Michael's childhood experiences gave him great empathy for children in dysfunctional homes. After some time Michael and Ruth began attending another church that many people came to for emergency food assistance. The Church and Pastor had little capacity to meet that need. Help was desperately needed. The crisis provided Michael with the opportunity he'd been looking for. This was a mission that he was made for. And he resolved to do it. He presently leads a significant, food-relief initiative aimed at ensuring that children in the area never go hungry. Michael and his team have literally helped hundreds of struggling families. Some of the people he serves have become followers of Jesus. Today, Michael's Mission Resolution includes feeding and housing people facing disadvantage as well as Pastoring a church in the poorest part of the City. Looking back, Michael can see that his past experiences were preparing him for his Mission Resolution. It was all part of the story.

VISION

In the field of vision, the word 'resolution' pertains to the fineness of detail that can be distinguished in an image. Great resolution means the image has great definition, clarity and sharpness. A great Mission Resolution will be expressed with those same qualities. It will help people clearly see what's up ahead.

Great leaders have the capacity to 'see' what the future should look like. Lincoln forecast the rise of a great democratic nation. His Vision was of a nation, under God, led by a government of the people, by the people, for the people. His Gettysburg speech was inspired by this outlook. He painted a word-picture of a preferable future. That Vision captivated the imagination of the people and strengthened their resolve to *together* bring that future into being. Lincoln's words framed that Vision. And, though he expected his own words to be quickly forgotten, they are long remembered for their potent portrayal of the aspirations of a young nation.

Godly leaders are, like Lincoln, the custodians of a Vision. We are painters with words. We are motivated by a God-given picture of a God-glorying future. God told Moses that he would lead Israel "into a good and spacious land, a land flowing with milk and honey" (Ex. 3:8). Think about that. What a vision for those oppressed people! That was the goal. And in all the ups and downs of the wilderness wanderings, faithful people like Joshua and Caleb must have held that picture close to their heart. It must have caused them to, in Lincoln's words, 'highly resolve' to take the next step towards the Promised Land.

You need to ask God for a picture of what he intends to do through you and your team in the foreseeable future. This picture will only be seen through the eyes of faith. That image may be blurry at first. It might take some time to come into focus. But you need to come to a point of conviction that God has shown you what he will do through you. Remember, the clearer the definition the deeper the resolution. Your Mission Resolution needs to paint a precise picture of what you will see at a definite point in the future. So, what should a Mission Resolution look like? It is:

- a word-picture that shows what the future looks like in real terms;
- a clear description of what you are aiming for;
- well defined;
- compelling;
- challenging;
- time specific;
- realistically aspirational;
- practically actionable;

- easily measurable.

A Mission Resolution completes the sentence, *'(This)* _____ *is what we will see by* _____ *(then)'*. Let me illustrate. I'm the lead Pastor of a church in Queensland, Australia. We have a Mission Resolution that paints a picture of a church that will be made up of 1500 people who are following Jesus and reaching people. We will direct the resources of our growing congregation towards starting 2 new churches aimed at reaching the least-reached in our City. Beyond that, we see 3 more missionaries from our church being sent to serve overseas in cross-cultural mission. People have been captivated and motivated by this Vision. We are resolved, under God, to do it. And, praise God, we are very close to seeing this Vision fulfilled!

Your Mission Resolution needs to portray the future as clearly as God reveals it to you. Sometimes you might not see it in high definition. Don't give up! God will reveal it as he sees fit. Just be sure to put what you see into words and then put your faith into action.

SCIENCE

In the fields of physics and chemistry, 'resolution' describes the act or process of separating or reducing something into its constituent parts; for example the prismatic resolution of sunlight into its spectral colors. This provides us with a detailed understanding of the nature of the subject. When it comes to discovering the exact nature of your Mission Resolution it helps to process your thoughts in a scientific manner. You can do this using a time-tested diagnostic tool that asks the following six questions: Who?; What?; Where?; When?; Why?; How? This sort of questioning is also used by journalistic reporters and police investigators. The maxim is that each question should elicit a definite answer — these answers are necessary to include for a report to be considered complete. When formulating a Mission Resolution you should be aiming for a scientific sort of accuracy. The resolution should be stated, if possible, in a concise sentence or short paragraph. This helps it to be conceptually accessible and easily memorable. Now, not every Mission Resolution will neatly conform to this six-question-formula, but it's worth a try!

I want to demonstrate how this works using one of the Biblical Mission Resolutions introduced earlier: the mission that Moses was given. Moses was to go to Pharaoh, bring the Israelites out of Egypt and lead them through the wilderness to the Promised Land (Ex. 3:8-10). I'll answer the diagnostic questions *from Moses' perspective*.

i) **Who** is the primary concern? **Answer:** The people of Israel. They are the main focus of the mission. I will lead this mission.

ii) **What** is to happen? **Answer:** They are to be freed from slavery and worship God on the way to the Promised Land. I can already see God's people settling down and enjoying that good and spacious land!

iii) **Where** will this happen? **Answer:** It will begin in Egypt and finish in Canaan by way of the wilderness.

iv) **When** will this happen? **Answer:** As soon as possible. As soon as Pharaoh lets God's people go. The mission will be accomplished when we reach the border of Canaan. I anticipate the desert leg of the journey will take six months at most.

v) **Why** will this happen? **Answer:** Because we are God's people. God had long-promised our forefathers that he would bring their descendants into the land he promised them. God has decided that that time is now. He is responding to all the misery-laden prayers and has determined to set his people free.

vi) **How** will this happen? **Answer:** By God's mighty hand, my leadership and a very long walk!

So, there you go. That's an attempt to demonstrate how the elements of Moses' mission correspond to and answer the diagnostic questions. If the Mission Resolution was to be stated in a concise sentence or short paragraph, it could read like this:

> In response to God's instructions, I am to lead the people of Israel from miserable slavery under Pharaoh in Egypt to freedom in the good and spacious land of Canaan. We will start as soon as possible and worship God along the way. With God's guidance, I see us traversing the wilderness and entering into the Promised Land before the end of the year.

Your goal is to create a Mission Resolution at least as specific as this one.

The 'Chat Room' Story

Following the murder in front of the church, we decided that we had to do something to help the vulnerable people around us. But there was so much need. We could not solve every problem. Where would we start? We began a process which didn't seem scientific at the time. Nevertheless, we asked ourselves the diagnostic questions. We did our research. There were already agencies providing food in Ipswich. Clothes and furniture were available cheaply too. We wanted to know precisely what we were going to do before we launched into anything. Here were our answers to the diagnostic questions:

i) ***Who** is the primary concern? **Answer:** 'At risk' people with no place to belong. These people live all around our church. We've identified around 60 such people. They feel isolated and are often victimized. We will love them and advocate for them.*

ii) ***What** is to happen? **Answer:** The mission is to be a compassionate presence for Jesus, being with marginalized people and loving them through all we do and*

> say. We won't major on providing food, housing, clothing and furniture. We will provide hospitality and 'community'. We will share the Gospel in word and deed.
>
> iii) **Where** will this happen? **Answer:** In a local, street-level community center. We need a place nearby that people can call 'home'. Most of them don't drive. The location needs to be easily accessible to them.
>
> iv) **When** will this happen? **Answer:** As often as we can provide a team to open the doors and our hearts to people looking for acceptance. Initially, we will be available during the day. We will find a location and foresee this ministry up and running within the next 2 years.
>
> v) **Why** will this happen? **Answer:** Because Jesus would do it! He walked with marginalized people while he was here on earth and demonstrated genuine compassion. We are following him to the streets!
>
> vi) **How** will this happen? **Answer:** By being compassionately present with people on the street. This ministry will happen with a team. We need to create and develop a team for the sake of accountability, sustainability and to model Christian community. This team will be trained in holistically serving the poor and people with mental health issues.

We separated things out into their constituent parts. We answered each question aiming for a scientific sort of accuracy. The following Mission Resolution reflects those answers:

> Jesus spent significant time with marginalized people. We see a team of well trained, open-hearted people from our church committed to creating a sense of community for 60 'at risk' people in our local area. Our aim is to create a space in a nearby building where people can feel at home and experience a sense of belonging. We will share the Gospel in word and deed. This ministry will happen during the day. We will begin with being open Mondays, Wednesdays and Fridays. Our goal is to start preparing immediately and we see ourselves settled in our community space within 2 years.

When your Mission Resolution gets 'as near to the central idea' as this one does then you will be most ready to create and develop an effective team. You need a formal statement like this to declare your intentions and galvanize resolve.

POLITICS

The word 'resolution' is also used of a formal statement of a decision or expression of opinion put before or adopted by an assembly such as the U.S. Congress. A Mission Resolution is, in this sense, a firm and formal written goal. The importance of a clear, concise and compelling statement cannot be over-estimated. When people know precisely what is being proposed they can choose to adopt it. They can support it confidently. This confidence is inspired by the fact that your intentions are written down for everyone to see and read. Your team can see and read it. Your leaders can see and read it. The people you are trying to reach can see and read it. And *together* you can resolve to do it. In the Implementation Elevators section at the end of the chapter you will be encouraged to do just this. It won't necessarily be easy. You won't always set the right tone the first time. You will need to work at it if you want to hit the right note.

MUSIC

Your Mission Resolution has to be well composed. It should sound right. When a piece of music resolves, the listener senses that the composer has hit the right note. There is a sense of completeness and relief. There is concord. Discordant music, on the other hand, sounds unfinished. Dissonant tones create tension. The listener senses that something is not right or sounds 'off key' and waits longingly for a melodious conclusion. The listener is actually waiting for the music to 'resolve'. Resolution is achieved when discord transitions to concord. When a piece of music resolves, it just sounds right and carries the note of completion.

What is true in the field of music can be transposed into the world of words. When you have articulated your Mission Resolution with precision it will sound 'right'; it will seem complete. There may well be a process involved to achieve that resolution. Interestingly, the difference between discord and concord can be just one note. Be patient. Lincoln reworked his Gettysburg speech until he sensed that he had reached the central idea to his own satisfaction. It might take you time to compose your Mission Resolution. You'll need to practice at it. You want it to be as short and sharp as possible. Lincoln wrote, "Give me six hours to chop down a tree and I will spend the first four sharpening the axe". The sharper your Mission Resolution the more it will cut through. Believe that the grinding investment will be worth it in the end. Keep going until you intuitively know it sounds right.

SUMMARY

We have now approached the task of formulating your Mission Resolution from five different perspectives. Each insight will help you in the process of producing a great Mission Resolution. Use the following Implementation Elevators to help you create a statement that is aspirational, actionable and achievable.

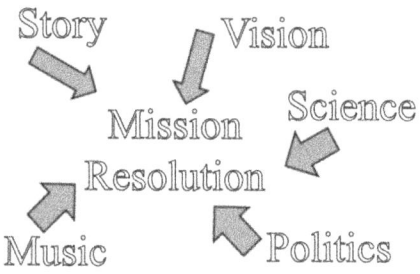

Implementation Elevators

REFLECTION

To be a great leader you need to be a '3%er'; that is you need to be among the 3% who have firm, written goals. Do you agree? What difference does having firm, written goals make?

EXERCISE # 1: YOUR STORY

What contribution does your story make towards discovering your Mission Resolution? How have past experiences, passions, gifting and present opportunities merged in your life to help shape it? Write down the most important and influential of these.

EXERCISE # 2: VISION

What picture has God given you of the future? When you have accomplished what you have resolved to do, what will you see in practical terms? Create a word picture. When will this future be brought into being? What's the time-frame? Write it down. Complete the sentence, '(This)_____ is what we will see by_____(then).'

EXERCISE # 3: SCIENCE

To help discover the exact nature of your Mission Resolution it helps to process your thoughts in a scientific manner. Use the time-tested diagnostic tool that asks the following six questions: Who?; What?; Where?; When?; Why?; How? Write down your answers to each question as accurately as possible.

EXERCISE # 4: POLITICS

Now formalize your Mission Resolution by drafting a statement that can be widely read and easily understood. You want as many people as possible to adopt what you are proposing. It will need to be something that will galvanize the resolve of a group. Make it clear, concise and compelling.

EXERCISE # 5: MUSIC

Now evaluate your Mission Resolution. Does it hit the right note? Does is sound right? If even a small section is discordant you will need to resolve it. When you think it's finished have other people read and critique it. Is it music to their ears too?

Chapter 3 MISSION RESOLUTION – PART 2

[Moses] started back to Egypt

(Exodus 4:20)

Moses knew what God wanted him to do. He was given his mission at Mt Sinai. That was foundational. But it wasn't enough. He needed to resolve to do it; to take the necessary steps to complete the mission. He took the first of these when he "started back to Egypt" (Ex. 4:20). In the last chapter we considered five nuances of the word 'resolution': they were associated with Story, Vision, Science, Politics and Music. These five variations on the theme helped you to formulate your Mission Resolution. You now have a precise word picture of what it is that God is asking you to do. Having a written Mission Resolution is necessary. But it is only the beginning. Now it's time to resolve to get it done. To this end, you must be determined and plan the actions steps required for success. To help you accomplish your stated mission we will consider two further meanings of the word 'resolution'. These concepts build on the first five. The word 'Resolution' also relates to:

    6) *Character* – the state or quality of being resolute; firm determination

    7) *Action* – resolving to do something.

CHARACTER

Abraham Lincoln was determined to appear at the Gettysburg ceremony. It was an opportunity to boost the Union's war effort and to solidify political support. But his personal circumstances at the time illustrate just how resolved he was to speak that day. At the last minute his son Tad became suddenly and seriously ill. Lincoln and his wife Mary had already lost two of their four children to disease so the situation was grave indeed. Mary was nearly hysterical in her entreaties that her husband should not leave. Nevertheless, Lincoln boarded the train bound for Gettysburg. His son's critical illness must have torn at is heart. Yet his resolve to honor the dead and fortify the living overrode even his most personal affections. Lincoln stood firm. He was a resolute leader.

The central word in Lincoln's emendation of his Gettysburg speech is "dedicate". The word appears five times in that short speech. It implies consecration; a pledge to God.[10] That kind of resolve is related to your character. That kind of dedication is forged deep within a person. Lincoln had this.

The Apostle Paul had this. The Bible records these words from Paul:

> "And now, compelled by the Spirit, I am going to Jerusalem, not knowing what will happen to me there. I only know that in every city the Holy Spirit warns me that

prison and hardships are facing me. However, I consider my life worth nothing to me, if only I may finish the race and complete the task the Lord Jesus has given me..." (Acts 20:22-24).

You need to have this sort of resolve as well. Once you know you have the right Mission Resolution you need to deeply commit to getting it done. Lincoln said, "Be sure to put your feet in the right place, then stand firm." When you are resolute you are ready to act in a courageous and disciplined manner. When you are resolute you are willing to do whatever it takes.

ACTION

Once you can see the future in specific terms, you must then form detailed action plans to bring that future into being. This is crucial. Your Mission Resolution isn't meant to be just a nice picture hung on a wall. Plans need to be made then action needs to be taken. You need to set out what has to be done, step by step, in order to reach your God-given goal. You should to do this with your Mission Resolution as the point of reference.

Moses, for example, needed to devise some strategies in order to fulfill the mission of leading the people of Israel into the Promised Land. It wasn't enough just to visualize God's people in the Promised Land. The Israelites were not 'teleported' from Egypt to the land of Canaan. There were action steps that needed to be taken along the way and in a certain order [below]. While God provided for Israel miraculously on many occasions, plans needed to be formulated and executed. For example:

- Moses needed to inform Israel's Elders of God's plan to deliver the nation.
- Pharaoh had to be confronted and persuaded to let God's people go.
- People needed to make. specific preparations for the journey.
- They needed to reach Mt Sinai.
- Deserts had to be traversed. *step by step*.
- Spies needed to be deployed.
- Battles were to be fought.

It quickly becomes apparent that a lot of methodical planning was required, even as Moses and the people relied on God each step of the way.

So with your Mission Resolution in front of you, create a detailed plan of action. One way to do this is to list the necessary action steps below each distinct part of your Mission Resolution. Below is a demonstration of what that might look like. I'll use the Chat Room's Mission Resolution as an example. Having stated the resolution I will break it down into its major constituent parts (**in bold**) and the set out the relevant action step or steps for each part. You are not only stating *what* action you will take but also *when* that action will be completed.

Mission Resolution

*Jesus spent significant time with marginalized people. We see **a team of well trained, open-hearted people** from our church committed to **creating a sense of community for 60 'at risk' people** in our local area. Our aim is to create **a space in a nearby building** where people can feel at home and experience a sense of belonging. We will share the Gospel in word and deed. This ministry will happen during the day. We will start with being open Mondays, Wednesdays and Fridays. Our goal is to start preparing immediately and we see ourselves in our community space **within 2 years**.*

Part 1: The team

Action steps:

1) Create Role Descriptions covering the range of essential functions for this ministry. To be completed within a month.

2) Work out the minimum number of leaders required to make this mission viable and sustainable. To be completed within a month.

3) Recruit the right people for this sensitive and specialized ministry. Have at least the minimum number recruited within 12 months.

4) Organize monthly, 3–hour training sessions in the lead-up to opening day. Thorough training day plans to be completed in 6 months' time.

5) Provide specific training in relating to people with mental health challenges. Part of training planning (above).

6) Follow through on all the levels of The Jethro Model (continually refer to the contents of this book). This will prove valuable in creating and developing the team.

Part 2: 'At risk' people

Action Steps:

1) Begin visiting local boarding houses and find out what issues people are facing. Visit 2 boarding houses per month for 6 months.

2) Find out what makes people feel comfortable. This will require ongoing learning.

3) Think about how best to share the Gospel with this people-group. Gather some resources that we can use from the start. Basic resources to be ready within 12 months.

4) Invite people along to their 'home away from home'. In the month leading up to opening.

Part 3: The location

Action Steps:

1) Find a suitable location that can accommodate 60 – 70 people. It will need to be available during the day. Found within 12 months.

2) What would fit-out cost? Seek advice and estimates. Exploration completed in 6 months.

3) Estimate costs of the facility and begin preparing a budget to cover associated costs.

4) Visit a similar ministry and learn what has made that venue 'work'. Within 6 months.

Of course, this is only an example of the process of creating Action Steps from a Mission Resolution. You will need to supply as much detail as possible so that progress will be made. One thing is for certain: you will not achieve your mission without taking the appropriate action steps. When you review your own performance as a leader, as well as the overall progress of your mission, your actions steps will tell the story. Did you make true and timely steps towards achieving your goals? Or did you just talk about it? 'Resolution' means action. It means resolving to *do* some things; to do the *right* things. The measure of your resolution is reflected in the magnitude of your actions. As Abraham Lincoln said, "Always bear in mind that your own resolution to succeed is more important than any other."

The measure of your resolution is reflected in the magnitude of your actions.

Joseph's Story

People in the Bible needed to plan. Their plans were often in response to things that God had shown them about the future. Their planning played an important part in fulfilling God's mission. The major principles taught in these two chapters on Mission Resolution are evident in the Biblical account of Joseph's life and mission as recorded in the Book of Genesis.

God gave Joseph some remarkable abilities – including the ability to interpret dreams. Through a series of divinely orchestrated circumstances, he was invited to interpret the dreams of the Pharaoh. These visions were clearly given to Pharaoh by God. Through them, God showed Pharaoh and Joseph what he was about to do. Here they are in full:

> "God has shown Pharaoh what he is about to do. Seven years of great abundance are coming throughout the land of Egypt, but seven years of famine will follow them. Then all the abundance in Egypt will be forgotten, and the famine will ravage the land. The abundance in the land will not be remembered, because the famine that follows it will be so severe. The reason the dream was given to Pharaoh in two forms is that the matter has been firmly decided by God, and God will do it soon.
> "And now let Pharaoh look for a discerning and wise man and put him in charge of the land of Egypt. Let Pharaoh appoint commissioners over the land to take a fifth of the harvest of Egypt during the seven years of abundance. They should collect all the food of these good years that are coming and store up the grain under the authority of Pharaoh, to be kept in the cities for food. This food should be held in reserve for the country, to be used during the seven years of famine that will come upon Egypt, so that the country may not be ruined by the famine" (Gen. 41:28-36).

God's Vision of the future was detailed and time-specific. The purpose was a saving one; God had graciously given this vision in order to ensure the preservation of Abraham's nation, as well to save many other peoples and nations (Gen. 45:6-7). Joseph's Mission Resolution could have read like this:

> *To provide emergency food for Egypt and the surrounding nations by creating a food bank, over the next seven good years, that will store enough food for distribution during the anticipated seven famine years that will follow. I see great storage barns being built in designated cities. I see the preservation of Egypt through this famine.*

That would have been a good Mission Resolution. But it wasn't enough to have the right picture of the future. Action was required in response to that Vision. Joseph set out a strategy (Gen. 41:33-36). The strategic Action Steps included:

> *1) Appointing the right leaders to oversee the collection of food.*
>
> *2) Collecting 20% of the crop yields and store it.*
>
> *3) Building storehouses to store all the grain.*
>
> *4) Distributing food during the famine years.*

Joseph's action steps were directly related to the Mission Resolution. His resolve was evidenced in deliberate actions. Right actions are a result of being on the right mission. As I said at the start, everything flows for knowing the mission and resolving to accomplish it. This resolve issues from a firm determination forged by character. And it all results in actions that intentionally progress you towards your God-given goal.

DIARIZE AND DELEGATE

Place these action steps into your diary and see that they are actioned on time. Space them out so that your deadlines are achievable. Delegate tasks to others as appropriate with accompanying deadlines. Here is where your resolve is really tested. The famous and successful coach John Wooden wrote, "It's the little details that are vital. Little things make big things happen." Resolve to take those small but significant action steps.

RESOLVING TO PRAY

Discovering your Mission Resolution and acting on it is a spiritual endeavor. Prayer, therefore, should be prominent: you would like to know your *God*-given mission. You are not asking God to bless your own plans. Abraham Lincoln rightly said, "Sir, my concern is not whether God is on our side; my greatest concern is to be on God's side, for God is always right." Pray earnestly, asking God to show you the right path and the right plan. In Psalm 31, David prays, "Since you are my rock and my fortress, for the sake of your name lead and guide me" (Ps. 31:3). Clearly, David didn't know exactly what to do and so he asked God to reveal it to him. If you only have a general conviction about something that needs to be done, ask God to make his precise will clear to you.

Following the murder on the doorsteps of the church, I had a general idea that something needed to be done. However, the needs on the street of that city were so immense and complex that it was hard to know where to begin. All we had was a general conviction that we knew would lead to some kind of action. Our initial response to the murder itself was to pray. A newspaper article cut-out from that time (which my wife found buried with some old photographs!) carries the headline, "Prayers at scene of murder". We prayed continually and open-heartedly for God's direction as to exactly how we should resolve to respond. God answered our prayers in the months that followed. Instead of putting up a big, barbed-wire fence around our property to keep the church people safe and secure from the dark and dangerous streets, we bought the building across the road as a refuge for at-risk people. The building was being used as a brothel but we transformed it into a refuge for people living on the margins of our community. This became an integral part of the overall mission of our church. We resolved to do this. Our general conviction was progressively clarified into a precise response to the need. Prayer was pivotal in this process.

DOES YOUR RESOLUTION RESONATE?

After you've articulated your Mission Resolution and created actions plans, you should seek confirmation that your aspirations and actions are the right ones. You want to know if they resonate with those that matter. Lincoln's short Gettysburg speech is considered one of the great speeches of history. This appraisal issues from the way his words resonated with the audience and captured the imagination of a nation. It articulated the crowd's *aspirations*. It galvanized their resolve to *action*. And it contributed to the *achievement* of two great outcomes; the abolition of slavery and the constitution of a democratic nation. There are three notable attributes of this speech that help explain why it resonated with so many people of the day:

1) Its opening words, "Four score and seven", struck a note of Biblical solemnity while its conclusion evoked God's name and acknowledged the need for his enabling.

2) It aligned with the general mood of the Union.

3) Its central idea was confirmed by discerning people; like the Reverend Edward Everett.

Ideally, you want your Mission Resolution to encapsulate God's intentions and capture people's imaginations. You're looking for confirmation from God and people that you are on the right track for spiritual success. You want your Mission Resolution to evoke a shared feeling and belief. Does your resolution resonate? Here are three 'resonances' to look for:

1) The Mission Resolution is consistent with Bible's teaching.

2) The Mission Resolution is aligned with the local church's overall mission.

3) The Mission Resolution has been confirmed by discerning people.

We will now look at each aspect in a little more depth. We'll start with the Bible.

1 THE BIBLE

Is your Mission Resolution consistent with God's will as revealed in the Bible? God often uses the Bible to reveal his particular mission for you. He might lead you to a verse or a theme in the Bible that helps define your particular mission. You might find yourself drawn by God's Holy Spirit to certain passages and subjects. This will help give you a Biblical context for the mission on which you will be deployed. One way or another, it's important to acknowledge that your mission will be a small but important part of God's bigger plan. Can you see how it could advance and enhance God's work in the world? And, is *the way* that you anticipate achieving it consistent with the Bible as well?

John's Story

Back in the 1960s, a movement called 'The Children of God' began. They had a mission to reach people with the gospel and many alternative lifestyle people (like 'hippies') joined in. John was part of it from the early days. His general impression was that the movement began soundly enough and the Bible was taken seriously. In the 1970s, however, the leader of the Children of God, David Berg, changed his name to Moses and things went badly from there! In 1974, he promoted a method of evangelism called 'Flirty Fishing' which sometimes used sex to 'show God's love' and win converts. This demonstrates the inappropriateness of thinking that 'the end justifies the means'. In Christian mission, we need to use the right means to the right end. The Bible guides us in both areas. The general idea of evangelism was right, but the methodology was abominable! Fortunately the practice was discontinued, but not until 1987!

I know this is an extreme example of a methodology that is contrary to the Bible's teaching. Probably you would never agree to such a glaringly wrong approach to achieving your Mission Resolution. Nevertheless, the story serves as a reminder that your actions are as important as your achievements. It also reminds us of the necessity of checking to ensure that everything that we dream and do for God is consistent with the teaching of the Bible. Can you provide Biblical support for both your mission and your methods; for your aspirations and actions? Does you resolution resonate with the Bible?

2 THE LOCAL CHURCH

The second consideration on our checklist is alignment with your local church's mission. God works through local churches. You can easily see that in the New Testament. The local church should be a hub of missional activity. And your Mission Resolution should be intentionally connected from your local church's mission. It should advance and enhance it. You need ask yourself, 'How does this Mission Resolution fit in with what God is doing in and through my church?' Better still share your Mission Resolution with your church's senior leaders. Do this in the early developmental stages. Invite their input. Seek their endorsement. Make sure that they share a belief in your stated mission. Confirmation that you are on the right track comes when *your* Mission Resolution resonates with *your church's* direction in mission.

3 CONFIRMATION THROUGH THE HOLY SPIRIT AND GOD'S PEOPLE

A third source of confirmation is through the council of godly people. The Bible says, "For the lack of guidance a nation falls, but many advisers make victory sure" (Prov. 11:14). In Acts 15, the Bible records a critical point in the mission of the Church. The lead-up to this crucial moment was the success of Paul's mission to the non-Jewish (Gentile) world. The mission had yielded extraordinary results! But it also created a significant challenge. Previously the church had been predominately Jewish. What was to be expected of these new Gentile converts? To protect the mission from disaster, and to find the positive path forward, it was decided that wise and godly people should gather in Jerusalem to discern what direction God wanted them to take (Acts 15:2). This gathering is sometimes called 'The Council of Jerusalem'.

> **The senior leaders said, "it seems good to the Holy Spirit and to us" (Acts 15:28).**

When you read the record of the Council of Jerusalem in the Book of Acts, there's no account of supernatural lightning from heaven or anything obviously miraculous. What we do note is that the Scriptures were open and wise leaders were debating the practical implications of what they were reading. They were trying to discern what the Holy Spirit was saying about the mission. When they emerged with their decision they could say that, "it seems good to the Holy Spirit and to us" (Acts 15:28). Confirmation came, as the Holy Spirit spoke to those senior leaders. This response resonated with all concerned. Never underestimate the value of the council of experienced, godly people. Does your Mission Resolution resonate with them? Do they share your belief in what you are proposing to do? Ideally, you will all come to the point where you can say that this seems good to us and to the Holy Spirit!

PERFORMANCE REVIEWS

The measure of your resolve is reflected in the magnitude of your actions. You need to *do* the kinds of actions that match the aspirational words in your Mission Resolution. Nothing will be achieved otherwise. In the next chapter, we will consider the importance of Role Descriptions. A Role Description should include measurable goals and planned action steps. You will need to write these down and see that they are done to the best of your ability. Team leaders will ask team members to do the same in the areas of their responsibility. In Chapter 9 we will consider the importance of reviewing everything and everyone connected with the mission. Progress towards the accomplishment of stated goals will form part of a performance review.

SUMMARY

We have now looked at seven variations on the 'resolution' theme: they were associated with story, vision, science, politics, music, character and action. It's time to state your mission and plan your actions. Before take-off, however, it might be best to perform a cross-check. Does your resolution resonate? Your Mission Resolution and associated actions should be:

    1) consistent with the Bible's teaching;

    2) aligned with the local church's overall mission;

    3) confirmed by the Holy Spirit and God's people.

Once everything is locked in, it's time to resolve to do what's required to enact your Mission Resolution. The following Implementation Elevators will help you do this.

Implementation Elevators

REFLECTION # 1

Think about Lincoln's determination to make that speech at Gettysburg. How resolved are you to accomplish your mission? Plot your level of resolve on the line below.

unresolved ←—————————————————————————→ *highly resolved*

What might increase your resolve?

EXERCISE # 1

Break down your Mission Resolution into its main constituent parts. These will serve as headings for EXERCISE 2.

EXERCISE # 2

Under each of the above headings, thoroughly plan the required action steps. These will need to be as time-specific as possible.

EXERCISE # 3

Diarize and delegate. Place these action steps into your diary and see that they are actioned. Delegate tasks as appropriate. Do this now. There's no time like the present!

REFLECTION # 2

John Wooden wrote, "It's the little details that are vital. Little things make big things happen." How convinced are you of this? What would increase your motivation when it comes to actioning your step-by-step plan?

REFLECTION # 3

Are your Mission Resolution and associated actions:

- consistent with the Bible's teaching?
- aligned with the local church's overall mission?
- confirmed by discerning people?

Chapter 4 ROLES

Jethro gave Moses a Role Description
(Exodus 18:19-22)

> I can do things you cannot, you can do things I cannot; together we can do great things.
>
> *Mother Teresa*

Agnes Gonxha Bojaxhiu (better known as Mother Teresa of Calcutta) founded the Missionaries of Charity. The Mission deploys thousands of women who have resolved to work in the world's poorest places, among the world's poorest people. It's a world famous mission. During her lifetime, Agnes was named eighteen times in the annual 'Gallup's most admired men and women poll'. How did she lead such a large and complex mission? Undoubtedly, her own faith in God sustained her. But there was another secret to her success: a genuine appreciation of the contributions of others. She said, "I can do things you cannot, you can do things I cannot; together we can do great things." This chapter will celebrate that truth!

As you work through this chapter keep your Mission Resolution at top-of-mind. Think about the amount of activity needed to achieve the mission. Think about all the different skill-sets and roles that will be required. You are going to need to create and develop a diverse and capable team to help you. The general rule is: the bigger the mission the bigger the team. Moses had a mission. He was to lead God's people to the Promised Land. The demands were enormous. He needed to know *who* was going to do *what*. You will need to know these things too.

DIFFERENT PEOPLE HAVE DIFFERENT ROLES

It needs to be acknowledged and celebrated that God has given people different passions, gifts and abilities. No *one* person can do everything. Admittedly, Moses tried to for a while. But it led to all sorts of problems. The mission was stalling as Moses tried to do everything for everyone. There was also the danger of lost expertise. Potentially hundreds of gifted leaders, who could have been fulfilling all sorts of vital roles, were not being given the opportunity to participate. Jethro, the veteran priest and leader, was acutely aware of these constraints. He understood that Moses needed a new, bigger vision of leadership and the roles that other people could play. There were many people whose complementary gifts and skills would help share the burden and ensure the success of the mission. Moses needed to create a leadership team. This was Jethro's mandate.

Nothing has changed. You need to create and develop a team to get things done. There are people who will play a role that will fuse with yours. The New Testament constantly reminds us that God has different roles for different people. This idea recurs in the Book of Ephesians. There, the Bible says things like:

> "For we are God's workmanship, created in Christ Jesus to do good works, which God prepared in advance for us to do" (Eph. 2:10).

"It was he [Christ] who gave some to be apostles, some to be prophets, some to be evangelists, and some to be pastors and teachers, to prepare God's people for works of service" (Eph. 4:11-12) [Emphasis added].

"From him [Christ] the whole body [the Church], joined and held together by every supporting ligament [*that is, Christian people with different, interdependent roles*], grows and builds itself up in love, as each part does its work" (Eph. 4:16) [Emphasis added].

The Bible pattern begins with the people appointed to the varied roles of apostle, prophet, evangelist, pastor and teacher. They developed and deployed God's people so that each person served in the area of their gifting. Clearly, Jesus' intent is that everyone discovers their different contribution and does their work. When each person knows their role, it all works wonderfully. When people either don't know their role, or don't like it, things start to break down. Paul addressed that problem directly when he wrote:

"Now the body is not made up of one part but of many. If the foot should say, "Because I am not a hand, I do not belong to the body," it would not for that reason cease to be part of the body...If the whole body were an eye, where would the sense of hearing be? If the whole body were an ear, where would the sense of smell be? But in fact God has arranged the parts in the body, every one of them, just as he wanted them to be" (1 Cor. 12:14-18).

When people aren't contributing according to their God-given role (i.e. hand, eye or ear) something is always lost. Things are not as God wants them to be. So, each person needs to play their part. And, just as importantly for us right now, no one can be the whole body! Moses, in a way, was trying to be the whole body. It seems that he wanted to do almost everything himself with all the effort he could summon. He needed to see things the way God saw them. Moses needed to know his specific role in God's mission. He needed a Role Description. Jethro provided one for him. It proved to be a teachable moment. Moses gratefully received the role recommendations of his father-in-law. Perhaps this is a teachable moment for you. You are ready to receive some inspired advice. What advice did Jethro give?

KNOW YOUR ROLE AS A TEAM LEADER

For a start, Jethro recognized that Moses needed a fresh perspective regarding his own, unique, leadership role. He knew Moses needed to get more focused. To this end, Jethro set out some boundaries regarding his son-in-law's responsibilities. His gave Moses what is essentially a Role Description.[11] A Role Description clearly states the specific contribution that someone will make to help accomplish the mission. It's created for ministry clarity. Moses had limited time and energy. Even a person with such an extraordinary capacity as Moses had

> **A Role Description clearly states the contribution that someone will make to help accomplish the mission.**

limits. His personal resources needed to be focused on the functions that only he could and *should* perform on behalf of the whole nation. And so, in Exodus 18:19-22, Jethro clearly listed for Moses the main areas that required his concentrated attention and concerted effort. The Role Description had four main parts:

1) Be the people's representative before God (Ex. 18:19);

2) Bring their *difficult* disputes before God (Ex. 18:19, 22);

3) Teach the nation the decrees and laws, and show them the way to live and the duties they are to perform (Ex. 18:20);

4) Select and appoint capable leaders to help lead the nation (Ex. 18:21).

If Moses continued to neglect these things the mission would be hindered. Conversely, if Moses attended to them properly, allowing other people to fulfill other roles, the mission would be accomplished. It's that simple. Jethro's advice helped his son-in-law become more self-aware as a leader and consequently more focused on his distinct leadership contributions. Moses needed to acknowledge his unique calling, particular gifting and specific contribution.

This ought to be your concern too. As team leader you need to determine what your role will be. If you are already leading a team, it may mean refining or redefining as you go. Your role will inevitably be a decisive one. Other people will merge into your team and play a necessary role. Nevertheless, your contribution will be pivotal. That's the nature of team leadership. The bigger the mission the more your role matters!

Sadly, many leaders don't get around to creating Role Descriptions. Moses, in the early days, was one of them. What had inhibited Moses from defining his role in the mission? Why hadn't he quite worked out what his role was exactly? We can't be certain. Nevertheless, there are some typical reasons for procrastination when it comes to describing a leader's role. Here are some common ones:

1) Too busy. Maybe Moses initially felt that he didn't have time to waste on thinking it through. He just wanted to get on with it. He was a man of action and perhaps the sort of reflection required to fashion a Role Description just wasn't his style. Maybe you feel you don't have time for all this Role Description stuff!

2) Too restricting. Maybe, Moses *liked* doing everything (for a while anyway). It certainly meant that he felt indispensable. Maybe you *like* the freedom of doing whatever you want whenever you want. Perhaps you subconsciously don't want to have to limit yourself by prescribing your role and sticking to it. That sort of self-indulgent free-for-all is not going to be helpful in team-building. The members of your team deserve to know what's to be done and who's going to do it. They also need to be assured that their contribution isn't going to be

made redundant because someone whimsically changes things or decides to do it themselves. Team leaders need to be disciplined and stick to the strategic things that they can do best and entrust other things to other people.

3) Too distrusting. Some leaders don't think that other people will be dependable enough to be trusted with a role. Highly capable leaders, competitive people and those with a perfectionist trait, often fit into this category. They are happy for others to play minor, supporting roles as long as they don't get in the way. A distrusting attitude undermines team-building. And, if you can't build a great team, you won't accomplish a great mission.

4) Too lazy! Maybe you're not naturally good with words. Moses certainly felt that way. Putting words together, therefore, requires a lot of effort and you don't feel you have the energy for that. Or, perhaps you're not a 'details' person and the thought of sitting down and writing Role Descriptions makes you suddenly want to go and clean the bathroom.

One way or another, there is a great temptation to procrastinate when it comes to writing Role Descriptions. Whatever your reluctance to draft a Role Description, I want to warn you: if you renege on the challenge to create Role Descriptions for you and your team then you're doing a great disservice to everyone involved. Your mission *deserves* a committed approach to this task. You need Role Descriptions. This takes discipline, not only to create a Role Description, but also to stick to it. Your efforts, nevertheless, will be rewarded! The powerful outcomes of this disciplined effort will be:

1) You will know your role, ensuring a sharpened leadership focus and increased effectiveness. Role Descriptions for each member of the team will help ensure the same for them. Moses, Israel and the mission benefitted greatly from this. So will you, your team and your mission.

2) You will better know what to say 'yes' or 'no' to and what to delegate, according to the role you will play on the mission. That kind of clarity is so liberating.

3) It will clarify the expectations that your team will have of you. Your leadership role will be clear to them. And, as you create Role Descriptions for each member of your team, your expectations of them will also be plain. This will lead to great team cohesion.

4) It will help you identify gaps. It will become more apparent to you what aspects of the mission will require the attention of other, gifted leaders – i.e. all the aspects you won't be directly involved in. This will help you when it comes to recruiting.

Hopefully, you are convinced of the importance of Role Descriptions. What things do you need to consider in the process of drafting one?

DISCOVERING AND DEFINING ROLES

So, how can you discover and define your role? And, how will you help others do the same? There are three major considerations that will help you in this process. They are:

1) Your gifts and skills mix;

2) The satisfactor;

3) The phase of the mission.

1 YOUR GIFTS AND SKILLS MIX

Spiritual Gifts

Knowing your spiritual gifts will really help you determine what your role should be. Spiritual gifts are God-given abilities for God-glorifying activities. Within you there is a certain combination of gifts and skills. You might have been given some obvious supernatural abilities. You might have been given natural gifts and skills that are enhanced by the Holy Spirit. One way or another, spiritual gifts are not randomly given but are received for a reason. They equip you for your unique leadership role in the team on the mission. No one has quite the same combination as you. Think of them as your spiritual fingerprint. There are many spiritual gifts recorded in the Bible. There is disagreement as to the exact number. We'll now consider just four of these gifts. We will explore the implications of each particular gift with regard to a potential role on your team. I have in mind general roles that most teams will require. I acknowledge, however, that each mission team will require specialist gifts appropriate to their particular goals. We'll start with an obvious one – leadership.

> **Spiritual gifts are God-given abilities for God-glorifying activities.**

　　i) **Leadership**. This gift gives a believer the confidence to step forward, give direction and provide motivation to complete a mission. Some of the Biblical references to this gift are as follows – Romans 12:8, John 21:15-17, 2 Timothy 4:1-5. This gift is uncommon. The logical reason for this is that God wants *most* people to willingly and intelligently follow his lead as it is expressed through gifted leaders. The Old and New Testaments confirm this theology of spiritual leadership. For example, the Book of Judges records these inspired words sung by the champion-leader Deborah:

> "When the princes of Israel take the lead,
>
> when the people willingly offer themselves –
>
> praise the LORD" (Judg. 5:2).

　　Clearly, Deborah is espousing that those who have the responsibility of godly leadership *ought* to take the lead. The people, for their part, should willingly volunteer their support. We find another example of this theology of leadership in the Book of Hebrews. There, the Bible says:

> "Obey your leaders and submit to their authority.
>
> They keep watch over you as men who must give an account.
>
> Obey them so that their work will be a joy, not a burden,
>
> for that would be of no advantage to you" (Heb. 13:17).

Leadership roles carry with them huge responsibilities. This is because of the far-reaching implications for all the people who are called to follow. That's why this gift comes with such a high level of accountability. It is, necessarily, a rarer gift. It follows that those with this gift ought to use it wisely and well. If you are called to lead, don't get caught up in things that will dull your leadership edge. Put 'leadership' at the top of your Role Description.

ii) **Administration**. This gift enables a leader to guide the people toward the accomplishment of God-given goals and directives by planning, organizing, and supervising others (the Greek word *kubernesis* means to steer or guide and refers to the work of a helmsman). Two of the Biblical references to this gift are 1 Corinthians 12:28 and Acts 14:23. This strategizing gift is crucial, as we saw in chapter 3. If you are a big-picture thinker and not into details, then you *need* someone fulfilling this role in your team. Factor that in early.

iii) **Service/ Helps**. This is a gift that enables a person to work gladly *behind the scenes* in order that God's work is fulfilled. Some of the Biblical references are Luke 23:50-54, Romans 12:7, 16:1-16 and Philippians 2:19-23. These people are humble and productive. They are the "willing volunteers" that Deborah sang about (Judg. 5:9). Many of these people are highly adaptable and can easily transition into other 'helps' roles as the mission requires.

iv) **Discernment**. This is a Holy Spirit-given ability to determine whether someone or something is of God or not. A person with this gift will spiritually analyze everything and help ensure the mission is heading in the right direction. In the context of a team this might not be a stand-alone role. Nevertheless, having someone on your team with godly wisdom and insight will be of great benefit.

Other spiritual gifts mentioned in the Bible are as follows:

- Prophecy
- Healing
- Teaching
- Exhortation
- Giving
- Mercy

- Wisdom
- Knowledge
- Faith
- Evangelism
- Pastor
- Hospitality
- Intercession
- Healing
- Miracles
- Tongues
- Exorcism

This Biblical list of gifts is not exhaustive and some people debate whether they are all in operation today. The point, however, is that the gifts people are given equip them for certain roles in God's mission. What are your spiritual gifts? If you're uncertain, then determine to discover them. There are many resources available that are designed to help you discover your spiritual gifts. One way or another, you need to know what they are because your Role Description will likely include some or all of them.

Skills

Acknowledging that there can be some overlap between spiritual *gifts* and God-given *skills*, I'll venture to offer a short list of skills that fit people for certain roles in teams. Some of these skills are mentioned or alluded to in the Bible. Here are ten capacity-building skills to look out for:

i) **Financial acumen.** Some people are not only trustworthy with money, they know how to invest it wisely and distribute it appropriately. This is an important skill because good use of financial resources will boost your ability to resource the mission.

ii) **Communication.** Communication plays a vital role in keeping people informed and unified. Some people are extraordinarily skilled at this. They seem to know who needs to know what and when. These people are clear and often creative in the way they communicate.

iii) **Second-in-charge.** It might seem strange to list this here, but it takes great skill to be a 2-I-C. There are many challenges around issues like loyalty, jealousy and the use of authority. It takes great humility and skill to lead in the shadow of another leader. These traits are, of course, needed on the part of every team member.

iv) **Gathering people.** The mission will include people. Where are they going to come from? Who will keep them together? Some people are highly skilled at attracting new people and integrating them into the group. Never underestimate the importance of this role!

v) **Church Planting**. Not many people can do this. It is very difficult to start something from nothing. People like this have an apostolic edge, are full of faith and very resourceful. It's a rare and valuable skill.

vi) **Artisan**. Artisans are highly creative people. We read about them in the Bible. These people might be skilled musicians or expert craftspeople. Creative skills like these help us in our worship of God.

vii) **Visionary**. Some people are especially skilled in seeing what the future should look like and knowing what needs to be done. They have the ability to sense *where* the Spirit is moving. Visionaries help reveal where God is taking us and what that will look like.

viii) **Networking**. Often the success of a mission will depend on meeting the right people. While these meetings are arranged by God, he will often use a human agency. There are some people who are great at getting the right people together in the room. These people usually have a high capacity for relationships and a great ability to make synergistic connections. Networking is a great skill.

ix) **Analysis**. Not many people have the ability to look analytically at a situation and come to a deep understanding of the underlying dynamics. Jethro had this skill. He observed what was going on with Moses and Israel and concluded that it was potentially damaging. He made the right recommendation that provided a solution.

x) **Group facilitation**. Most of what happens in teams and through teams will involve a number of people meeting at the same time. Further, many churches have small group ministries that meet to study the Bible and provide mutual support. Managing group dynamics in environments like these requires great skill. Skilled facilitators will manage group dynamics such that all interactions are inclusive, safe and mutually beneficial. Not everyone can do that.

This list is far from exhaustive. Hopefully it will stimulate your own thinking. It's a useful exercise to write down all the different skills you can think of. Think about your own skills. Be creative and adventurous. Write down skills that you know God has given you. Your skills, along with your spiritual gifts, will help shape your Role Description. Knowing these from the start will help you when it comes to designing and developing your team.

2 THE SATISFACTOMETER

Ideally, your role should be a satisfying one. You'll want this to be the experience of your team members as well. This should be a big consideration when drafting Role Descriptions. Longevity in leadership is often linked with a sense of personal fulfillment. So don't discount the importance of this. Your aim is that leading "will be a joy, not a burden" (in the spirit of Hebrews 13:17). Moses' burden was significantly alleviated when he implemented The Jethro Model. He was able to lead in the areas of his strengths and in accordance with his particular leadership calling.

So, what are the signs that someone's leadership role is a satisfying one? Here are seven significant indicators:

S kills and gifts used optimally;
A ffirmed by others;
T eam is integrated and motivated;
I nvigorated by the role;
S tanding the strain;
F uture looks fruitful;
Y ielding good results.

satisfactometer

When you and your team are serving in the right areas then you will be able to respond affirmatively to these indicators. In the 'Implementation Elevators' section at the end of this chapter, there's an exercise with which you can rate your leadership role on the 'Satisfactometer'. It will help you assess the suitability of your Role Description.

3 THE PHASE OF THE MISSION

As your team grows, roles will probably need to be adjusted. Even your own role will need to be adapted as the mission and the team grows and develops. The advantage of a larger team is the possibility of specialization. You go from pragmatically filling necessary gaps in your team's gifts-and-skills set to mainly doing the leadership things you love and do best. Specialization is fantastically satisfying! It means that you have the opportunity to operate almost exclusively in the area of your strengths. My own leadership role has developed from the start-up, generalist phase to a specialist phase.

My Story

At the time of the murder at the doorsteps of my church, I was a Pastor with less than a year's experience. Being the only full-time Pastor usually means that you do almost everything. I visited people in homes and hospitals, prepared and preached sermons, wrote reports, led almost every church meeting, did the work of an evangelist, led worship, served at working-bees, married people, dedicated their children, buried people, mentored leaders, encouraged new people to stay, encouraged older members not to leave...you get what I mean. I was the team leader of a church of a little over one hundred people and I filled a lot of gaps. I didn't resent it. It was just the phase we were in. I did whatever I could to help the church grow! Some of these things I was good at, and some of them I wasn't. In the early, developmental phases of the mission, your role is often to do a lot of things that others simply can't or won't do.

But as time went on and I got to know people, I began to identify their gifts, skills and potential. I began to see how people and roles could fit together. I began designing a Dream Team. I'll show you how to go about this later in the chapter. Then I began recruiting people on the basis of the roles they could enthusiastically and effectively fulfill. As time passed other people came on board with all kinds of expertise that I didn't have. Then I increasingly had the freedom to specialize in the areas of my own expertise. It was a very liberating process.

These days, my Role Description contains a short list of things that God has shaped me to do and do well. It is certainly the most fulfilling phase of my leadership journey so far. But usually, it's not like that at the start. When you begin, you are usually very 'hands on'. Perhaps 80% of your role will be taken up with doing practical ministry while 20% will be spent leading and developing your team. This can't continue indefinitely. A mission team leader needs

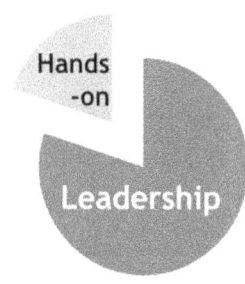

to be aware of what developmental phase their team and mission is in and adapt their role accordingly. As a general rule, once your team has been created and is developing satisfactorily, a team leader's Role Description should entail an 80% team leadership-and-development component with only 20% of the role taken up with delivering the 'hands-on' ministry. This leadership shift will be essential to achieving team synergy, efficiency and building capacity.

Imagine the possibilities. Instead of being overwhelmed by the demands of personally attending to every little problem and detail, you have around you a group of capable people who are willing and able to share the load. They are happily doing most of the work. They are also looking to you to lead them; to lead the mission. Their amazing contribution affords you the opportunity to look up and look ahead. You have an 80%–leadership-role. You can sharpen the arrow! You can identify the targets. You still lead by example. You still do some of the ministry: 20% of your time is spent serving people in practical ways. Leaders should always do some of the hands-on work. But now you are giving a confidence-inspiring lead by attending to those few big things as a team leader should. Drafting Role Descriptions (*starting with that of the team leader*) is one of those 'big things' that needs attending to.

ROLE DESCRIPTION TEMPLATE

What are the essential elements in a Role Description? I've listed them below along with the reasoning behind the inclusion of each element.

> **NAME OF THE MISSION TEAM** – This is for simple identification purposes.
>
> **MISSION RESOLUTION** – Everything flows out of the mission. This role is being intentionally designed in order to help fulfill it. Consequently, the Mission Resolution provides the frame of reference for the role.

NAME OF THE TEAM MEMBER – A Role Description is, in a sense, a covenant. The team member is committing to making a certain contribution. The team leader is committing to provide support. It is a very personal document. The team member and team leader may choose to sign the document (this optional element would be included at the end).

LEADERSHIP STRUCTURE – Who reports to whom? The leadership connections need to be clear. This is essential for The Jethro Model to work effectively. Lines of support and accountability need to be documented.

ROLE TITLE – This is for simple identification purposes.

A DETAILED DESCRIPTION OF THE SPECIFIC ROLE – This is the central purpose of a Role Description. It's essential to articulate the exact nature of the contribution that will be made. Remember, be thorough. Role Descriptions will form the basis for reviewing the performance of each member of the team (see Chapter 9). So, make sure this section is completed comprehensively.

CULTURE-CARRYING COMMITMENTS – What values must be upheld? What are some of the important 'intangibles' that need to be embodied in this role and as part of this team?

GOALS AND ACTION STEPS– What are the specific performance and role related goals? Action steps will need to be planned in accordance with the stated goals. The review process will include an evaluation of progress and success in achieving them.

TIME COMMITMENT – Realistic expectations help to ensure a rewarding experience. Carefully calculate the time required to fulfill the Role. Are the regular demands sensible and sustainable? It should be acknowledged that there will always be times of extraordinary sacrifice. Nevertheless, it's good to establish the normal time commitment. The figure may relate to hours per day, week or month depending on the nature of the mission and the particular role.

DURATION OF THE COMMITMENT – This could be a semester, a year, when the mission in accomplished or whatever is negotiated as reasonable.

ROLE REVIEW TIME-FRAME – The performance of the team member should be reviewed with reference to the Role Description only. This should take place at least every twelve months. The time of the review should be negotiated so as to be acceptable to the reviewer and the one being reviewed. At the time of review, the Role Description can be adjusted and renegotiated so as to be satisfactory to all concerned.

SUPPORT PROVIDED – What can be expected in terms of support? Who will check up on the team member and how will that be done?

(OPTIONAL) SIGNATURE OF TEAM MEMBER

(OPTIONAL) SIGNATURE OF TEAM LEADER

In APPENDIX 3, I've provided a sample of a completed Role Description.

DESIGNING YOUR TEAM

Many action films, including classics like The Dirty Dozen and Mission Impossible series, are built around the idea of putting a team together. The assignment set is daunting. The challenge requires the assembly of a multi-gifted team. If even one of the required skills is missing the whole mission will fail. The team leader usually has the responsibility of assembling the right mix of talents. They might need a skilled driver, an electronics expert, a computer-hacking genius, a strong-arm guy, a shooter and whatever. The team leader, who is usually the brains behind the operation, designs the ideal team. He starts by *imagining* the types of talents and temperaments needed. Once he knows what he's looking for he then goes about the task of recruiting the right people for those roles.

You have a similar task. And it's *not* mission impossible. Once you start working on your own Role Description, it will become increasingly apparent to you the role-gaps that you need to fill.

> **While some heroes in the Bible accomplished their mission alone, most people went on mission in teams.**

You will begin to discern the *other* roles that are required. These roles will complement your own contribution. Without them, your mission will fail. You are starting to see the bigger picture. Now, with a bit of imagination and inspiration, you can commence designing the kind of team you'll need – your Dream Team. This sort of team engineering reflects God's designing of things. It is God's intention that people should normally work in teams. While some heroes in the Bible accomplished their God-given mission all alone (think of Jonah sent to preach to the people of Nineveh), most people went on mission in teams. Our focus is on the development of teams that will accomplish a God-glorifying mission.

God often links people in teams in order that his mission is accomplished. Moses served with Aaron (Ex. 4:14-16). Later, there would need to be many other people chosen for different but complementary roles; from skilled craftsmen (Ex. 31:1-11) to the Levites who would serve exclusively in and around the temple (Num. 18:5). Deborah and Barak would team up (Judg. 4). Joab was King David's right hand man on many a mission. Jesus banded together the twelve disciples. Jesus and the disciples were supported by a team of wealthy women (Lk. 8:3). On one occasion, Jesus sent out thirty-six mission teams comprised of two people per team (Lk. 10:1). The Apostle Paul had travelling companions on his mission trips (Acts 19:29) and is linked with Barnabas (Acts 13:2), Phoebe (Rom. 16:1-2), Timothy, Titus and many others. Everyone had a contributing role. Paul, for example, didn't baptize people much. This decision was deliberate (1 Cor. 1:15). Baptizing, it seems, wasn't listed in his Role Description. Other people did the baptizing. That was fine. Paul understood that. "The Lord assigns to each a task", he wrote (1 Cor. 3:5). Each works together to accomplish the ultimate mission that more people come to believe in and follow Jesus. Paul wrote:

> "I planted the seed, Apollos watered it, but God made it grow...
> the man who plants and the man who waters have one purpose...
> For we are God's fellow workers" (1 Cor. 3:6-9).

The thing is that each understood his role as they resolved together to fulfill the one mission. This is so important! We are different by design. *You can't do everything.* So when it comes to forming a team, you can happily presume that there are people out there who are *made* to do the things that you can't do. You need to acknowledge this deep down. Then there's the designing part.

One of the most creative facets of team leadership is the designing and developing of your team. When you start out with no one but you, there's a fair bit of holy imagination required. When you've got your team going, there's always room for development. Here's how I think about this task from the outset.

Designing your Team

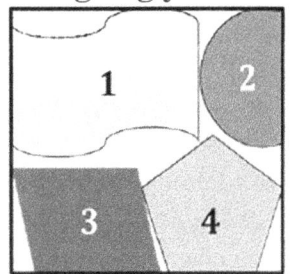

First, having discovered and documented my gifts and skills, strengths and weaknesses, I create my own Role Description based on my strengths. I then imagine how my role fits in terms of the overall mission. Let's say, using the 'Designing your Team' diagram, I'm piece number one. I might then consider my weaknesses and create complementary Role Descriptions that will make up for those. Those pieces are represented by pieces two and three in the diagram. One of those pieces might be, for example, administration. The other might be pastoral care. The point is that *some* of these major roles will be determined by what I'm *not* good at.

But, beyond just compensating for my own weaknesses, there will be other capacity-building roles that will be required. Piece four on the diagram represents one such role. It might be evangelism, for example. The mission that you are on will probably require specialist gifts appropriate to your particular goals. You might need a communication specialist or someone great at vision-casting. You might need a gifted healer or a finance expert. There are so many exciting possibilities! These roles will need to be incorporated into the team composition. My point is this: to some extent you need to imagine what your Dream Team will look like *before* you go recruiting. You need to have a good idea about the kinds of roles that will need filling. Your best guess will suffice at this point because it is realistic to expect some loose ends. If you are observant, you can see that there are still gaps in my 'Designing your Team' diagram. The gaps serve as reminders that you rarely cover off on every role from the start. It's also worth acknowledging that roles rarely fit together perfectly. Refinement will be necessary as you go along on the mission.

But if you can see the big, basic bits and see how they might fit from the start, then you're well on the way to creating something special.

RE-DESIGNING YOUR TEAM

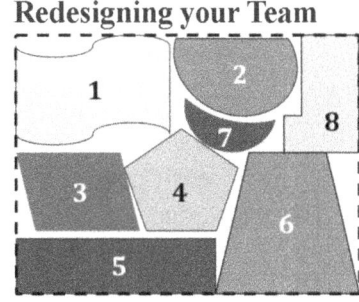

Redesigning your Team

For those who are leading an already-existing team, you'll be aware that this designing task never ends. There's always a natural flow in and out of teams as people come and go. It is rare for a team to stay the same for long. So it's important to be attentive to the changing shape of the required roles, and reconfigure roles from time to time to fit the new scenario. Of course, if your mission is expanding, there will be new opportunities that require perhaps previously unimagined roles. If this is the case, you'll need to design a bigger and better Dream Team.

HAVING THE RIGHT APPROACH IS REQUISITE TO SUCCESSFUL TEAM DESIGN

It's one thing to understand team design conceptually; it's another to do it well. The right approach is important. Here are some tips that will help you get your approach right.

1) Make sure you are absolutely convinced of the necessity of Role Descriptions for team harmony and efficiency. Be prepared to champion this in the face of resistance. Each team member needs to know their role and fulfill it. Your approach will need to be upbeat!

2) You don't want two of you. Don't have another role that's the same as yours or even close. This could unwittingly lead to competitiveness.

3) Be humble. Celebrate the contribution of others. Design so that others will shine. Harry S. Truman said, "It is amazing what you can accomplish if you do not care who gets the credit."

4) If you're not particularly creative, you might need a little bit of help with this task. Approach someone gifted in this area, someone who understands you and your mission, and ask for their insights. Involve other trusted leaders in the design process.

5) Don't over-design your team at the start. Four or five people fulfilling big-block roles will often be enough. Once the team has bonded, revisit and refine their Role Descriptions. Then go on a fresh round of recruiting to fill the gaps.

6) Having established your own Role Description, recognize that you still may need to fill some small gaps in order to cover-off on everything your mission requires. Make sure you make an allowance for the time commitment that this might entail.

7) Do unto others as you would have them do unto you. You naturally want your role to be as satisfying as possible and make optimal use of your gifts and skills. You ought to want the same for your team members. Don't just give people the jobs you don't want to do. Give them the roles they were made for.

8) Once your team is up and running, keep returning to the 'design table'. It would be wrong to approach this as a once-off or even occasional task. Experience suggests that constant development will be required.

9) Be thorough. Role Descriptions will form the basis for reviewing the performance of each member of the team. So, make sure they are as comprehensive as possible.

By making the right approach to this task you will increase your chances of success. The context you are in will require you to adjust your approach accordingly. Bear in mind, however, that the way you approach the task of creating Role Descriptions will largely determine whether your team builds and bonds or buckles and breaks.

BACK TO THE START

Jethro was alarmed by Moses' attempt to lead the mission alone. He knew intuitively that Moses needed to focus on his own unique role as leader of Israel. To this end, Jethro drafted a Role Description for his son-in-law. Moses, for his part, needed a fresh appreciation of the leadership roles that others could play. There were hundreds of latent leaders in Israel. These people had the leadership capacity to address all but the most difficult of problems. Moses needed to design an effective leadership team. Jethro's mandate and model were timely and helpful! Perhaps, you're aware that this advice is timely for you as well. You see the importance of Role Descriptions for your team and in your church. You already know your mission. Now it's time to know your role and work on your team design. The Implementation Elevators will help you do this.

Implementation Elevators

REFLECTION QUESTIONS:

What are the benefits of having Role Descriptions?
What are the problems that Role Descriptions help avoid?
Are you motivated to conscientiously draft Role Descriptions for you and your team?
Review the Role Description Template provided in this chapter. Are there any changes that need to be made to maximize the benefits for your team and mission?

EXERCISE # 1: COLLATE RELEVANT MATERIAL TO HELP DRAFT YOUR ROLE DESCRIPTION

SPIRITUAL GIFT IDENTIFICATION

What spiritual gifts have you been given? Make a list. If you are uncertain, find a resource designed to help you discover your spiritual gifts and complete the inventory. Make a list and then rate them from strongest to weakest.

SKILLS IDENTIFICATION

What skills have you been given? Make an exhaustive list and then rate them from strongest to weakest.

GIFTS AND SKILLS MIX

Group the highest ranking of your gifts and skills together and imagine how they can be incorporated into your own Role Description.
Ask a trusted third party to confirm that you are on the right track.

EXERCISE # 2: DRAFT YOUR OWN ROLE DESCRIPTION

Because you are the leader of the team, your role will be a decisive one. To a large extent your team will be designed around you. Using the Role Description Template, now draft your own Role Description.

EXERCISE # 3: TEAM DESIGN

Having described your own role, think about what your Dream Team might look like in terms of the other roles required.

In Exercise # 1, you identified your strongest gifts and skills. What other gifts and skill-sets will be required to ensure a balanced team?

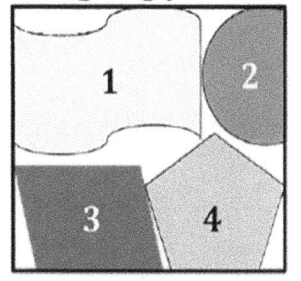
Designing your Team

What are some essential roles that will urgently need filling? Make a list.

What are some non-essential roles that would, nevertheless, be of great benefit? Make a list.

EXERCISE # 4: DRAFTING ROLE DESCRIPTION FOR TEAM MEMBERS

Using the Role Description Template, first create draft Role Descriptions covering the essential roles that will need filling. Then do the same for the non-essential ones.

At this point, your team design is taking shape.

REFLECTION QUESTIONS:

Now imagine your Dream Team is assembled and working together to fulfill the mission. Take time to think about the different, real-life challenges that will confront you. Would this be a team that is able to respond to anticipated, mission-related situations?

Will the experience be satisfying for all involved? You will get some indication of this as you answer the following questions:

Are your skills and gifts used optimally in this role?

In the exercise of your role, are you being affirmed by others?

Is your team integrated and motivated?

Do you feel invigorated by your role?

Are you all standing the strain?

Does the future look fruitful?

Is the mission yielding good outcomes?

Chapter 5 RECRUITING

Select capable people

(Exodus 18:21)

> **If you can't recruit people to the mission, your goals will probably need to be downgraded and your effectiveness will be diminished.**

I believe that recruiting is *the* most undervalued of the leadership tasks. Recruiting is a game-changer and yet it doesn't often appear at the top of a senior leader's priorities list. A good leader might have great personal gifts and passion. A good leader might generate some interest and spawn a Cheer Squad. Nevertheless, I'm convinced that the ability to recruit well is something that distinguishes a good leader from a great one. You shouldn't underestimate this. You might have captured God's mission in words and you might have designed great Role Descriptions, but if you can't recruit people to the mission, your goals will probably need to be downgraded and your effectiveness will be diminished. NFL coach Pete Carroll said, "Recruiting is the lifeblood of any program, so you can't put anything above that". You will find that the enduring success of great teams, including great churches and mission agencies, is largely due to their ability to recruit the best people to their mission. Don't get me wrong, the mission needs to be the right one and this is especially true in the case of Christian mission. Nevertheless, the ability to recruit the best available people will prove to be pivotal. A mission rises or falls according to the people who are leading it.

You see this in the Bible. God called the nation of Israel to be his own, special people. He invested his love and his power into that group of people. He had a mission for his nation – that through them, the whole world would be blessed. But time and time again we read that the fortunes of the nation and its mission turned on the quality of the leaders (see Judg. 2:7-15). When the leaders were great, things flourished. When the leaders were trash, everything went to the refuse tip. Your goal is to raise up a real Dream Team.

WHO DO YOU RECRUIT?

Moses was instructed to "select capable men from all the people" to be leaders, and he made his choices (Ex. 18:25). The brevity of the account belies the gravity of those decisions. The word 'select' or 'choose', used in this context, has the meaning of "look out for".[12] Moses was instructed to look for the right people. They were to be judges. The word 'judge' isn't used in a strictly legal sense. Rather, these people were to be *champion-leaders* as is the case in the Book of Judges. These leaders would fulfill influential roles that Moses couldn't (Ex. 18:21). Jethro mandated that Moses appoint leaders who demonstrated the following three essential qualities. They had to be:

1) wise and discerning;
2) respected by the community;
3) able to judge impartially.

Similar qualities are required of church leaders in the New Testament (1 Tim. 3:1-13).[13] Sometimes, this selection process is fairly straight-forward. Some leaders seem to 'choose themselves'. By this I mean that they are already proven and are just waiting to be deployed. These people are a great gift from God! Moses seems to have had the benefit of hundreds of leaders who were ready, willing and able. In Deuteronomy 1, Moses recalls, "So I took the leading men of your tribes, wise and respected men, and appointed them to have authority over you" (Deut. 1:15). Many of these people were already part of Israel's family and tribal structures.

> **Get these leadership selections right and your burden will be lightened, people will be satisfied, needs will be met and your mission will be accomplished. Get these choices wrong, and the strain on you will increase as dissatisfactions grow and the mission stalls.**

Of course Moses had *overlooked* them until his 'Jethro-moment', so it's worth me making the point. You need to be on the look-out for experienced people like this.

In some situations, however, you'll need to take a closer look at a potential recruit. There are three main reasons for this. One reason would be that a leader is emerging and shows great potential but has little experience. They might be raw and unproven. A second reason is that, for some reason, you're not quite convinced that they have the character qualities required. And a third reason for taking a closer look at a potential recruit is that the role you have in mind for them is a very influential one. You therefore need to be certain that they have the character and capacity for such a significant role on the mission. Sooner or later, decisions need to be made. This calls for great discernment. Get these leadership selections right and your burden will be lightened, people will be satisfied, needs will be met and your mission will be accomplished. Get these choices wrong, and the strain on you will increase as dissatisfactions grow and the mission stalls.

So, how do you choose the right leaders? This chapter will feature six filters designed to aid you in the selection process. The six filters are:

1 Committed to Christ;

2 Character;

3 Capability;

4 Controlled by the Spirit;

5 Cooperativeness;

6 Culture-Carrier.

If you run a potential recruit through these filters, you will be in a good position to make a decision as to their appropriateness for a role on your mission. These filters reflect the qualities that Jethro deemed critical. I wouldn't make a recruiting decision without referring to them.

 # 1 PEOPLE WHO ARE COMMITTED TO CHRIST

Select people "who fear God", advised Jethro (Ex. 18:21). Reverent respect for God is essential because the mission we are on is *his* mission. The parallel passage in Deuteronomy puts this into perspective: "Do not be afraid of any man for judgment belongs to God" (Deut. 1:17). This reminds us that the leaders we choose must have a personal sense of direct accountability to God for their lead (2 Cor. 1:12). We need to be confident that they will lead "in Jesus' name". They need to be born again and personally committed to Christ (Jn. 1:43; 3:3). So ask yourself, 'Does this person have a reverent respect for God?' If a leader doesn't, then it won't end well.

Moses and the people of Israel learned this the hard way. Moses apparently made some bad leadership selections at a critical moment in Israel's journey. Moses recounts the disaster that followed, in Deuteronomy 1. The people of Israel were poised on the edge of the Promised Land. They were ready to enter into Canaan and take a great stride towards 'mission accomplished'. They were so close! I'll let Moses take it from here:

> "Then all of you came to me and said, "Let us send men ahead to spy out the land for us and bring back a report about the route we are to take and the towns we will come to." The idea seemed good to me; so I selected twelve of you, one man from each tribe" (Deut. 1:22-23).

Perhaps you already know that the story ended badly because most of the chosen leaders were unfaithful (Num. 13:26-33). If only Moses could have gone back and made those selections again! Did he really look closely enough at those original recruits? Maybe he did. Whatever the case may be, ten of the twelve that he chose *feared people* more than they *feared God*. Their commitment wavered when so much was at stake! Their report was defeatist. They lamented, "The people are stronger and taller than we are" and the result was that they made God's people lose heart (Deut. 1:28). This had dire consequences for the whole nation because none of that generation entered into the Promised Land except Joshua and Caleb. Why did those two go in? They  entered in because they feared the Lord and followed him wholeheartedly (Deut. 1:36, 38). They had a reverent respect for God. The Bible says, "But in your hearts set apart Christ as Lord" (1 Pet. 3:15). This is the first thing to look out for when you are recruiting for your mission. You want people who trust God and take him at his word. They need to demonstrate spiritual commitment.

So ask a potential leader to share the story of their salvation and their journey with God. Does it seem genuine? Ask for examples of times that they have put God first at the risk of public ridicule. Have they stood for Christ in the face of opposition? You want to choose leaders who are seriously committed to Christ.

2 PEOPLE WHO EVIDENCE A GODLY CHARACTER

Never compromise on character. A person's character is the combination of qualities that distinguish a person. Jethro knew the importance of appointing leaders with godly character. Moses, for example, was advised to select quality people who were trustworthy (Ex. 18:21). Those leaders needed to have a reverent respect for the Lord. The Bible says that the fear of the Lord keeps people from sinning (Ex. 20:20). You want to recruit people whose lives evidence a deep alignment with God's truth. They may not be perfect, but they are trustworthy. They will make mistakes but they have integrity. What are the marks of godly character? Here's my list:

C hrist-Centred;
H umble;
A ctive prayer life;
R ead their Bible regularly;
A ppropriate with opposite sex;
C areful with their words and actions;
T rue to their word;
E vidence trail of faithful service;
R eputation inside and outside the church is good.

Let's explore each of these a little further. Looking for Christ-centeredness in a potential leader covers off on the first point I made with regard to Christian commitment. For someone with godly character, Jesus is the source, the center and the ultimate goal of everything.

The next mark follows supernaturally – humility. We're not born with a lot of this. The greatest, godly leaders have possessed the greatest humility. Moses, who is a standout leader in the Old Testament, is described as being "more humble than anyone else on the face of the earth" (Num. 12:3). The first two marks, Christ-centeredness and humility, have to do with *the inner life*. Evidence of these attributes should be discerned before appointing leaders and giving them spiritual authority.

The next two marks have to do with *activity*. When you are considering a potential recruit, ask yourself questions like: "Does this person show evidence of dependence on God by being a person who prays?" and "Do they demonstrate openness to the Truth through regular exposure to God's Word, the Bible?" Better still, ask the candidate these questions in the course of discussions about a possible leadership role. Their answers will provide insights into their Christian character. These spiritual disciples build spiritual character.

The next two attributes of a godly character relate to *relationships*. Because what we do is all about people, it follows that the way we treat people either qualifies or disqualifies us for a leadership role. The people we lead are *God's* people. The way we relate to others, therefore, must demonstrate the highest standards of dignity. Ask questions like, "Would this potential leader value and protect a vulnerable person?" and "Do they relate to the opposite sex in a healthy, holy way?" Few things compromise a mission more than sexual misconduct. Not only is it just plain wrong, it's also a massive momentum stopper! People entrusted with leadership roles need to interact carefully with people. Trust can be broken so easily by a careless word or action. Good, godly leaders are acutely aware that the things they do and say impact people. If you don't choose carefully here, things will inevitably get messy!

The final three marks are linked to *lasting influence*. Ask questions like: "What sort of impact has that leader had on people so far?" "Have people found them to be reliable?" And "do they follow through on the things they say they'll do?" Try to do some background evidence checks. Is the evidence trail positive or negative? What does the past suggest about this recruit's future? The answer might encourage or discourage your pursuit of that recruit. The final mark of a godly character comes straight from the Bible. The Apostle Paul's recruitment advice to Timothy was that a high-influence leader "must have a good reputation with outsiders" (1 Tim. 3:2-7). Clearly, credibility in the wider world was not-negotiable. A big part of our mission will be reaching out to unbelievers. This mission is severely compromised when unbelievers have very good reason to disrespect an inconsistent Christian. This is exaggerated when that person has been elevated to a leadership position. You can't overlook a person's reputation! Truthfulness, faithfulness and being worthy of respect are marks of godly character.

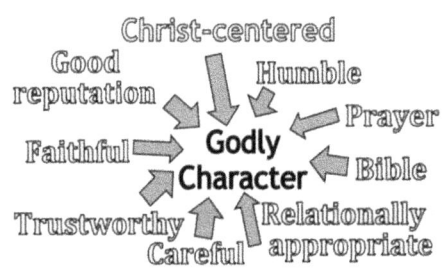

So there are my nine attributes of a godly character. This provides a checklist when discerning the suitability of a potential leader. Come up with your own list if you like. One way or another you will need to be satisfied that you're recruiting the right people. Of course, having a godly character isn't required only of leaders. This is something God wants for everyone. But, you can't lead without it. And to recruit someone to a significant leadership spot when you have a big question mark over any of these character traits is a BIG mistake. As I said at the top, never compromise on character!

3 PEOPLE WITH CAPABILITY

Jethro told Moses to select *capable* leaders. A potential recruit should be committed to God and demonstrate godly character. These essentials notwithstanding, *capability* in leadership is another important consideration. Not everyone can lead at the same level. Some have the capacity to lead thousands, others hundreds or fifties or tens. The ability to discern *who* has the capacity to lead *at what level* is a skill that is required of a high-level leader. Pray for competence in this area. Moses had this gift and it must have come into play in the selection process. But be cautious because there are some traps here for inexperienced leaders. If you elevate someone inappropriately they will be out of their depth. There is an often-repeated saying in the Armed Forces that goes: "He was promoted to his level of incompetency". In other words, his career ambitions have exceeded his ability to perform. The person promoted was incapable of leading at that level. This scenario causes a lot of grief for the leader and for those he cannot ably lead.

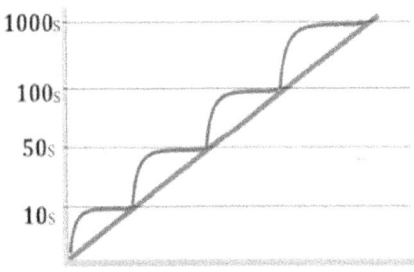

The thing is that leaders have different capacities. It is sometimes difficult to accept this if you are made to lead tens and you're looking with envy at those who lead more. It's easy to make the mistake of thinking that the 'higher' leader is somehow better than you. But, there's absolutely no correlation between the level of lead you're given and your own personal worth. The love God has for you and your value to the mission is off the charts irrespective of where you might be plotted on the graph above. Just as each of us should know our role and stick to it, so we should find the level at which we were made to lead and then "govern diligently" (Rom. 12:8). We all need to fulfill our supporting role in the big scheme of things. This sort of thinking is in the spirit of the teaching set out in Ephesians 4:16:

> "From him [Christ] the whole body [the Church], joined and held together by every supporting ligament [Christian people with different but connected roles], grows and builds itself up in love, as each part does its work." [Emphasis added]

Now, this doesn't invalidate a holy ambition to exercise a greater lead. The Bible says, "Here is a trustworthy saying: If anyone sets his heart on being an overseer, he desires a noble task" (1 Tim. 3:1). Sometimes, a person needs exposure to a higher level of leadership to test their capability. People need the opportunity to stretch and see. Leaders *can* learn and grow. You might even surprise yourself with the discovery that God has made you a leader of thousands. However, if someone stubbornly clings on to a leadership appointment that exceeds their competency, everyone suffers. It's best to simply acknowledge that that person's sphere of influence is smaller, though no less essential. When a leader leads positively and diligently *at the right level* it is a great gift to the mission. When a leader who is out of their depth graciously relinquishes their role it will provide opportunity for the right person to rise up and take it on.

Sylvia and Carolyn's Story

Sylvia led our Sunday Kids' Church. She was also a standout leader on one of our church oversight teams. When I was called to the church to serve as lead Pastor, I quickly began teaching The Jethro Model. Sylvia is a keen learner and was one of the early adopters of the principles taught in this book. She articulated the Mission Resolution, created Role Descriptions and recruited an effective team. The Jethro Model helped ensure success.

During the growth period that followed, Sylvia was well able to manage the increasing number of relationships with team members and children. Things continued to flourish. But after a few demanding years of growth, Sylvia began to feel the strain of leading, managing and recruiting so many leaders. She understood that this pressure was not going to abate. Her leadership experience had taught her that as the mission grew, more leaders would be needed. On top of that, the team ranks would continuously need replenishing due to the natural turnover of contributors. Sylvia was conscious that this recruiting challenge demanded greater attention than she felt able to give. She was also growing agonizingly aware that she was missing the steady pastoral interaction with a small group of children at Kids' Church. After all, that was the reason she started serving in Kids' Church in the first place. Sylvia was beginning to discern that the overall leadership role wasn't her best fit.

During an informal review of Kids' Church, we began talking about the kind of leader needed to take the Kids' Church mission to the next level. That leader would need to focus on the ongoing implementation of The Jethro Model with a special emphasis of recruiting the right people. That leader would probably not have much ongoing pastoral interaction with children on a weekly basis. That person would need to focus almost solely on leading and developing the Kids' Church team. Was Sylvia the one to do this? Did she have the capacity? Did she even want to? In the course of that conversation, we both came to the conclusion that Sylvia's time as overall leader was soon coming to an end. Someone else was needed to take things further. There was a certain sadness to this conclusion. It was the end of a special era. Sylvia understood the need to have the right people in the right roles and so she was willing, whatever her personal feelings, to step aside and let someone else take the lead. She knew it would be for the best. This would allow the Kids' Church to grow bigger and better and Sylvia could lead at her ideal level. Win, win! But it was still a courageous decision. It was Sylvia's understanding and acceptance of The Jethro Model that prepared her for this transition.

We didn't have anyone in mind to take over at that point. We just knew it was the right call to make. So we established a succession plan. We developed a Role Description that articulated what would be required of the new Kids' Church leader. We advertised the position in our church notices. We prayed and waited, believing that God was preparing the next leader. In the meantime, Sylvia continued to lead faithfully.

Carolyn read the advertisement. She was immediately drawn to the possibility of applying for the role but waited for God to show her what he wanted her to do. The notice stayed in her handbag for a week or two. She had already applied for a paid position with a Christian organization at the time and was waiting for an offer. Nevertheless the thought of the Kids' Church role continued to excite her. Strangely enough, Carolyn had just thrown the notice in the bin when I called her and asked her if she was interested in applying. She was and she did! It turned out that Carolyn was ideal for the role. What happened next simply demonstrates the power of The Jethro Model principles:

- *Because Sylvia knew that the Mission Resolution was more important than her position, she was willing to step aside and help establish Carolyn as the overall leader of Kids' Church.*
- *Because the Role Description was clear, Carolyn was able to confidently step into her role and make a great start.*
- *Sylvia is thriving in her smaller leadership role and enjoying direct interaction with children.*
- *Carolyn is building on Sylvia's work, recruiting a great team and pioneering new opportunities for reaching children.*

Sylvia and Carolyn's story demonstrates a number of the advantages of implementing The Jethro Model. And the Kids' Church mission is going better than ever!

So, how can you assess a leader's capability to lead at any given level? I think the three foremost indicators are found in Exodus 18 as well as in the progress towards entry into the Promised Land. These are the three capability-indicators:

1) The people they are leading are consistently satisfied (Ex. 18:23);
2) The leader is personally coping with the strain of her/his role (Ex. 18:23);
3) The mission is progressing toward accomplishment (Exodus – Deuteronomy).

If ongoing problems arise in any one of these three areas, I think the signs are there that the leader is not capable of leading at the current level. Now I need to be clear here. I've referred to ongoing problems as an *indicator*. Everyone has challenges from time to time that aren't quickly or easily resolved. That's a given in any leadership role. But if genuine problems remain unresolved or the same issues constantly reoccur or no progress is being made, you shouldn't ignore the signs. It might be a matter of increasing the leader's support or it might be a matter of reducing their level of lead. Senior leaders need to discern this. Sometimes some leadership coaching or bolstering of the ranks can turn things around. But sometimes no amount of help will compensate for the deficiency because the leader is simply in the wrong spot. They're not a bad person or a complete failure. Not at all! They are just not capable of leading at *that* particular level. That's all that is being indicated. Conversely, if the people being led are genuinely satisfied, the leader is personally managing the strain, and the mission is steadily being accomplished, then you can happily conclude that the right leader is in the right spot!

A mission leader needs to ensure that the leaders they are recruiting are capable of the lead they are entrusted with. This is vital for the health of the people and the success of the mission. If you can get the right leaders operating at the right levels then all three indicating lights go green!

#4 PEOPLE CONTROLLED BY THE HOLY SPIRIT

> **Moses said, "I wish that all the LORD'S people were prophets and that the LORD would put his Spirit on them" (Num. 11:28).**

In the Bible, the exercise of leadership is often connected with the ministry of the Holy Spirit. The power of God's Holy Spirit was in operation, directing and enabling them in their lead. This meant that the work of the Holy Spirit was superimposed over and above any natural capacity a leader might have. That was the decisive thing. This was the case for Old Testament champion-leaders (Judg. 3:10, 11:29, 15:14), Kings (1 Sam. 10:9-10, 16:13), Prophets (1 Sam. 19:20; Is. 48:16) and craftsmen (Ex. 31:1-3). The Book of Numbers records that Moses and seventy of his key leaders experienced the Holy Spirit resting on them and working through them (Num. 11:25). Moses couldn't have been happier. Moses said, "I wish that all the LORD'S people were prophets and that the LORD would put his Spirit on them" (Num. 11:29). They didn't perform miracles all the time. But they were able to provide Spirit-inspired leadership. That's what we want!

In the New Testament, leadership is connected with the ministry of the Holy Spirit (Acts 11:22-24, 13:2-4, 16:6, 20:28; Rom. 12:6-8; Eph. 3:5; 1 Thes. 1:5). When you are recruiting, you should be looking out for people whose leadership dynamism emanates from more than just their human faculties. I look for evidence that the Holy Spirit is functioning in their life and leadership. What should you be looking for?

1) Look for evidence of the things that the Holy Spirit produces when someone is controlled by the Spirit – love, joy, peace, patience, kindness, goodness, faithfulness, gentleness and self-control (Gal. 5:22-23). This fruit is largely borne out in healthy relationships. Can you observe these attributes in their relationships?

2) Look for a spirit of wisdom. Joshua, Moses' successor, was given this and he needed it (Deut. 34:9)! Leaders are challenged with all sorts of problems, burdens and disputes. We need wisdom by the bucket-load! Solomon asked for it. He prayed, "Give me wisdom and knowledge that I may lead this people" (2 Chr. 1:10). You should ask for it too. And, you should certainly look for it in the people you are recruiting.

3) Look for God's power at work in and through the person. Are there signs of God's supernatural enablement? Do extraordinary things happen that indicate the Holy Spirit is in control? Is God's power displayed in their lead?

One way or another, I'm looking for some substantiation of their spiritual, leadership credentials. You should be looking out for Spirit-controlled people.

5 PEOPLE WITH A COOPERATIVE SPIRIT

When Jethro observed Moses attempting to single-handedly meet the needs of two million people, he was understandably shocked. He could see "all these people" and quickly concluded that what Moses was trying to do was "not good" (Ex. 18:14, 17). It was a valiant but misguided endeavor. The leadership situation was totally unsatisfying. So, by divine inspiration, Jethro laid out a leadership structure involving layers of leaders. One huge advantage of this organizational arrangement was that leaders with different capacities could each operate at a level that was comfortable for them. Jethro instructed Moses, "have them *bring every difficult case to you*; the simple cases they can decide themselves [*each at their level*]. That will make your load lighter, because they will *share* it with you" (Ex. 18: 22) [Emphasis added]. These ideas of *referring* and *sharing* are important here. It requires a spirit of cooperation.

In a larger mission involving a lot of people you're going to need a lot of leaders. In Moses' case, there must have been *thousands* of leaders with a variety of roles, leading at different levels. For me, that would be a logistical nightmare! But even in the team I lead, I need that spirit of cooperation. The different levels of leaders need to be connected so that things are shared, *up and down the levels*, and the appropriate information is referred to the 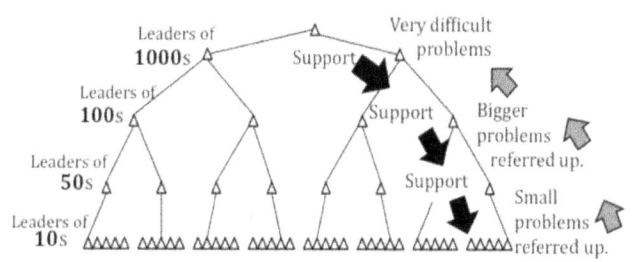 right person in the right place. For Moses, managing the whole structure would have become unwieldy if the leaders didn't share the leadership burden or appropriately refer the difficult cases to people with the required expertise. No doubt this spirit of cooperation would have been a consideration when recruiting and appointing the leaders.

The Jethro Model won't work well if leaders aren't willing to humbly ask for help when they are dealing with a problem they find too difficult. Unwittingly, they might do more harm than good. Why is it that some people don't refer difficult things on to others with more expertise? Why don't some leaders truly share the leadership responsibility? Sometimes a leader doesn't refer problems on to those better equipped because of the sin of pride (Gal. 5:20). They don't want to accept or admit that a burden is too big for them. Perhaps, they want to be seen as the 'savior' in that situation. If a case that's too difficult for them doesn't get referred on, I can assure you it won't go away. Unresolved problems are like time bombs. It's

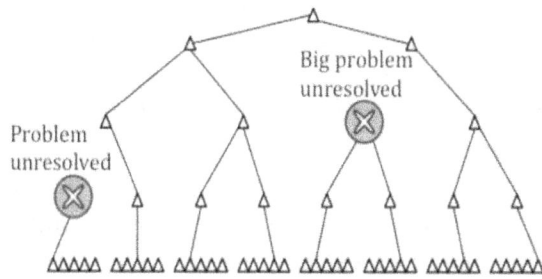

going to blow up sometime and it could be messy. That's why recruiting the right sort of leader matters so much. When a leader operates in isolation, and tends to keep things to themselves, all sorts of problems arise. Don't recruit such a person to a significant level of influence. Another reason why someone may not refer or share is that they might have a selfish ambition to be the sole leader. In a case like this a grasping leader will subtly or openly try to usurp proper leadership authority. Moses experienced such attempts (Num. 12:1; 14:4). It can get nasty. So, if you're suspicious that the recruit you're considering is motivated by selfish ambition, don't recruit them. It's better to be safe than sorry.

The thing is to make sure this spirit of cooperation is part of your deliberation over the suitability of a potential recruit for a leadership role. Don't attempt to shove a lone-ranger into a genuine team even if they are spectacularly gifted. If you do, you can expect problems. However, when you assemble a leadership team made up of leaders who are willing to seek assistance and truly share the leadership burden then you've helped create something special.

6 PEOPLE WHO WILL BE CULTURE-CARRIERS

The people you recruit need to *embody* the goals and values of your team and church. They will need to agree with the things you are trying to do and with the way you are trying to do them. This is important because these people will become influencers and help shape an environment in which you do mission. You need to recruit people who will carry the right culture. This happens best when you've clearly articulated what culture you are celebrating and cultivating. Often, the values that you hold dear are not spelled out. Perhaps you assume that people will pick them up intuitively. Perhaps you're hoping that your example will rub off on others. Happily this is often the case. Nevertheless, to avoid any misunderstanding, I think it's important to write down the things you value so that potential recruits will be clear on that right up front. Your Role Descriptions ought to include these things.

Lindsay's Story

I have led a church music team for about 10 years, and in that time have always tried to model the kind of attitude, and create the kind of culture that I want to see in my team members. I have heard many times about "leading by example" and how this is the best way to create a culture and a team that follows this example. I believe I have done that kind of "example leading" consistently, but my experience is that this has not led to the kind of culture intended. While the culture has not been a bad one, it just hasn't been the kind of extra-mile stewardship that I've tried to model, and I've ended up busy doing most of those extra miles myself. This shows me that many people do not catch on from the example only, but need more explicit direction and encouragement. Part of this direction has been to put in place explicit Role Descriptions that highlight not just the things people need to do but the attitude and culture that we are seeking in the team. Having these things written down on paper and discussed with new team members as they join means that they are aware of them right from the start and have something to aspire to and that we can remind them about as appropriate. With this clarity of expectation along with leading by example, I trust that we will become the kind of team we aspire to.

So make sure your potential recruits know the culture that they are entering. Recruit those who espouse those things that you and your church value. And provide continual coaching regarding your culture.

HOW DO YOU RECRUIT?

So, we have six Bible-based filters that will help team leaders choose *who* to recruit. You're looking to populate your team with people who are committed Christians, who display godly character, are capable to fulfill a role, are filled with the Holy Spirit, have a cooperative spirit and can carry your culture.

The next question is, 'How do you recruit?' How do you get the right people onto your team? I believe that there are five important ingredients to attracting the right people:

1) Having a clear and compelling Mission Resolution;

2) Having your essential Role Descriptions pre-drafted;

3) Having an integration process that offers a potential recruit the opportunity to experience the mission (and allows you the opportunity to run them through the six filters);

4) Taking the long view in developing an emerging leader with potential;

5) Praying for the right people.

Let's look at each of these in a little more detail.

1 HAVE A CLEAR AND COMPELLING MISSION RESOLUTION

You maximize the possibility of attracting the right people to your mission team when your Mission Resolution is clear. When you have a clear and compelling Mission Resolution the right people will get on board. People naturally want to know where a plane is going. When I'm flying home, I'm glad my boarding pass is double-checked because home is where I want to go. I wouldn't want to board a plane that's going to fly around aimlessly unless I had a lot of vacation owing! Who knows where that journey will end up? The idea of going *anywhere* might seem OK, until you end up in the middle of *nowhere*! You've got to be clear about the destination *then* the right people will get on board. Can you provide a clear destination for those who would take the journey with you?

Let them know where you're going.

The destination also needs to be compelling. By that I don't mean *nice*. Serving homeless people who haven't showered for weeks isn't nice. Taking teens on a mission trip isn't nice – not if you like sleeping! These missions aren't nice, but many people find them compelling. Sometimes, the bigger the mission and the more extreme the challenge, the more great leaders want to get on board. I've found that the most capable leaders are attracted to the most compelling missions. Great leaders don't really want to join a team that's just 'ticking along' or embark on a mission to nowhere. When you have a clear and compelling mission to accomplish, then the task of recruiting gets a bit easier!

2 HAVE ESSENTIAL ROLE DESCRIPTIONS PRE–DRAFTED

If you've done the design work that was encouraged in the last chapter, then you should have a reasonable idea of the big-block roles that need filling. You should draft these up and have them at the ready to give to potential recruits. There are a number of good reasons to do this:

i) It's confidence-inspiring for a potential recruit to see that you have thoroughly thought things through.

ii) It gives a potential recruit something to take away and consider prayerfully. When I am launching a mission I might give someone who's interested *all* the Role Descriptions. That person might not fit any one of the Roles exactly, but they will have an idea of what is needed and the sort of time required to pursue the mission.

iii) Some people might erroneously assume that their gifts and abilities wouldn't fit your mission. They have a preconceived idea of what and who you're looking for and it's the *wrong* idea. For example, quiet people with administration skills may easily assume that the crazy youth mission team would not be looking for someone like them. They can't immediately see a role for their gifts and skills. How great would it be to put a pre-drafted Role Description into the hands of the administrator you're looking for? That's one big way to impress an administrator. Gotcha!

3 HAVE AN INTEGRATION PROCESS

Try before you buy! That's what they say. You want to test it before you commit to it. That's a perfectly reasonable approach to making many big decisions. You should expect that someone interested in your mission would want to take a closer look. That's how you will recruit people. You give them the best experience of the mission that you possibly can. You allow them to "taste and see". That's a very important strategy.

So, think about how you can do that. Here are some things that might get the creative juices flowing:

a) Invite them to hang out with your mission team on a social occasion. It helps a potential recruit get a feel for team dynamics.

b) Invite them to a one-off event.

c) Invite them to come along for a month as an observer.

d) Ask them to help out for a while and make a decision then about whether to commit.

e) Ask them to participate in some small way that allows them to use their gifts and skills.

f) If that was a positive experience, ask them if they are prepared to do a little more.

g) Debrief with them after the experience. Ask them to critique what they did or observed.

Whatever way you do it, *have* a process. And, as team leader, make sure you are personally involved. This will help you establish a relationship with that person and allow you to observe them in action. All the while, you should be running them through the six filters. After all, 'try before you buy' works both ways.

4 TAKE THE LONG VIEW AND DEVELOP EMERGING LEADERS WHO SHOW POTENTIAL

I want to finish this chapter on recruiting with a focus on the future. As I said at the start of this chapter, some leaders are almost ready-made for a role on your God-given mission. You need to look out for them. Some leaders, however, you've got to nurture into service.

Moses looked to the future. This shows the measure of his great stature as a leader. It seems that even in his earlier years as the leader of Israel, he began raising up the next generation of leaders. He did this most notably by nurturing a relationship with an emerging leader named Joshua. Great leaders invest themselves in the kinds of people who will fill roles and lead on into the future.

A lot of team leaders wait for the right people to come along. They are only looking for the people who are already developed. In other words, they are waiting for leaders that *other* people have invested in to the point that they are ready and able to lead. Thankfully, these already-developed-leaders are often around and you'd be crazy not to recruit them. But think about it for a minute. If your God-given mission massively expands, who will populate your leadership ranks? Who will be there to share the leadership load? And, who will carry the mission forward in the future? Great leaders see the big picture. They think long-range. They are capable of looking beyond their immediate needs and even their anticipated intermediate

> **Great leaders see the big picture. They think long-range. They invest in emerging leaders.**

> **God arranges circumstances whereby an emerging leader comes to our attention.**

requirements. They prepare for the expansive future. They invest in emerging leaders. This is a rarer gift. Praise God for the people who have this sort of foresight. You need to develop this gift. You need to become that sort of leader.

Moses had the foresight to make a long-term investment and it paid off. He took Joshua on as an apprentice. Joshua eventually succeeded Moses in the leadership of Israel and he succeeded as a leader. The Bible says, "The people served the LORD throughout the lifetime of Joshua" (Judg. 2:7). Moses played a big part in setting Joshua up for this great achievement by mentoring him across a lot of years. This was one of Moses' great legacies. So, who are you relating to when it comes to potential future leaders? If you're not, maybe you'd like some answers to questions like; "What should you be looking for in an emerging leader?", and, "How can your relationship with them assist them to fulfill their God-given potential?" I'll try to give some answers to these questions.

When we first meet Joshua in the Bible, he's been ordered by Moses to fight a battle (Ex. 17:8-9). Whether he carried any official sort of rank we cannot be certain. Regarding the circumstances surrounding his choosing, we know nothing. There's no point guessing. From our perspective, he just suddenly appears on the scene in the Bible. One way or another, he came to Moses' attention. But that's often how it happens. God arranges circumstances whereby an emerging leader comes to our attention. There could be a thousand reasons why. When I was a young man in my twenties, I was in a larger church and going along pretty much unnoticed by the people who were leading. I wasn't a remarkable person and I've managed to remain that way. But, there was this girl in the church who was a highly regarded leader and I happened to like her. A lot! Once we started going out, I suddenly came to the attention of the leaders. I emerged from obscurity and they began choosing me to lead things. It can all appear to be very random, but God has his way of bringing emerging leaders to the attention of the people who can develop them. Who is God bringing to your attention?

If you read the account in Exodus 17, you'll quickly realize how formative that initial leadership experience was for Joshua. It showed him a lot about the nature of spiritual leadership. He was down in the valley fighting the Amalekites but the real battle was being fought supernaturally. Up on a hill, overlooking the valley-of-the-battle, Moses was raising the staff of God towards heaven. As long as that staff was held high, the battle was being won. Whenever that staff came down, the enemy gained the upper hand. The battle was fought and won *spiritually*. Post the victory, Moses was instructed to, "Write this on a scroll as something to be remembered and make sure that Joshua hears it" (Ex. 17:14). Joshua was to learn the lesson early! It's good to get emerging leaders straight into the battle. Give them something to get stuck into. In the early days, you'll be like a Moses to them. They will fight 'under' you. Their efforts will be acknowledged – the victory, on one level, was ascribed to Joshua's sword (Ex. 17:13) – but the triumph really depended on Moses prevailing in the spiritual realm. This is one thing that they can learn from you if you are an experienced campaigner. They can learn how to accomplish a mission by prevailing spiritually. Moses needed the soldiers *and* the staff of God. This principle was laid down early in Joshua's development. It made for an excellent start.

Joshua was considered a young man at the time of his emergence as a leader (Ex. 33:11). Exactly how old he was we're not sure. Perhaps there were other older, already-developed-leaders around. Moses nonetheless sees Joshua's potential and takes the long view. That's what great leaders do. When you're looking for an emerging leader, look out for a young person. Don't completely overlook older prospects. Moses was eighty years old at the time of the Exodus and his best years lay in front of him! But an investment in youth will, in all likelihood, bring long term benefits. Moses made that personal investment in Joshua. What exactly consolidated their leadership relationship we're not sure. Perhaps it was Joshua's willing service and early success. You should certainly look for those things. Gifted, emerging leaders will *want* opportunities and they will gain you some ground. Moses gave Joshua the gift of his time. They began doing things together (Ex. 24:13). Joshua became part of Moses' small circle of personal care. Moses helped Joshua get closer to God (Ex. 33:11). This is a major way that your relationship can assist an emerging leader. Spiritual leadership flows out of knowing God. Whatever skills and structures an experienced campaigner has to teach, nothing tops helping an emerging champion know God better.

The next big lesson that Joshua learned from Moses was that spiritual leadership isn't a competitive sport. There isn't just *one* champion-leader. In fact, the more champions the better! We all need to be in this together. In Numbers 11, God gives the Holy Spirit to seventy of Moses' senior leaders. God took the Spirit that was on Moses and put the Spirit on seventy elders (Num. 11:25). Before this sharing of the Spirit took place, we assume that Moses alone experienced the personal presence and power of the Holy Spirit in that special way. Joshua was alarmed when he learned that other leaders had received the Holy Spirit. He thought this shared anointing might threaten Moses' lead over the nation. When he heard that other leaders had received the Holy Spirit and were prophesying, '"he spoke up and said, "Moses, my lord, stop them"' (Num. 11:28). But Moses' response taught Joshua an important lesson about the interrelatedness of spiritual leaders. 'Moses replied, "Are you jealous for my sake? I wish that all the LORD's people were prophets and that the LORD would put his Spirit on them"' (Num. 11:29). We need all the

Great leaders demonstrate great generosity of spirit. We need to become just a link in a great chain of leaders.

great leaders we can get! Perhaps, someday, a protégé of yours will exceed your lead. For me, I hope that will be the case in many instances. Great leaders demonstrate great generosity of spirit. We need to become just a link in a great chain of leaders. This principle was taught to Timothy by his mentor the Apostle Paul. "And these things you have heard me say", wrote Paul, "entrust to reliable men who will also be qualified to teach others" (2 Tim. 2:2). Joshua learned this leadership principle from Moses.

So Moses made an investment in this future leader. He had a long range view. He gave Joshua the gift of time. He mentored him. They forged a long-lasting, leadership relationship. Then along came the payoff. Some time down the track, as Moses grew older, he must have been pondering the big succession question; "Who will carry the mission forward in the future?" He took the question, as any experienced campaigner should, to God. He asked the Lord:

> "May the LORD, the God of the spirits of all mankind, appoint a man over this community to go out and come in before them, one who will lead them out and bring them in, so the LORD'S people will not be like sheep without a shepherd. So the LORD said to Moses, "Take Joshua son of Nun, a man in whom is the spirit, and lay your hand on him...Give him some of your authority so the whole Israelite community will obey him" (Num. 27:15-20).

Joshua had emerged under the tutelage of Moses. He was commissioned for a significant lead in the mission (Num. 27:23). This was made possible because a great leader had the foresight to invest in a future leader. And the senior ranks of Israel's leadership received a man who would lead them on for the next generation. So again, who are you relating to when it comes to potential future leaders? If you're a leader now, don't just wait for already-developed-leaders to come along. Forge a friendship with a promising emerging leader.

5 PRAY FOR THE RIGHT LEADERS

This whole process should be saturated with prayer. Jesus said we should pray for willing workers (Lk. 10:2). Jesus modeled this for us. The Bible says that before Jesus chose the twelve disciples, he spent a night praying on a mountain (Lk. 6:12-16). Ask God to guide you in the recruiting process.

The L'Abri Story

The L'Abri community was founded in Switzerland in 1955 by Dr. Francis Schaeffer and his wife, Edith. L'Abri is a French word that means shelter. According to their website, "The L'Abri communities are study centers in Europe, Asia and America where individuals have the opportunity to seek answers to honest questions about God and the significance of human life. L'Abri believes that Christianity speaks to all aspects of life." Today, the L'Abri movement has centers is Australia, Brazil, Canada, England, Germany, Holland, Korea,

Massachusetts, Minnesota, Sweden and Switzerland. What interests us here is how they recruited workers in the early years. Here's how Edith told the story:

> We also prayed that if it grew, God would send us the workers of His choice, rather than us trying to advertise or get people to help us... So not to advertise, but simply pray that God will send those of His choice, and keep others away, is a different way of doing things.
>
> We don't say that everyone ought to work this way, we simply say that we feel led by God to do this as a demonstration that He is able to bring the people to a place – even a tiny out-of-the-way place... and only to bring the ones he wants to have there for His purposes.[14]

I agree with Edith that not everyone ought to work that way. Nevertheless, it remains a powerful story of how God can and does assemble the right leaders in the right place in order to accomplish his mission.

SUMMING UP

In this chapter, we've considered the six filters through which we pass every potential recruit. Only people who pass the test comfortably should be allowed to serve in the significant roles on your mission. That filtering process will go a long way to answering the question, "Who should I recruit?" We've also considered 'how' you should go about it. It starts by applying what you already have learned as part of The Jethro Mandate. Get your mission clear and the big-block roles drafted. Make sure you have an integration process. Develop emerging leaders. And pray for God to bring along the right people for the right roles. Doing these things will help ensure success in the recruiting process.

Implementation Elevators

PREREQUISITE CHECK LIST
☐ Have you got a clear and compelling Mission Resolution?
☐ Have you got pre-drafted Role Descriptions, especially covering the essential roles?

EXERCISE # 1: PUTTING A POTENTIAL RECRUIT THROUGH THE SIX FILTERS

Recruiting people will always involve some subjective judgment. It can be hard to assess a person's suitability objectively. Nevertheless, the following matrix will prove helpful in assessing whether a potential recruit is really the sort of person that you are looking for. The idea is to rate them from 1 to 10 [10 being the highest and best score] according to each of the six filters taught in this chapter. Shade in their score against each of the filters and a helpful picture will emerge.

	1	2	3	4	5	6	7	8	9	10
Christian Commitment										
Godly Character										
Capability										
Controlled by Spirit										
Cooperativeness										
Culture Carrier										

While this sort of chart and exercise can seem a bit unsophisticated, the discernment process isn't an easy one and thorough consideration requires some sort of systematic approach. Completing this exercise will not, of course, mean your decision will necessarily become an easy one. You will still need to decide how to respond if someone doesn't rate well in one or more areas.

EXERCISE # 2: DEVELOP A PATHWAY THAT ALLOWS A POTENTIAL RECRUIT TO 'TRY BEFORE THEY BUY'

First impressions matter. If someone expresses interest in joining your team and you have a clear pathway by which they can take their first steps, it inspires confidence. Develop an obligation-free pathway that allows a potential recruit the opportunity to experience the mission.

EXERCISE # 3: CREATE AN INTEGRATION PLAN FOR SUCCESSFUL RECRUITS

Prepare an integration plan for your successful recruits. How can you make it as easy as possible for them to assimilate into your team? Create an orientation process.

EXERCISE # 4: TAKE THE LONG VIEW AND NURTURE EMERGING LEADERS

List some of the emerging leaders that you are aware of. What potential do they hold? How can you develop them as great future leaders? Make a practical plan to personally nurture one or two of them. Take the long view!

Chapter 6 RELATIONSHIPS

*You led your people like a flock
by the hand of Moses...*

(Psalm 77:20)

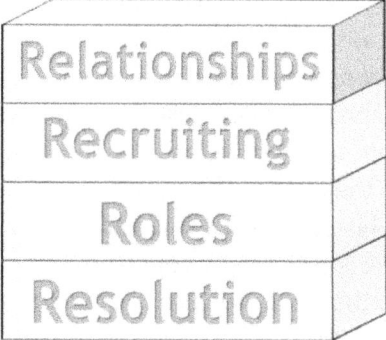

> **God's mission is planned. He knows the ultimate destination and he knows the right way to go about getting there. It's the way of love.**

It's all about people. God's concern is for people. When God mandated that Moses implement the Jethro structure it was for the benefit of his people and their leaders. It was God's desire that the genuine needs of his people be satisfied though a relational network of caring leaders *and* that those leaders not burn out in the process (Ex. 18:23). It was a perfect plan conceived by a God who is concerned about *the way* that his mission is accomplished. This is because people are at the heart of the mission. People matter to God. And, therefore, people should matter to us too. If you are a godly leader, then you'll lead people in a way that pleases God.

LOVING PEOPLE IS THE MISSION

God's mission is planned (Ps. 33:11). There's nothing random about it. He knows the ultimate destination and he knows the right way to go about getting there. It's the way of love. It has to be that way because God is by nature love and his plans will be consistent with his nature (1 Jn. 4:8). Therefore, the right way of getting there is as important as the destination itself. These two things are divinely intertwined and you dare not separate things that God has joined together! God's loving plan for the people of Israel was that the ongoing needs of his people be met *while* the overall mission was being accomplished. It wasn't a case of one or the other. Moses didn't have to ask himself, "Do we care for people or do we get on with the mission?" He didn't have that option. And we don't either. People are the mission. God's intention is that we leaders care for the existing people entrusted to us *while* reaching ahead for more that he has in store. These things can and *should* happen concurrently.

We see these mutual objectives unified in the ministry and mission of Jesus. He genuinely cared for those around him, including his twelve disciple-leaders, while stretching forward to reach more people still (Mk. 1:38). In John's Gospel, Chapter 10, there's a passage which all Christian leaders should study. It's a passage in which Jesus teaches about the nature of spiritual leadership. The idea being explored is that of the strong bond between a leader and the people he or she leads. The imagery Jesus uses is that of a shepherd and his sheep. He is the shepherd, his people are his sheep. The good shepherd-leader, Jesus teaches, valiantly protects the sheep from trouble. He cares for the sheep. He's willing to put his life on the line for the people (Jn. 10:11). His people are enfolded in his care. Jesus is the definitive good shepherd-leader. His care for people is contrasted with bad shepherd-leaders who don't really care about those they lead. They run at the first sign of trouble or when they don't get what they want (Jn 10:12). Jesus, by contrast, sacrificially cared about those that were already entrusted to him. That's part of the message of the passage. The other

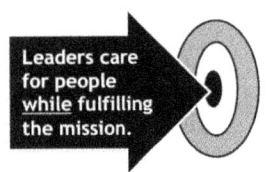
Leaders care for people while fulfilling the mission.

part consists of the reality that there were still *more* sheep out there. The mission wasn't complete. His care for those already in the 'sheep pen' did not lessen his concern for those he had yet to reach. Jesus resolved to reach them too. This objective is stated in verse sixteen where Jesus is quoted as saying, "I have other sheep that are not of this sheep pen. I must bring them also" (Jn. 10:16). This is, I believe, a defining verse for any mission leader. It keeps two important things together: we've got to love the people around us *as* we reach out to others in the hope of bringing them in. This is the way of Jesus. This is the way of love.

Unfortunately many senior Christian leaders *do* separate what God had joined together. They may not do this intentionally but this is what happens in practice. They either focus their love on the people in the church already *or* fixate on the mission to reach those outside. Let's consider a leader who emphasizes caring for the people around them at the expense of being on the wider mission. Leaders like this effectively scrub verse sixteen out of John, Chapter 10. To them, there are no "other sheep"! All their energy is dispensed on the people immediately around them on the 'inside'. They are happily occupied because God's people in their small circle still have needs to be met. Disturbingly, there's no love lost on people beyond those confines; there is for them no outreach mission. Many churches and missions have stagnated under a shepherd-leader who cares for their own to the exclusion of everyone else.

Other leaders make the opposite mistake. They are on a personal mission to reach *another* target group. To them, the insiders are invisible. Their sights are trained only on what is beyond. They don't really care too much about God's people unless they can be of use in accomplishing the outreach mission. God's people become 'mission-fodder'. It's a toxic situation. These kinds of leaders are careless shepherds. Driven-type personalities will really need to watch out for this. Of course, the above scenarios I've presented are the extremes. Nevertheless, leaders do tend to congregate at each end of the spectrum.

The Jethro Model keeps things in balance. The Jethro Mandate is healthy because it affirms that people matter along with accomplishing the overall mission. Every person matters. Relationships are vital. In Jethro's structure, as it was originally taught, everyone was to be intentionally connected through an organizational structure that valued individuals and leaders. This demonstrates to us that a management framework can and *ought* to be both rigorous *and* relational. These things are not mutually exclusive. God wants these things to coexist. We've already examined the organizational framework side of things. Now, I want to explore with you ways of maintaining the relational side of things. How can you ensure that the team you've recruited, and the people that you serve, are relating well *as* you press forward together on your mission? All that I will say here is premised on the conviction that

> **The Jethro Mandate is healthy because it affirms that people matter along with accomplishing the overall mission.**

the heart of the team is the strength of the team. You cannot *overestimate* the power of strong relationships in creating and maintaining a healthy team. Strong relationships encourage loyalty and longevity. And you shouldn't *underestimate* the significance of the team leader's role in shaping that heart. Here's a four-point 'to do' list that will make sure you get to the heart of things.

1) You've got to be there with the people that you lead and serve.

2) You've got to communicate.

3) You've got to create a sense of 'team'.

4) You've got to personally provide some pastoral care.

I'll present these things from a team leader's perspective, although I believe that every leader at every level will benefit from doing these things.

1 YOU'VE GOT TO BE THERE WITH THE PEOPLE THAT YOU LEAD AND SERVE

Nothing beats being with the people you love and lead with. You've got to be there with them and for them. I love the way the psalmist put it: "You led your people like a flock by the hand of Moses..." (Ps. 77:20). There's a personal directness about it. The leader was with his people. There are all sorts of reasons as to why a leader's presence is so powerful. For instance, it's probably the most intimate way of showing that these people matter to you. You're giving them precious gifts – the gift of your time, the gift of your attentiveness. Jesus, the definitive shepherd-leader, gave these gifts to his disciples. He spent three years in close contact with them. He was very accessible to them. There was a lot of direct interaction between them. Occasionally they did things separately, but mostly they were on the mission together. This is the ideal leadership environment, I think. Nothing strengthens the relational side of things more than regular, close interactivity. Being with the disciples was a priority for Christ and not just because of their future role in the Great Commission. Jesus loved them, for them! I imagine there was a lot of laughing, and we know there was a lot of learning. He wanted to be in their company. When his time to leave this world was approaching, Jesus said some things to reassure his disciples of this. John's Gospel records these words:

> "Do not let your hearts be troubled. Trust in God; trust also in me. In my Father's house are many rooms... I am going there to prepare a place for you... I will come back and take you to be with me that you also may be where I am" (Jn. 14:1-3).

When the team that you love and lead *knows* you like being with them, when they can see that is a priority for you, it makes a massive difference. Maybe you don't want to build a mansion and move in with them all right now, but they've got to know that you like serving alongside them. Nothing beats being there.

Being there has other benefits. A lot can be learned from just being around other leaders. We can teach each other as iron sharpens iron (Prov. 27:17). If you're a team leader, you've probably got a lot to offer. Others will learn from your example. The people you lead *will* be watching you!

> **Just as time spent with Jesus is the making of a spiritual leader, so people will learn a lot in the presence of a godly leader.**

I know I've learned a lot from being around outstanding leaders. This is often the best leadership school. It can exert an astonishing influence on people. Peter and John got their best tuition this way. They didn't go to Old Testament College or attend a formal leadership training school. They had simply been with Jesus. His influence on them was remarkable. They had learned to lead like him. They showed great poise under pressure. They had become outstanding leaders. This transformation was acknowledged by their opponents. In Acts, Chapter 4, the Bible gives an account of an occasion when Peter and John were hauled before the hostile religious leaders who had the power to beat them, imprison them or even sentence them to death. The religious leaders were intent on intimidating the two disciples so that they would stop talking about Jesus. But the disciples were not intimidated and responded assertively, stating their resolve to continue with the mission. The Bible says that, "When they saw the courage of Peter and John and realized that they were unschooled, ordinary men, they were astonished and they took note that these men had been with Jesus" (Acts 4:13). They had learned how to lead courageously from Jesus' example. Time spent with Jesus is the making of a spiritual leader. That's why reading the Bible, praying and remaining Christ-centered are absolutely essential for Christian leaders. And as you are shaped by Christ's example, so you will inevitably shape your team. People learn a lot in the presence of godly leaders.

Another benefit of being there is that you can see for yourself what's going on. When you're with people, you can see the problems and suggest solutions. There's no doubting that Moses benefitted from Jethro's first-hand observation. It was a game-changer. While Jethro was living back home in Midian, he could not have pictured the mess that Moses was in. Jethro heard things – the Bible says, "Now Jethro, the priest of Midian and father-in-law of Moses, heard of everything God had done for Moses" (Ex. 18:1) – and everything sounded good. However, when Jethro came to Moses in the desert and observed things directly, he saw the other side of the picture – "When his father-in-law saw all that Moses was doing for the people, he said, "What you are doing is not good"" (Ex. 18:14, 17). Being there made all the difference. Jethro surveyed the situation and then recommended a solution. He could not have done that from his armchair back in Midian. He was able to serve Moses directly because of his close proximity. Of course, when you're around, it's not just trouble that you're looking for. You will be looking out for the positives. You'll be constructive too. There will be many things that you can observe and commend people for. Don't miss those opportunities. The chapter on Rewarding will develop this idea further. When you're *there* to encourage people it will build great, relational rapport. That's a big part of a team leader's job. So, be there!

2 YOU'VE GOT TO COMMUNICATE

Good communication is essential for your team. Bad communication is detrimental to your team. Good communication brings clarity and cohesion to your team. Bad communication breeds confusion and conflict. Communication counts! The Bible highlights the negative and positive power of words (Jam. 3:2-6).

> **Leaders ought to be wise stewards of words. This takes great discipline but yields great rewards.**

Your success as a team leader will be greatly determined by the things you say. So, you've got to say things *well*! Let me be clear about what I'm going to concentrate on here. I'm going to restrict my advice on communication to words – written and spoken words. Communication of course encompasses a lot more than words; for example, we send powerful messages through our body language. Nevertheless, we'll consider how best to use words. I'm going to focus on the kind of intentional, word-based communication that brings clarity and cohesion to your team.

Words are a means by which we communicate ideas, instructions and questions (among other things). So, words are worthy of great respect. Of themselves, they are mostly benign, but when you put them together their impact can either be constructive or destructive. From a team perspective, they can create cohesion or cause conflict depending on how they are wielded. Therefore, leaders ought to be wise stewards of words. This takes great discipline but yields great rewards. Now, not every leader is linguistically gifted. Moses apparently wasn't. He could write, thank God – the beginning of the Bible is attributed to his quill (Deut. 31:24). But, he couldn't speak fluently for some reason (Ex. 4:10). Since good communication counts for so much, this was a legitimate impediment to Moses' role. But, God promised help and Moses received it (Ex. 4:15). This is something that you can pray for too. Ask God to help you be a great communicator.

If you think about it, you've already seen the value of words in the context of your team. Hopefully, this became increasingly obvious when you worked on your Mission Resolution and Role Descriptions. Mission Resolutions and Role Descriptions are forms of communication designed to bring clarity and cohesion to your team, and the more precise you are with the words you use to create them, the greater the possibility of comprehension on the part of all parties concerned. That *comprehension* will be essential to *cohesion*. If your Mission Resolution is arrow sharp, you and your team know exactly what you're aiming for. If your Role Descriptions are specific, everyone knows precisely what's expected and can get on with it. That's got to be good for your team! That's the power of words! Great discipline here will yield great rewards.

But, there will be other things to say and write. How should you approach them? One thing I've learned is to not say or write something important that's not first clear in my own mind. Good communication emanates from a good comprehension of what exactly it is you are trying to get across. If you're still confused about it, you'll just transmit your confusion if you start using words too soon. I like to write things down, wait a while, and then rewrite them until I'm clear in my own head about what it is I'm trying to say. Once I

The recipients have got to be able to comprehend your message to the extent that they can transmit it accurately to a wider audience.

think I have clarity, I'm ready to make an announcement. I'm also asking myself, 'How will my words be received and understood?' This is important because not only do I want the people I'm directly communicating with to understand what I'm saying, I will often want those people to pass the message on. This will be the case for you too. The recipients have got to be able to comprehend your message to the extent that they can accurately transmit it to a wider audience. If you get this right it will unlock a whole world of shared information. It will mean that there are increasing circles of common knowledge. This will act like glue for your team!

We see this 'transmittable idea' principle playing out in the way that The Jethro Mandate was communicated. Jethro advised Moses concerning a leadership structure that was ultimately authorized by God (Ex. 18:23-24). Moses then explained it to the people. This communication task was obviously successful because Moses confidently asserted, "I told you everything that you were to do" (Deut. 1:18). The clarity of that transmittable idea facilitated cohesion for the whole nation. Hopefully, you've grasped the importance of this, and if you do it well, then everybody will know what's going on. Of course, *The Resolute Leader* is an exercise in communication. Its success will be determined by people's ability to get hold of the ideas and put them into practice. I've designed The Jethro Model to be a transmittable idea. The book is intended to create a common pool of leadership principles and a shared leadership vocabulary.

Great leaders are also great listeners. Are you listening? Listening is a necessary element in the communication process. Not all the words need to come from you. Not all the good ideas need to come from you. They shouldn't. There needs to be a constant flow of communication between leaders. If you're a leader, you need to make sure you listen.

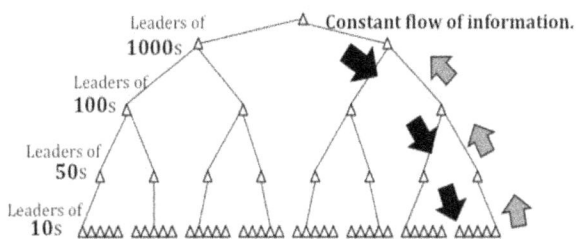

Moses, the greatest leader in the Old Testament, knew how to listen. He listened to God (Ex. 19:3), and to his father-in-law (Ex. 18:24), and his ears were also open to the concerns of the people (Deut. 1:17). Listening is an act of love. It's highly relational. Listening is an expression of concern and respect for those being listened to. It's a great way to communicate that you care. It also creates the kind of environment where the leadership load can be truly shared and problems referred on (Ex. 18:22). The effectiveness of The

Jethro Model depends on great communication. Have you been really listening to the people you lead with and serve?

I want to get really practical now. When it comes to communication, you've got to do well and do it *often*. How often? Here's a 'Communication Calendar' that works. Use it to stimulate your own thinking and planning.

1) **Weekly**. I want to suggest that you should communicate with your whole team once a week. This should be short and sharp. If it's too long people won't absorb it. It should be mostly 'need to know' stuff. Prepare your team for what is immediately ahead. Share encouraging stories. Is someone's birthday this week? Heard something funny? Keep your team *informed* and *inspired*.

2) **Monthly**. Every month you need to communicate more thoroughly. Report on progress towards your Mission Resolution. Share some helpful resources that will build the capacity of your team. Keep a strong stream of information flowing. Take the time to report on progress regarding your immediate Action Steps. Address a team-wide problem or potential problem (never use this as an opportunity to tackle something that should be done personally; Mat. 18:15-17).

3) **Annually**. In Chapter 9, I will encourage you to conduct annual reviews not only of team members but also of the whole mission that you are on. There needs to be an honest and in-depth appraisal of progress over the past year. Think of this as an Annual Report to your team. What were the highlights? What were the struggles? You should encourage input from the team in the preparation of your Annual Report. This is also a great opportunity to look forward to some of the big goals for the year ahead.

4) **Opportunely**. Fresh news is often the best news. Let your team be the first to know when something remarkable has happened. This could be in the case of a sudden crisis or a startling success. The immediacy of a 'News Flash' will keep your team up to speed.

5) **Feedback Channels**. Great communicators listen to those they lead and serve. As you communicate weekly, monthly, annually and opportunely, ensure that the recipients can respond as directly as possible. When you initiate communication it starts a conversation. Provide obvious and open channels for feedback.

Remember:
    Good communication is essential for your team.
    Bad communication is detrimental to your team.
    Good communication brings clarity and cohesion to your team.
    Bad communication breeds confusion and conflict.

Find the right words and say them at the right time. Be disciplined in your communication. Create an annual Communication Calendar. Words are your most precious commodity in communication. Make sure you use yours wisely. They can be like glue when it comes to team building and bonding.

3 YOU'VE GOT TO CREATE A SENSE OF 'TEAM'

It ought to mean something to be part of your team. There ought to be some real solidarity. Great teams feel almost tribal. Team leaders are responsible for creating a sense of team. They need to create a culture of belonging. When you do this, others will sense this and want to be part of the action. How can you bond individuals in such a way that they work with and for each other? Here are four team-builders to stimulate your thinking.

Firstly, teams bond around a compelling mission. Your team should know that they are making a difference, changing lives and shaping destinies. Your Mission Resolution ought to have a galvanizing effect. You ought to be heading towards that 'Promised Land' *together*. When you have compelling Mission Resolution it will help unite your team around a common Cause. Of course, when you're traversing the desert on the way to the Promised Land it can be a grind. Not every week on mission is an adrenalin rush. Jethro heard about the tribes of Israel including "everything the LORD had done to Pharaoh and the Egyptians for Israel's sake *and about all the hardships*" (Ex. 18:8). Moses and the people of God had many long-haul days in the desert. Your team will go through times when it feels like that. But there should be a deep-down conviction that 'we are going to get through this together and we *will* reach God's goal'. A team leader needs to exemplify this resolve. It will strengthen the heart of your team! And, as I've said, the heart of the team is the strength of the team.

Another way to engender a sense of team is to turn *adversity* to *advantage*. A bad experience can be a bonding experience. The hardships we go through can be a godsend. Israel's exodus and wilderness experiences created a national bond. They were melded together in that fiery desert heat. The same thing can happen to a team. Relationships can be fortified by the fires of adversity. A team can acquire a steely resolve to work for each other and for the success of the mission. The determination of the early Thessalonian Christians to keep sharing the gospel despite severe opposition epitomizes this. The Apostles Paul wrote of them, "in spite of severe suffering you welcomed the message with the joy given by the Holy Spirit. And so you became a model to all the believers in Macedonia and Achaia. The Lord's message rang out from you not only in Macedonia and Achaia – your faith in God has become known everywhere" (1 Thes. 1:6-8). I imagine that when Paul wrote those words he had goose bumps. It's a great example of unity in adversity. The challenges they faced steeled their resolve and supercharged the mission. A challenging experience can be the making of a team.

> **A bad experience can be a bonding experience.**

A third way to promote solidarity in your team is to celebrate the differences. If you've been creative in designing your team and have been recruiting accordingly, you're going to have an interesting mix of people on your team. Those people will likely possess different gifts and skill sets, different personality profiles and different backgrounds. The Mission Resolution may well be the only thing that brought this diverse group of people together. Well, Viva la Difference! Those differences will bring their challenges but also vitalize your team. Celebrate those differences. "Make every effort to keep the unity of the Spirit through the bond of peace" (Eph. 4:3). Honor each contribution. Don't show preferences (Deut. 1:16-17). Here are 4 practical ways to celebrate the differences:

1) Do a personality profiling exercise that helps team members better understand themselves and those they serve alongside.
2) Share hospitality. We tend to appreciate people more when we've spent quality time with them over a meal or a cup of coffee.
3) Ask each team member to share an appreciation story that commends someone in a role that's different from their own.
4) Allow room for different people to share their particular slant on things. Use that different perspective as a catalyst for team discussion. Different ideas won't diminish your mission but narrow thinking will. Not every idea needs to be incorporated but all should be considered.

I suggest that you plan at least one major team-building exercise each year.

A fourth way to build a team involves doing intentional team-building exercises. These can be simple and informal or adventurous and intense. There are many easy-to-do team-building games and exercises that are readily available. If time and money are in good supply then there are many adventure-style, day or weekend packages that your team can participate in (things ranging from canoeing and gentle hiking, to paintball and boot-camps). Find something appropriate *that you can all do*. If someone can't possibly participate in a team-building exercise then it diminishes the value of the process. Intentional team-building exercises will help your team bond. I suggest that you plan at least one major team-building exercise each year.

Unity in diversity is what God desires. A team leader is responsible for team cohesion.

 # 4 YOU'VE GOT TO PERSONALLY PROVIDE SOME PASTORAL CARE

As I wrote at the top of this chapter, people always matter to God. Therefore, people should matter to us too. The Bible says, "You [God] led your people like a flock by the hand of Moses..." (Ps. 77:20) [Emphasis added]. Moses' leadership directly expressed God's personal care. Spiritual leaders should reflect God's love. After all, we lead *on God's behalf*. We find this charge to be 'under-shepherds' (of the Chief Shepherd, Jesus) in the New Testament. The Apostle Peter wrote:

> "Be shepherds of God's flock that is under your care, serving as overseers... not lording it over those entrusted to you, but being examples to the flock. And when the Chief Shepherd appears, you will receive the crown of glory that will never fade away" (1 Pet. 5:2-4).

Spiritual leadership is spiritual care. That's why as a team leader, you've got to provide some pastoral care. It should be on your 'to do' list not because you must, but because you are willing. How can you practically provide some pastoral care? The size of your team and the nature of your mission will largely determine *how* you provide care and *who* you personally care for.

Here's what I mean. Let's say you lead a team of musicians and singers who lead worship on Sunday mornings. If that team consists of up to twenty people, then it would be reasonable to expect that you could offer some direct, basic pastoral care to all your team members. I'm not suggesting high-level, crisis care here. There should be other people in your church who have that role. I have in mind some of the more common problems and burdens that people experience from time to time. That sort of pastoral care should be both manageable and sustainable. If, however, you lead the team that oversees pastoral care for the *whole church*, then the expectations would be very different. If the congregation consists of more than one hundred and fifty people, then you couldn't possibly offer personal pastoral care to everyone. That would be unmanageable and unsustainable. Most of us don't have the kind of capacity that is required to lovingly deal with the problems, burdens and disputes of that many people. We all have our limitations. As a team leader, you need to approach the pastoral care challenge with a purposeful and practical plan. If you don't, people will either miss out or you will burn out. It's that simple.

Moses tried providing pastoral care for every individual in Israel and he almost burned out in the process. It proved to be impractical, and impeded the mission. Even Jesus, while he was

> **The Jethro Mandate is, at heart, a system of pastoral care.**

on earth, couldn't attend to every need (Mk. 1:37). He was limited to time and space just as we are. There are two, similar pastoral strategies that will help you use your limited time and energy most effectively to deliver pastoral care. The first strategy that I will set out comes from the example of Jesus. The second strategy is the one that Jethro transmitted to Moses. The Jethro Mandate is, at heart, a system of pastoral care.

Jesus, during his time in this world, had human limitations. He had limited time and energy. He could only be in one place at one time. His circumstances were much like our own. Yet he really cared about *all* his 'sheep', including the ones he was yet to bring in (Jn. 10:16).

He was truly called the Good Shepherd and he fittingly bears the title of 'Chief Shepherd' (1 Pet. 5:4). So, *who* did Jesus give pastoral care to, given the limitations of his humanity? And what could we learn from that that could help us construct our own pastoral care strategy? What we learn from the Gospels and the Book of Acts is that Jesus provided pastoral care and leadership within four, general yet identifiable circles. We read that Jesus concentrated extra time and energy on three disciples who appear to have been closest to him – Peter, James and John (e.g. Mat. 17:1). We'll call them 'the circle of three'.

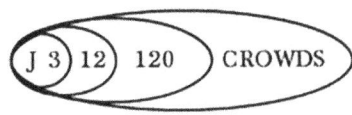

Beyond (though including) those three, Jesus spent the bulk of his three ministry years with the twelve disciples – 'the circle of twelve'. Further out from 'the twelve', we read about a group of people loosely numbered between seventy (Lk. 10:1) and one hundred and twenty (Acts 1:15). We can't be sure who all these people were, but probably people like Mary, Martha and Lazarus were numbered in 'the circle of one hundred and twenty' (Jn. 11:1-3). Further out, receiving less personal and ongoing attention from Jesus, were 'the crowds' (Jn. 6:5). The people in crowds were, nevertheless, recipients of his care.

What we observe is this: Jesus invested heavily in the circle of three. They were a special focus of his care and concern. Then, it was the twelve. Outside of those inner circles, his interactions with people became increasingly intermittent. It wasn't that Jesus cared *less* for those in the crowds. His love is limitless! But his relational space during his life on earth was limited. That's just the reality of the situation that we find ourselves in. Love might have no limits, but life practically demands them. The Chief Shepherd's strategy in managing his relationships was to draw some lines around all the people he loved. The smallest circles received the largest input. That was the strategy. It's as simple as that. No doubt he prayed for wisdom as to the right people to include in those smaller circles (Lk. 6:12-16). I'm sure that discernment was still required as those circles got bigger. But he cared enough to make the choices and he went deep with those people closest to him.

This, I believe, is an excellent pastoral care framework for a team leader. It's a valuable exercise to actually draw those circles and place some appropriate names within them. This framework offers a mechanism whereby you can deliver strategic, manageable and meaningful levels of pastoral leadership. Your leadership and care strategy will then reflect something of Jesus' own approach. You'll be following the example of Jesus.

The second pastoral care strategy is the one that Jethro transmitted to Moses. Allow me to reiterate: The Jethro Model is, at heart, a system of pastoral care (Ex. 18:23). It's designed to help every person by providing access to different levels of pastoral expertise. Simple problems can be easily handled by most leaders. The higher level leaders will be able to offer higher levels of pastoral care. The most intense, difficult pastoral problems are meant to be handled by senior leaders (Ex. 18:22). The Jethro Model helps people access appropriate levels of care. The team leader who really cares will champion the implementation of this system. Here's how it can look if you implement The Jethro Model.

The model below illustrates what a pastoral care leadership structure might look like if care was being provided for three hundred people. In accordance with The Jethro Model, people who care for ten or so people would be supported by people who oversee fifty, and so on. The leaders in the upper tiers provide personal care and support for those below them and they also handle the difficult problems that are referred up to them.

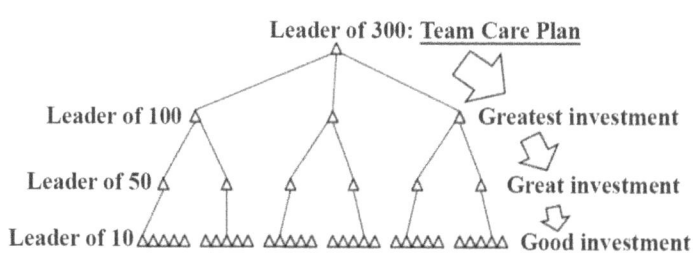

Thinking about this with Jesus' model in mind, the team leader (in this case, the overseer of three hundred people) would probably include the three leaders of one hundred in their 'circle of three'. It is reasonable to expect that they would recieve the greatest investment from the overall leader. Following this line of logic through, the leaders of fifty would recieve a great level of personal investment from the overall team leader (similar to Jesus' 'circle of twelve'). The 'circle of investment' necessarily widens from there. One way or another, The Jethro Model is totally scaleable: if you are leading a team of five on a mission that reaches one hundred people, or if you are leading a team of fifty to reach one thousand people, the principles are the same. With good planning, this organizational structure can provide care for the crowds *and also* for the leaders.

So, incorporate these care concepts into your team structure. Find an arrangement that works for you and your team. Make team care part of your team culture. Understand that, as team leader, you have to provide some

Make team care part of your team culture.

pastoral care! You have to do this personally and sustainably. If the team that you lead is smaller, then you can probably care for everyone on an individual basis. If your team is large, then you'll need a strategy and structure to ensure that care is provided for everyone concerned. Jesus' model and The Jethro Model show the way. This will mean that you will have to make choices concerning the levels of care that you give to different people. Some people find this strategy a little harsh and these choices hard. At some point, nevertheless, you need to reckon with the realities of your human limitations just as Jesus did. In the Implementation Elevators section you will go through the exercise of deciding what level of care you will provide for the people you lead and serve. Remember: love has no limits *but you do*. Plan your pastoral care strategy.

SUMMARY

So here is a four-point 'to do' list that will help make sure your team relationships are healthy and helpful:

>1) be there with your team;
>
>2) communicate well and often;
>
>3) create a sense of 'team';
>
>4) provide pastoral care.

 *Implementation Elevators*

EXERCISE # 1

Where would you plot yourself on the continuum below?

I tend to focus on the people already around me. *I tend to focus on the mission in front of me.*

◄───►

At the start of this chapter, I suggested that there are different challenges for leaders at each end of the spectrum. Given where you have plotted yourself on the line above, reflect on those approaches and attitudes that might need to be monitored or even adjusted.

REFLECTION QUESTIONS

Why is it important to be with the people you lead and serve?

What does this mean practically for a team leader? How will you do this?

EXERCISE # 2: CREATE A COMMUNICATION CALENDAR

- ❏ I have a plan for my weekly communication.
- ❏ I have a plan for my monthly communication.
- ❏ I have a plan for my annual communication.

REFLECTION QUESTIONS

If you lead a team right now, what rating out of 10 (10 being the highest and best) would you give for 'team cohesion'?

What would help your team bond more?

EXERCISE # 3: DEVISE A TEAM–BUILDING STRATEGY FOR THE YEAR

Plan your team–building strategy with reference to the following questions:

1) Is your mission clear and compelling enough to unite your team?

2) Is there an adversity that you can turn into an advantage?

3) How can you accentuate the positive aspects of your team's diversity?

4) What intentional team-building exercises will you do this year?

EXERCISE # 4: MAKE A DIAGRAM OF YOUR APPROACH TO PROVIDING PASTORAL CARE

Use the diagrams below to help you determine who you will invest in, and in what measure. Put names or roles in the circles or on the levels. Think about how that will play out in practical terms.

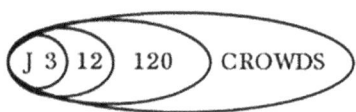

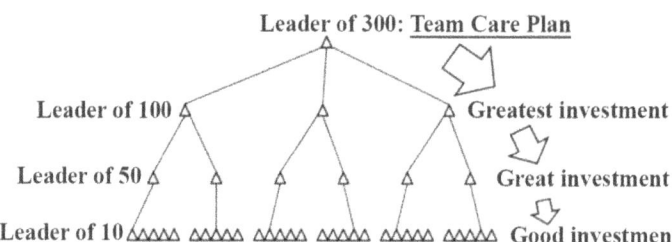

Chapter 7 REWARDING

Encourage him

(Deuteronomy 3:28)

Rewarding
Relationships
Recruiting
Roles
Resolution

By now, you're well and truly underway. The mission is clear, roles have been described, people have been recruited for those roles, and you're relating well together. Perhaps, you're already experiencing some success. The people you serve are generally satisfied. You and the team are meeting their needs. The leaders you are serving with are standing the strain. So far so good! You're finding that you are enjoying what you're doing. Your rigor in systematically building up The Jethro Model, level by level, is paying off! You can see for yourself how it builds clarity, cohesion and the capacity to care for people. Hopefully, it has been a rewarding experience for you as the team leader. It should also be a rewarding journey for your team.

A lot of the rewards that people receive while doing God's work are intrinsic. Most of the people who are serving with you on your mission are volunteers. They're certainly not doing it for the money! They are doing it because the mission is compelling. God has called them to it and they know he will reward them for it. They are serving because it's spiritually satisfying; they are making a difference; meeting some sort of important need. So their motivation is essentially spiritual and altruistic. That can be reward enough. Nevertheless, you need to demonstrate your gratitude to the people who serve on your team. Those amazing people who are fulfilling such important roles deserve to be appropriately rewarded for their contributions. So do that! And as you honor people for their hard work it will build esteem – esteem in the individual and esteem in the team. This will boost morale and motivation. Some people think that the recognition and rewarding of people's efforts is unspiritual. They think that it's just a human, motivational technique. They think, 'We do it for God and that should be reward enough'. I agree that offering your service to God *is* the main thing. But, there's much more to it than that. We see this time and again in the Bible. Great team leaders openly acknowledge the great contributions of others. They find creative ways of honoring contributors tangibly. There are many ways that you can and should reward your team. We'll explore the main ones in this chapter. But first, let's reflect on the fact that when we reward people we are following a practice exemplified by God himself.

THE GOD WHO REWARDS

God is the great Rewarder. He recognizes and rewards faithful service. God will not miss the opportunity to give credit where credit is due. This is an expression of his love for us and his appreciation for the work we do for him. He has given us a role in his mission and will reward us according to the *quality* of our contribution. That's why the principles in *The Resolute Leader* are important; things like knowing your God-given mission, fulfilling your role, building capacity and leading with love. The levels and principles in this book will help improve the build-

> **God will reward us according to the quality of our contribution. *The Resolute Leader* will help improve the build-quality of your life's work.**

quality of your life's work. You will be eternally grateful! Think about this in the light of 1 Corinthians 3:10-14:

> "By the grace God has given me, I [Paul] laid a foundation as an expert builder, and someone else is building on it. But each one should be careful how he builds. For no one can lay any foundation other than the one already laid, which is Jesus Christ. If a man builds on this foundation using gold, silver, costly stones, wood, hay or straw, his work will be shown for what it is, because the Day [of Judgment and Reward] will bring it to light. It will be revealed with fire, and the fire will test the quality of each man's work. If what he builds survives, he will receive his reward [from God]." [Emphasis added]

We all want to receive a reward. We all want to have something to show for the life we've lived; something to carry with us into eternity. We aspire to hear the Master's ultimate commendation, "Well done, good and faithful servant! You have been faithful with a few things; I will put you in charge of many things. Come and share your master's happiness!" (Mat. 25:21). In eternity, we will enjoy God's reward. The rewards for faithful service are not, however, only reserved for the next life. God rewards his people in this life in various ways. Caleb, one of the faithful spies sent out by Moses, was rewarded with a large land-holding because he followed God wholeheartedly (Josh. 14:9). In the New Testament, Jesus gave assurance that his disciples will be more than compensated for the price they pay when following Jesus on his mission. Jesus said:

> "no one who has left home or brothers or sisters or mother or father or children or fields for me and the gospel will fail to receive a hundred times as much in this present age (homes brothers, sisters, mothers, children and fields – and with them, persecutions) and in the age to come, eternal life" (Mk. 10:29-30).

Those rewards might be tangible or intangible. The blessings might be material or spiritual in nature. But they are rewards nonetheless! God looks for every opportunity to express gratitude. The Bible says, "The eyes of the LORD range throughout the earth to strengthen those whose hearts are fully committed to him" (2 Chr. 16:9). Nothing will be overlooked. Not a word of comfort or a cup of water will be missed. Jesus said, "I tell you the truth, anyone who gives you a cup of water in my name because you belong to Christ will certainly not lose his reward" (Mk. 9:41). God is the great Rewarder.

HOW TO REWARD THE PEOPLE

When we reward people we reflect the heart of God. We need to look for every opportunity to do this. Our eyes should be searching for an opportunity to encourage. So, in what ways can we reward people? I think there at least are four excellent ways to express our appreciation for a job well done. Here they are.

1 WORDS OF COMMENDATION

We've already considered the power of words in Chapter 6. Words have great impact. They can be very constructive. Think about some of the positive things that people have said about you. Consider what those words have meant to you and the positive impact that they've had. Reflect on the way those words have motivated you. Those words have yielded great reward in your life, haven't you? Jesus said, "Do to others as you would have them do to you" (Lk. 6:31). Make sure you say things that will be rewarding to others.

Every leader is a steward of words. The people who respect you will pay close attention to what you say. Your words carry weight. People take your words to heart. Your commendation, written or spoken, will be of great encouragement.

> **You might *think* someone's doing a great job. That's good for you. But when you *tell them* they are doing a great job, it's good for them!**

It will lift esteem. The commendation will generate feelings of satisfaction. So, don't just think it, say it! You might *think* someone's doing a great job. That's good for you. But when you *tell them* they are doing a great job, it's good for them! You don't have to over-do it, just don't under-do it! The Apostle Paul made a habit of listing people worthy of 'special mention' at the end of his letters. Here are some examples:

> "I commend to you our sister Phoebe, a servant of the church in Cenchrea. I ask you to receive her in the Lord in a way worthy of the saints and to give her any help she may need from you, for she has been a great help to many people, including me" (Rom. 16:1-2).

And then there's:

> "You know that the household of Stephanas were the first converts in Achaia, and they have devoted themselves to the service of the saints. I urge you, brothers, to submit to such as these and to everyone who joins in the work, and labors at it" (1 Cor. 16:15-16).

And, what about this one:

> "I hope in the Lord Jesus to send Timothy to you... I have no one else like him, who takes a genuine interest in your welfare... you know that Timothy has proved himself... he has served with me in the work of the gospel" (Phil. 2:19-22).

Paul didn't hold back. He gave credit where credit was due. He wrote down these commendations in letters that were widely circulated and eventually incorporated in the Bible. So, don't miss the opportunity to praise the people around you. Here are the kinds of things I look out for:

C aring for people
O n time
M ajor successes
M inor successes
E xtra-mile effort
N ew ideas
D iligence
A ttitude
T eamwork
I nitiative
O wning mistakes
N ever giving up!

Some people do this so naturally.

Barnabas' Story

Joseph was a Cypriot and a Levite who knew how to encourage people. It was in his nature. He was the type of person who saw the best in people (Acts 15:37-38). He endorsed Paul when many were uncertain of his credentials (Acts 11:25-26). I think he would have been the kind of guy who noticed the great things that other people were doing and praised them for it. His reputation for seeing the good in people was such that the apostles gave him the nickname 'Barnabas'; which means Son of Encouragement (Acts 4:36). Being around Barnabas would have been a rewarding experience.

We all need to be more like him. Some people even have the prophetic gift of encouragement (1 Cor. 14:3). But even if you're not so good at commending people right now, don't make the mistake of thinking that it doesn't matter or that it's someone else's role. If you are a team leader you have got to *become* good at this. It's a skill that can be learned. Perhaps you could start by keeping the 'CHARACTER' list handy (from Chapter 5) and practice becoming *attentive* to the great things that your team is doing and being *active* in telling them so. An excellent way of rewarding people is through words of commendation. And next, there's celebration!

2 CELEBRATION

Celebrate the good things! There are all sorts of good things to cheer about. It might be 'mission accomplished'; a strategic goal reached; a significant breakthrough; a victory; someone becoming a Christian; or surviving another year! There are so many reasons to thank God and let your hair down. The people of Israel knew how to party. They sometimes wrote songs especially for the occasion. In the early stage of the Exodus, the Israelites were being hotly pursued by the Egyptian army. They came to the edge of the Red Sea and the Egyptians were behind them and closing in. The Sea had halted their progress forward and all seemed lost. But, God miraculously parted the waters to let them through and they safely crossed over to the other side. There, from the safety of the shoreline, they watched their bitter enemies drown when God caused the water to close back in. To the Egyptian army it would have seemed like two massive storm-surges converged on them from opposite directions. It was a great victory for God's people. It was party time! Out came the tambourines and the women started dancing. [That apparently, made for a good time back then.] Even Moses sang a song (Ex. 15:1). That worries me a little because he admitted he couldn't speak very well, so what made him think he could sing! Anyway, the point is they didn't miss the opportunity to celebrate.

Heaven knows how to party! In a series of parables recorded in Luke 14, Jesus emphasized the point that when lost people are found, heaven celebrates. He said:

> "There is rejoicing in the presence of the angels of God over one sinner who repents" (Lk. 15:10).

> "Quick! Bring the best robe and put it on him. Put a ring on his finger and sandals on his feet. Bring the fattened calf and kill it. Let's have a feast and celebrate. For this son of mine was dead and is alive again; he was lost and is found... near the house he heard music and dancing" (Lk. 15:22-25).

Maybe tambourines and dancing aren't your thing. Maybe you'd prefer to crack open a fizzy can rather than kill a fattened calf when you feel like celebrating something good. Whatever way you want to do it, celebrate with your team. It will be a rewarding experience. The alternative isn't very exciting. It can be pretty *unrewarding* for a team, if meeting blends into meeting, week into week and year into year, and all that the team leader ever talks about is what's got to be done next. Don't be so locked into the future that you overlook the current successes. Sometimes the good things going on just seem to get breezed over. It's very de-motivating. Learn how to celebrate the moment. Think about some reasons why you could host a party for your team. Here are some great reasons for a celebration that will stimulate your own thinking:

C risis averted!
E vangelistic success
L aughter is just plain good for you
E veryone has a birthday
B reakthrough moments
R etiring team member
A nother leader joins the team
T arget is reached
E nd of another great year

So, bake a cake, crack open some cans, crank up the music, go out for a meal, hold a party, have tea and coffee or whatever. Just don't let all those great moments go past without saying 'thanks' to God and to each other. These sorts of celebrations are memory-makers, morale-boosters, God-moments, team-builders, and they will remind people of all those things that make being part of this team so rewarding. So ask yourself, "What can we celebrate?"

3 EXPANDED OPPORTUNITY

Another way of rewarding a faithful leader is to expand their leadership opportunities. This could be thought of as a kind of leadership promotion. They will be given the opportunity to increase their sphere of influence. This is a fitting reward for faithful, effective service as is illustrated by the parable that Jesus told concerning a good and faithful servant: "You have been faithful with a few things; I will put you in charge of many things" (Mat. 25:21). Moses learned to be faithful in the small things too. This was part of his divine preparation for the task of leading Israel.[15] Proven perseverance and productiveness precede promotion.

If we think about the Jethro structure, with its layers of leaders, it's not hard to imagine what the promotion system may have looked like back in that day. As the first generation died in the desert new leaders would have been raised up (Num. 32:13). An emerging leader might have been entrusted with the responsibility of leading and caring for ten people. If he did this satisfactorily, he might have been entrusted with responsibility for fifty people. If he proved faithful and capable at that level, his opportunities could have been expanded to oversee hundreds or, maybe, even thousands of people. For a capable and energetic leader, this increasing authority and responsibility would have been a rewarding experience. The expanding opportunities would have been stretching and stimulating. Conversely, being perpetually locked in at the level of leading ten would have had a retarding effect on his development and mindset. The same principle applies today. I know myself, that I have appreciated expanded opportunities and leadership responsibilities.

Proven perseverance and productiveness precede promotion.

My Story

Within the movement that I'm a part of (Queensland Baptists in Australia), I've been given an increasing sphere of influence. Initially, I was offered the opportunity of coordinating the Pastors in my local area. As a result of my service there, I was invited to take up a role on the Board of Queensland Baptists. This involved leadership-oversight of one hundred and eighty churches that cared for something like twenty-eight thousand people. After some years, I was invited to be the Chairman the Board. This involved chairing meetings involving hundreds of people. I've not taken this lightly. But, I've appreciated the stretching and stimulation that have accompanied these leadership roles.

There are people around you who will find bigger challenges very rewarding. Don't withhold that from them. Give them a greater opportunity to lead.

So, how do you know if someone's ready for an expanded opportunity? I think you're looking for someone who is succeeding. Often, it's just obvious. The things that God will be doing through that leader will make the decision easy. The people they are serving will be super-satisfied with their lead. You can tell that God has a great sphere of influence in store for them. They are easily coping with their current role. Sometimes, God will do something amazing through an up-and-coming leader that proves to be a leadership turning point. As a result of a spiritual achievement of some magnitude, people's respect for that leader will go through the roof. People will be convinced that that leader is worth following! This was the case for both Moses and Joshua. God did things through them for the purpose of winning the allegiance of the people. He exalted those leaders in the eyes of the people.

Joshua's Story

The crossing of the Jordan River was a defining moment in Joshua's leadership journey. Moses was dead and the people were looking at Joshua and wondering if he had the credentials to take them forward. As God's people were preparing to cross the river, the Lord said to Joshua, "Today I will begin to exalt you in the eyes of all Israel, so they may know that I am with you as I was with Moses" (Josh. 3:7). Well, it took an action step of faith, but God parted the waters of the Jordan River and the people went across. What was the outcome of all that for Joshua? The Bible reports, "That day the LORD exalted Joshua in the sight of all Israel; and they revered him all the days of his life, just as they had revered Moses" (Josh. 4:14).

> **When you believe in someone enough to give them a chance to shine brighter it just may prove to be the making of that leader.**

So, God made it clear to everyone that Joshua was ready for the big lead. It was time for him to step up to the front. A little support in the background didn't go astray though. Moses had encouraged him back in the early days (Deut. 1:38; 3:28). And a little encouragement from you could go a long way in helping another leader realize their full potential. Maybe someone in your team would like to have a bigger lead but they are too humble to push themselves forward. They are waiting and wanting you to give them your blessing. They want you to show faith in them. They want *your* encouragement. When you believe in someone enough to give them a chance to shine brighter it just may prove to be the making of that leader. Who knows what they may go on to do? And, one day, when you look back on their life's leadership legacy, how rewarding will it be to think that your encouragement expanded their opportunities. So, who around you deserves the reward of a bigger sphere of influence?

In most team situations, commendations, celebrations and expanding opportunities will be reward enough for the people involved in your mission. But there is one other reward worthy of mention – a resource boost.

4 A RESOURCE BOOST

A resource boost is a reward distributed at the discretion of a senior leader or leaders. By 'resource boost' I mean the deployment of *extraordinary* resources to a team that is experiencing unusual success. In some cases a resource boost might even be given to a team member who is like a Joshua in their generation. The resources deployed might include more money, extra people-support, extra promotional opportunities and extra investment from the senior leadership group. The circumstances will dictate this. This sort of reward is worth considering although it can be a controversial one. There are some challenging implications to this. A resource boost will usually require the *redirection* of precious resources from somewhere else. There's the crunch! This is where all sorts of misunderstandings can occur. The extraordinary rewarding of one area through the redirecting of resources can be interpreted as penalizing the sources from which those resources came. This can easily be the perception though nothing of the kind is intended.

> **A 'resource boost' is the deployment of *extraordinary* resources to a team member, team or mission that is experiencing unusual success.**

Resources are always finite. In miracle situations you might have more than enough but this is not normally the case. Let's take the time and attention of a senior leader by way of example. A senior leader can only be in one place at one time. In the days of the New Testament Apostles, having an apostle around would have been a huge boost (Acts 4:33)! The apostles were THE senior leaders of the church. But even they couldn't have been everywhere at once. Now, think about this – God had to deploy his apostolic resources strategically. Some cities received the Apostle Paul's ministry, some cities missed out. The Spirit of God prevented Paul from entering Bithynia even as the door to Macedonia was opened (Acts 16:6-10). What a beginning for the church in Europe! I assume that the opportunities in Macedonia and Greece were such that, from God's perspective, Paul's time was best spent there. I make this assumption based on another account in the Book of Acts. There it is recorded that God spoke to Paul in a vision and encouraged him to stay in Corinth (Southern Greece). "I have many people in this city", he said (Acts 18:10). The Bible says that Paul stayed on for a year and a half, teaching them the word of God (Acts 18:11).

The city of Corinth received an extraordinary proportion of Paul's time (a year and a half!) because many people would be won to faith there. God deployed Paul in that one place, for all that time, *because* his ministry would experience unusual numerical success *there* and *then*. The circumstances dictated this. This was the expedient thing to do. The city of

Corinth received a timely boost of apostolic resources. Consequently, other people and places missed out, but they were not being penalized. It was just that the limited resources had to be used optimally. That is how the principle of a 'resource boost' plays out in the Bible. It will also play out in your own local church. It certainly has in the churches that I have led.

A Local Church's Story

Northreach Baptist Church's buildings stand on eight acres of land in the Australian tropics. During the summer Wet Season, the grass grows fast! Managing a property of this size is very demanding. It takes many hours of work each week just to keep the grass under control, not to mention all the other tasks like gardening and maintaining the car parks. So, when it came to Budget time we included a line-item that provided a salary for a part-time grounds-person to undertake the major maintenance of the property. When the allocation of funds for this purpose was presented to our Board, the Leader in charge of the grounds enthusiastically endorsed the proposal! That was understandable. I'm sure the whole grounds team breathed a collective sigh of relief. In six months, they anticipated, there would be someone employed to do the majority of this work.

In the meantime, however, our Children's ministry experienced a period of extraordinary growth that showed no signs of slowing up. In fact, it became apparent that the growth trajectory was excitingly steep! God was moving in the lives of children in our church. From a senior leadership perspective, this was something that required extra resources as soon as possible. These resources had to come from somewhere. During one of our Senior Leadership meetings it was recommended that:

> *Due to the rapid growth of Children's ministry, the allocated funding to the budget for a part-time grounds-person be re-prioritized for the purpose of employing a part-time Children's Ministry Coordinator.*

Now, as you can imagine, the grounds leader and team were probably not as enthusiastic about this decision as the Children's Ministry team obviously were. Thankfully, those people working hard to look after the property could see the bigger picture. They were better able to come to terms with this decision for reasons that I will set out below. It was the right decision to give the Children's Ministry the resource boost even though it came at the expense of much-anticipated support for the grounds team. We were not penalizing them. We just needed to re-prioritize the resources because of the extraordinary success of the Children's ministry.

If you are a church leader or a mission team leader, you will occasionally need to make controversial decisions. One of them will be to redeploy resources according to the principle of *maximum effectiveness* rather than strict *democratic 'fairness'*. Paul didn't spend equal amounts of time with every person in every place. Sometimes you have to make a decision that closes the door for someone or something even as it opens the door for another. If you are a church Pastor or part of the senior leadership team you will regularly need to make decisions like these. To distribute resources equally everywhere, with no consideration of their optimal use, is simply leadership weakness and/or laziness. Budget setting time ought to at least raise the tension levels with reference to the 'resource boost' principle. Senior leaders need to ask, 'What people and teams need rewarding because God is doing extraordinary things through them?' And you need to make strategic decisions with regard to the distribution of the limited resources that God has entrusted to you.

> **To distribute resources equally everywhere, with no consideration of their optimal use, is simply leadership weakness and/or laziness.**

CHAPTER SUMMARY

Serving on a ministry team ought to be a rewarding experience. Team leaders need to do all that they can to ensure that this is the case. Any rewarding that we do is only a reflection of God's own desire to reward his faithful servants. For the members of the team that you lead, many of the rewards will be intangible. Nevertheless, there are a number of ways that you can express your appreciation for all that they do. They are:

1) Words of Commendation.

2) Celebrating the Wins!

3) Expanded Opportunity for an Effective Leader.

4) A Resource Boost.

My advice is, never miss an opportunity to express your appreciation for those who lead well. This will ensure that serving on your team is a very rewarding experience.

 *Implementation Elevators*

FOR REFLECTION

God rewards *everything* that we do for him. How does that motivate you? In what ways has God rewarded you already?

Think about some of the most memorable commendations that you have received and how that encouraged you. Imagine how your commendations could encourage others.

EXERCISE # 1: PRACTICING THE ART OF COMMENDATION

How readily do you offer encouragement to others? Where are you positioned on the continuum below?

I rarely encourage other people. *I am constantly rewarding people for commendable actions and attitudes.*

◄─────────────────────────────────►

What habits could move you further towards the right end of the continuum?

Who could you commend right now?

How could you appropriately express your appreciation for their actions and/or attitudes?

EXERCISE # 2: PLANNING TO CELEBRATE

What does success look like for your team and mission? What will be the milestones that you can celebrate? What will you do when you reach those significant markers? This would be a great topic for team discussion!

Find out how your team likes to celebrate. Think about things like timing, location and atmosphere. Spontaneity is great. Nevertheless, pre-plan whenever you can. This will go a long way to ensuring that the experience is rewarding.

EXERCISE # 3: IDENTIFYING A LEADER WHO'S READY TO BE REWARDED BY GREATER OPPORTUNITY.

Some leaders want to be rewarded with the opportunity to have an increased sphere of influence. How do you evaluate whether a person is primed for such an opportunity? Proven perseverance and productiveness precede promotion! I've listed below the indicators that I look for. My confidence concerning a leader's readiness for an expanded opportunity depends on how I rate them against these 6 criteria. So, when considering someone for a greater leadership role, go through this exercise of rating them out of 10 (10 being excellent) in each area. Add any other relevant measure specific to your context.

Shade in their scores. This will help you better 'see' the suitability of a person for a bigger role.

	1	2	3	4	5	6	7	8	9	10
#1 Are they faithful in things big and small?										
#2 Are they persistent and consistent?										
#3 Are they successful in their present role?										
#4 Are they easily coping with the responsibility?										
#5 Do they have a holy ambition for a bigger lead?										
#6 Are the people that they are leading and serving satisfied with their performance?										

REFLECTION QUESTIONS: IS THERE A CASE FOR A RESOURCE BOOST?

Is an area within your ministry or church experiencing the kind of extraordinary, spiritual success that should be rewarded with a resource boost?

If so, how should limited resources be reprioritized in order to make the most of this opportunity?

Chapter 8 RESOURCING

By faith Moses left Egypt

(Hebrews 11:27)

Resourcing
Rewarding
Relationships
Recruiting
Roles
Resolution

> You are acutely aware that in order to achieve this mission you are going to need resources. Maybe a lot of resources! And, you're wondering where they are going to come from.

The people of Israel had been slaves in Egypt. It was impossible to accumulate wealth. With nearly all the able men slavishly working on Pharaoh's ambitious construction projects (Ex. 1:11), there would have been barely adequate food stocks. As they prepared for the exodus and embarked on their mission, resources were scarce. They just assembled what little they had and trusted God to provide for their needs. This was their introduction to faith-mission. The question was, 'Where are the resources going to come from?' The answer had to be, 'God will provide!' And God did (Ex. 12:36).

You are embarking on your mission with a firm determination. You have a team to mobilize, each member fulfilling a crucial role. Strong bonds are forming. It's been a very rewarding experience so far. You continue to carefully develop everything. There is continual improvement right across the board. You are aiming to accomplish this big, God-glorifying mission. But you are acutely aware that in order to achieve this mission you are going to need resources. Maybe a lot of resources! And, you're wondering where they are going to come from. This chapter will offer you some practical advice on how to attain some of the resources required. But none of these recommendations will negate the need for faith. You are on a faith-mission. That's exactly the way that God wants it to be. He wants us to trust him to supply what is needed to accomplish the mission. The Bible says, "And without faith it is impossible to please God" (Heb. 11:6). It also says, concerning Moses, "By faith he left Egypt" (Heb. 11:27).

FAITH

Faith is impossible to learn in a classroom, or from a book. It's learned on the ragged edges of life on mission with God. Sure, you can think about faith as a theological construct.

> Faith is learned on the ragged edges of life on mission with God.

Maybe you already know the verse, "Now faith is being sure of what we hope for and certain of what we do not see" (Heb. 11:1). You understand its meaning conceptually. But you only get to exercise faith and learn what that really means when you're stuck between the Egyptians and the deep Red Sea (Ex. 14). Or when the God-ordained command comes in the middle of the night, "Up! Leave... Go" (Ex. 12:31) and you have precious little to go with. That's where you learn what it means to trust and obey. There's no other way.

Most of us, truth be told, struggle in this area of having the right amount of faith. It might sound strange to talk about a 'quantity' of faith, but a number of passages in the Bible indicate to me that we can think about faith this way. One of them is found in the Book of Romans: "We have different gifts, according to the grace given us. If a man's gift is prophesying, let him use it in proportion to his faith" (Rom. 12:6). There are also many examples of Jesus

reprimanding the disciples for not having enough faith (Mat. 14:31, 17:20). And there's a special affirmation of a woman who had a lot of it (Mat. 15:28)! The Bible also records the confession of a man who knew he needed more faith. He said to Jesus, "I do believe; help me overcome my unbelief" (Mk. 9: 24)! This verse has proved to be really helpful for a lot of people because it brings to the surface our deep desire for a larger faith. We want that sort of faith, but we aren't always sure where it is going to come from.

7 RESOURCE GENERATORS

Encouragingly, there are a number of things that will help your faith to grow. I'll teach them here in the hope that it will be helpful for team leaders who need resources. I am, however, well aware of the limitations of outlining these faith-concepts. While it's good to know these things in theory, you need to experience them on your mission. That is the classroom that counts for big-faith learning. God intended it to be this way. So, what are some faith-building ideas that could prove helpful when you face those inevitable circumstances where the requirements are huge, but the resources are few. Let's look at six faith-builders.

1 BIG FAITH COMES WITH A BIG VISION OF GOD

Our faith is in God the Father, God the Son and God the Holy Spirit. In the end, it gets down to that. A reverent respect for the awesomeness of God is the right faith-foundation! If our view of God is huge, it puts into perspective any comparatively small resource-challenges we might have. That doesn't mean the challenges we face aren't real. It just means we're looking at them from the right viewpoint. Our faith *isn't* in our own capabilities even though we might be capable people. Moses was charged to select capable people, for sure, but the qualification was that they *also* feared God (Ex. 18:21)! Their view of God needed to be the overriding factor in the lead that they gave. So, our faith shouldn't be in our own capacity or that of our team. Our faith *isn't* in The Jethro Model either, even though it is a very helpful resource. Moses received the Jethro Structure as inspired mandate (Ex. 18:23). It was given to him because the leadership requirements were so huge and he was trying to meet them himself. The situation was unsatisfactory. The pastoral-care life of Israel was, consequently, under-resourced. Jethro's leadership resource came just in time. Perhaps, for you, The Jethro Mandate will prove to be both timely and beneficial. I certainly hope so! But it won't negate the need for ongoing faith in God.

> **If our view of God is huge, it puts into perspective any comparatively small resource-challenges we might have.**

If God gives you the mission, he will supply the *necessary* resources. Moses repeatedly experienced this. God provided. God provided food in the desert. Miraculous meals arrived when all that the people could see were vast stretches of sand. Even Moses struggled to have enough faith to believe God could do that. Despite all the miracles he had already seen, his faith needed to increase. Moses asked God somewhat doubtfully, "Where is the food for these two million, desert-surrounded people going to come from?" There will be times when you have your own variation on that question; "Where will the money come from?" or, "Where will I get enough leaders for this?" or, "How can we possibly meet all these needs?" Moses needed a bigger view of God and we do too. God's reply to Moses' food-question was succinct and classic:

"Is the LORD's arm too short?" (Num. 11:23)

My wife is Dutch and a very generous person. But there's a saying about Dutch people that goes: 'Short arms, deep pockets'. In other words, they are reluctant to dig down deep and extract the resources for the purpose of distribution. Apparently the 'arms are too short'. This isn't actually true of the Dutch people I know. And it certainly isn't true of God either! When you are on your God-given mission, and what you require totally overwhelms whatever resources you might possess, God will supply *in his way* and *in his time*. Do you have a mental picture of God that portrays him with short arms? If you do, you can expect to be short on faith. If you have a big, Biblical view of God, then your faith will become proportionately expansive. Peter had the faith to say to the lame man, "Silver or gold I do not have, but what I have I give you. In the name of Jesus Christ of Nazareth, walk" (Acts 3:6).

2 FAITH COMES FROM A CONVICTION THAT YOU ARE ON GOD'S MISSION

I believe that every Christian should seek to know what their God-given mission is. I also believe that we should discover the role we are to play on that mission. This book is premised on those convictions. I believe that God can impress upon us, and guide us to, exactly what it is that he wants us to do. This revelation will not usually come through hearing God's audible voice. Rather, I would expect that we will be led by God to discern his will by means already described in this book. What does this all have to do with faith? My point is this: when you are *convinced* that you know the mission and your role in it, when you have great certainty about that, then your confidence in God's provision escalates. This is a big reason why prayerful and careful application of the Implementation Elevators in chapter two will prove so advantageous. Your faith grows in proportion to the confidence that you have when you are doing exactly what God wants. If a team leader can say in all good conscience that, 'God made me for a leading role in this mission', then that leader will be able to exercise great faith. Big faith will flow from a conviction that you are on God's mission.

> **When you are *convinced* that you know the mission and your role in it, when you have great certainty about that, then your confidence in God's provision escalates!**

3 THE IMPORTANCE OF PRAYER

The Bible records many instances when heaven opened in response to prayer. God's provision was released through prayer. In response to prayer, God miraculously provided what was lacking; be it crops, a child, evangelistic boldness, victory against the odds, or even prosperity. Here are just a few examples:

> "I prayed for this child and the LORD has granted me what I asked of him" (1 Sam. 1:27).

> "Jabez cried out to the God of Israel, "Oh, that you would bless me and enlarge my territory! Let your hand be with me, and keep me from harm so that I will be free from pain"" (1 Chr. 4:10).

> "Judah turned and saw that they were being attacked at both front and rear. Then they cried out to the LORD... God routed Jeroboam... and delivered them into their hands" (2 Chr. 13:14-16).

> "Now, Lord... enable your servants to speak your word with great boldness... After they prayed, the place where they were meeting was shaken. And they were all filled with the Holy Spirit and spoke the word of God boldly" (Acts 4:29-31).

> "Elijah was a man just like us. He prayed earnestly that it would not rain, and it did not rain on the land for three and a half years. Again he prayed and the heavens gave rain, and the earth produced its crops" (Jam. 5:17-18).

When the opportunities are great but the resources are few, then we need to pray. Jesus said, "The harvest is plentiful but the workers are few. Ask the Lord of the harvest, therefore, to send out workers into his harvest field" (Lk. 10:2). Resources flow in response to believing prayer.

4 RESOURCES WILL FLOW WHEN INDIVIDUALS WITH THE GIFT OF GIVING BELIEVE THAT YOU ARE DOING GOD'S WORK

In the New Testament, one of the spiritual gifts listed is the gift of giving. The Apostle Paul wrote: "if it is contributing to the needs of others, let him give generously" (Rom. 12:8). Some people are blessed with resources for the purpose of generously supporting the needs of the church and its mission (1 Tim. 6:18-19). They help provide resources. Perhaps you don't have the necessary means available to meet the challenges, but they do. It's their *role* to give. This is powerfully illustrated in the circumstances surrounding the ministry and mission of Jesus. We presume Jesus worked for a living in the years leading up to his three-year mission focus. He was probably a carpenter. We have no indication that he amassed any sort of financial reserves in his career as a tradesman. Back then, no one got wealthy performing manual labor! This means that, subsequent to his baptism and calling to full-time ministry, Jesus had no way of supporting himself. His disciples were not earning a living either. This was the ultimate faith-mission! How did they survive? How was the mission resourced? The Bible informs us that:

> "Jesus travelled about from one town and village to another, proclaiming the good news of the kingdom of God. The twelve were with him, and also some women who had been cured of evil spirits and diseases: Mary (called Magdalene) from whom seven demons had come out; Joanna the wife of Cuza, the manager of Herod's household; Susanna; and many others. These women were helping to support them out of their own means" (Lk. 8:1-3).

Wealthy benefactors have often resourced Christian missions.

These women had the gift of generosity! They resourced Jesus' mission as he and the disciples rolled through town after town in the course of this fulltime preaching and healing ministry. If your mission is compelling enough, and you're being effective in meeting needs, your mission could well attract the support of people of means. This is one way that God resources the mission. Wealthy benefactors have often resourced Christian mission. There is an important aside to this story that should not go unnoticed; I wonder if you picked it up? Curiously, it was the very people that Jesus had reached out to and helped *in the course of the mission*, who ended up being significant contributors. This is not uncommon. It's not the reason *why* we help people but it can be one of the positive consequences. As your mission helps more people, more people will get behind you. Some of those people you reach will end up being your greatest resourcers.

5 RESOURCES WILL FLOW WHEN THE CHURCH BELIEVES THAT YOU ARE DOING GOD'S WORK

This section is written primarily for team leaders who lead missions that support the overall mission of your local church. You will need to provide your church's decision-makers with a reasoned and compelling case to support your mission. It's ideal when the local church gets financially behind the local mission. God's desire is that each local church has a generous heart toward mission. In the earliest days of the church, this pattern was set. The church in Jerusalem exemplified this ideal of the local church collaborating to connect the resources to the needs. The Book of Acts reports that:

> "All the believers were one in heart and mind. No one claimed that any of his possessions were his own, but they shared everything... There were no needy persons among them. For from time to time those who owned lands or houses sold them, brought the money from the sales and put it at the apostles' feet, and it was distributed to anyone as he had need" (Acts 4:32-35).

While this expression of generosity appears to be similar to the situation above (in which wealthy individuals gave personal support to people on mission), it is appreciably different. In the case of the Jerusalem church, the resources were 'collected' by the apostles, who were the leaders of the local church. The apostles then distributed those resources as 'from the church', rather than from individual, wealthy benefactors. Many contemporary local churches follow this pattern. The financial offerings from the whole church are collected (perhaps on Sunday) and the church leaders distribute what is given to resource the church's missions and meet as many needs as possible. Most churches have annual budgets that guide decisions with regard to the distribution of funds. If your local church, through its leaders, believes that your mission fits in with God's purposes and is meeting real needs, then it would be reasonable to expect that appropriate resources be channeled into your mission. This being understood, there are four important considerations to keep in mind:

> **If your local church, through its leaders, believes that your mission fits in with God's purposes then it would be reasonable to expect that appropriate resources be channelled into your mission.**

1) If your church has an established budget-setting process, then you need to find out how it works and make a reasonable submission for financial support of your mission. The support you've been looking for could well be provided by the local church through its general giving. Senior leaders will make a decision concerning the amount of resources they will direct toward your mission, a decision most likely based on how compelling your mission is and evidence of its effectiveness.

2) Keep the finance people informed with regard to the progress of your mission, whatever it is. I would suggest writing a monthly report to your senior leaders even if that's not normally required. Paul knew the importance of keeping supporters informed. The letter to the Philippians included an up-beat update as to the progress of his mission (Phil. 1:12-14).

3) This distribution of resources will be needs-based and there are always many competing needs. Be aware of this if your resource request is downsized some. No disrespect will be intended. It's not easy to keep everyone happy when drafting a church budget! So try to be understanding if you don't get what you requested.

A final note on resource support from your local church: it's incumbent on team leaders to foster good relationships with the senior decision-makers in their local church. Support them. Pray that they will have wisdom in apportioning financial resources.

6 IT TAKES A STEP OF FAITH

There are moments that define leaders. They almost always have to do with a step of faith. Many of God's miracles were preceded by a moment when a leader put everything on the line. I've been led by people who have remarkable faith. I've heard stories of what God has done through other leaders. But I know now what you know too: it feels different when *you're* the leader. Being a team leader isn't easy. And when resources are depleted and some sort of miracle is required, all eyes are going to be on you. People look to their leaders; that's just what people do. God looks to his leaders too. And we leaders need to look back to God!

Joshua had looked on as God had done amazing things while Moses was in the lead. Moses had been instructed to hit a rock and water had come out. Moses had been asked to pray and plagues were stopped in their tracks. The list of miracles went on. Moses was a man of amazing faith and everybody knew it! Joshua would have been the first to affirm what the Bible says of Moses at the close of the Book of Deuteronomy:

> "Since then, no prophet has risen in Israel like Moses, whom the LORD knew face to face, who did all those miraculous signs and wonders... For no one has ever shown the mighty power or performed the awesome deeds that Moses did in the sight of all Israel" (Deut. 34:10-12).

But by the time the Book of Joshua begins, Moses is dead, and Joshua is about to commence his rookie year as the leader of all Israel. His calling to leadership is appended with an assurance that God would be with him wherever he went (Josh. 1:9). That principle holds true for every leader that God calls to head up a mission. And you need to know that, because sooner or later, we will all face a Jordan River of some kind. For Joshua it didn't take long at all (Josh. 3:9-17).

This was the situation; the people had to get to the other side of the Jordan River to enter the Promised Land. But it seemed like the wrong time and the wrong place to make this crossing. The time was spring, when the Jordan River floods and the waters rage wildly toward the Dead Sea (Josh. 3:15-16). The place happened to be just north of the Dead Sea (Josh. 3:16), where the mountains fall sharply into the Jordan River system creating treacherous conditions. Wrong time, wrong place! There were no natural means by which this river could be crossed. Where was Moses when they needed him? All eyes turned to Joshua.

If you are a team leader, expect to experience this sometimes. Maybe, it's *your* rookie year and you're facing a seemingly insurmountable hurdle with the mission already. The mission appears doomed from the start! You're facing a Jordan River. Perhaps as you've been reading *The Resolute Leader* and calculating all that needs to be done, you feel overwhelmed by the challenge and tempted to abandon the mission. Or it may be that you're facing a significant resource shortage right now. You might be in desperate need of finances or someone to fill a necessary role. You might be beginning to think that it's the wrong place and the wrong time to attempt this mission here and now.

You really need to trust the Lord in this. If, in all good conscience, you believe that what you are doing is right, then believe for a miracle and take a step of faith. Joshua commanded the people to get ready to cross the turbulent waters of the Jordan River. He took the lead. According to God's instructions, the priests and the Ark of the Covenant were to be out in front of the people. I believe this was meant to signify that God was going before them. And

> **If, in all good conscience, you believe that what you are doing is right then believe for a miracle and take a step of faith.**

the Bible records that as soon as the priests who carried the ark *set foot in the water*, the waters were "cut off" and stood "up in a heap" (Josh. 3:13). God turned a 'wrong time, wrong place' scenario into a 'right time, right place' miracle. What it took was a step of faith. God provided the means when the leaders had the faith. Your resource-miracle might await your step of faith.

The epilogue to the story is instructive. The rookie leader gained great credibility in the eyes of the people. The Bible says, "That day [when the step of faith was taken and God's miracle ensued] the LORD exalted Joshua in the sight of all Israel" (Josh. 4:14)[Emphasis added].

7 RESOURCE YOUR TEAM BY DESIGNING AN ACHIEVABLE, ANNUAL TRAINING PLAN

In the chapter so far, we've considered ways in which God can arrange the supply of extraordinary resources that are needed for your mission. In the cases that we've considered, it has been assumed that the resources

> **Your team is one of your greatest resources.**

required needed to be sourced from outside the team and mission. But what about building up the team itself? After all, your team is one of your greatest resources. God gave you this team. He does some of his most powerful work through people. Remember: God led his people by the hand of Moses (Ps. 77:20). Moses did this with the support of a huge leadership team! Building the mission-capacity of your team will go a long way to accomplishing your God-given mission. Team leaders need to resource their teams with ongoing training and development opportunities. Below, I've listed some practical suggestions for building a team's capacity.

R ead relevant books and access expert teaching in your mission area. Circulate what's best.

E xposure to a similar mission in another setting.

S eminary-type training. Do rigorous and relevant coursework. Earn a substantial qualification.

O utsider input. Invite an expert to bring fresh inspiration.

U tilize expertise within your team. Get capacity-building input from each other.

R egular on-the-mission training spots. Don't underestimate the power of short, sharp input.

C onferences can be a catalyst for growth.

I mplement The Jethro Model thoroughly. Ensure all team members read this book.

N etwork & learn from other leaders in your church who have embraced The Jethro Mandate.

G roup-work. Reflect regularly as a team. Discuss ideas. Encourage synergy.

As team leader, you need to consider the time and financial constraints of your team members and design an achievable, annual training plan. In the Implementation Elevators section you will be encouraged to design a training plan that will help ensure your team receives ongoing leadership development. Your team is your greatest resource.

CHAPTER SUMMARY

So, there are seven, resource-generating ideas that could prove helpful when you face those inevitable circumstances when what is required vastly exceeds what is at hand. Here they are again:

1) Big faith comes with a big vision of God.

2) Faith comes from a conviction that you are on God's mission.

3) Prayer is central.

4) Resources will flow when individuals with the gift of giving believe that you are doing God's work.

5) Resources will flow when the church believes that you are doing God's work.

6) It takes a step of faith.

7) Resource your team by designing an achievable, annual training plan.

I could do no better than finish this chapter on resources with these words from the Apostle Paul: "My God will meet all your needs according to his glorious riches in Christ Jesus" (Phil. 4:19). AMEN!

 *Implementation Elevators*

REFLECTION QUESTIONS

What are the resources that you feel most in need of now?

What have you personally learned about faith on your journey so far?

'God will provide'. How do you respond to that statement?

RESOURCE—GENERATING EXERCISES

EXERCISE # 1: COMPARING YOUR VISION OF GOD WITH THE CHALLENGE YOU FACE

Write down all of your resource challenges in a column. List the least challenging at the top and the most challenging at the bottom. Draw 2 vertical lines down both sides of the column and one across the bottom so that the words look like they are piled in a mine shaft. Now, over the top write the question, 'Is the LORD'S arm too short?'

Prayerfully ask God:

    i) to show you if these are *necessary* resource needs;

    ii) to help you see and believe that nothing is out of his reach.

EXERCISE # 2: RATING YOUR 'MISSION—CONVICTION' LEVEL

Your faith in God's *provision* for your mission often correlates with the strength of your conviction that you have *precision* regarding the mission. Use the continuum below to plot the strength of your conviction.

Very uncertain   *Completely convinced*

⬅———————————————————➡

What do you think would help you move further towards the right end of the scale?

Get your team members involved this exercise. If the team is collectively sure that God has ordained this mission, then your faith will combine and you will trust God for big things *together!*

EXERCISE # 3: PRAYER EXERCISES

The absolute importance of prayer is a recurring theme in this book. When it comes to trusting God for an extraordinary provision of resources, we need to pray, believing that God can and will do it!

1) Ask God to help you overcome your unbelief (Mk. 9:24). Pray for a faith-increase. In Luke 11:13, Jesus taught that God will give the Holy Spirit (in greater measure) to those who ask him. Don't conclude that the amount of faith that you have is fixed. Pray for *more faith* in the all-powerful Lord of the mission!

2) Pray together as a team. The Bible has many examples of people praying in unity for God's miraculous provision. This will sometimes happen spontaneously. That's great! However, there are many times recorded in the Bible when God's people deliberately set aside time to wait on Him in prayer (e.g. Acts 1:14; 3:1; 4:24). When would be the optimal time(s) for your team to pray together concerning God's provision for the mission? Disciplined praying strengthens a disciple's faith!

EXERCISE # 4: RAISING AWARENESS OF YOUR MISSION WITH GIFTED DONORS

There are people who have the gift of giving (Rom. 12:8). Ideally, they are attentive to the Holy Spirit's directives and they give generously to mission endeavors. It may well be God's intention that *your* mission be the recipient of needed resources through people with the supernatural gift of giving. Prepare for this eventuality.

In this exercise, imagine that a generous person is enquiring about your mission because they are considering making a financial contribution. What would you say to them? How would you make them aware of the opportunities you have and the resources required? Make a specific list of things that a generous person could procure for you. Write it down in faithful readiness!

EXERCISE # 5: SUPPORT FROM YOUR LOCAL CHURCH

Most churches prepare annual budgets. Consequently, team leaders will need to do the following:

1) Find out how your church's budget process works. You'll need to know things like:

   a) what leadership group prepares the budget;

   b) the deadline for budget submissions;

   c) the acceptable format for budget submissions.

2) Make your budget submission as organized and compelling as possible. You need to provide the decision-makers with a reasoned and compelling case to support your mission.

3) So, as part of your application include things like:

   a) your Mission Resolution;

b) evidence of success so far (anything that might encourage 'investment' in your mission);

c) a detailed inventory of how the funding will be used, including researched cost projections;

d) a mutually satisfactory accountability pathway (usually a written report) that will provide proof that the funds have been spent appropriately.

REFLECTION QUESTION

What step of faith is God asking you to take?

EXERCISE # 6: DESIGNING AN ACHEIVABLE, ANNUAL DEVELOPMENT PLAN

In this chapter, I suggested a number of capacity building options. They are listed below.

R ead relevant books and access expert teaching in your mission area.

E xposure to a similar mission in another setting.

S eminary-type training.

O utsider input.

U tilize expertise within your team.

R egular on-the-mission training spots.

C onferences.

I mplement The Jethro Model thoroughly.

N etwork and learn from other leaders in your church.

G roup-work.

Now with consideration of the availability of time and finances, design an achievable, annual plan for you and your team that will help resource your team with a variety of training experiences. Remember, your team is one of your greatest resources.

Chapter 9 REVIEWING

*For no one has ever shown the mighty power
or performed the awesome deeds that Moses did*

(A Review of Moses' life; Deuteronomy 34:12)

Reviewing
Resourcing
Rewarding
Relationships
Recruiting
Roles
Resolution

So, you know what your mission is, you've recruited people who know their role, the team is growing closer, your team members are finding it a rewarding experience and everything seems to be developing well. Sure, there are some challenges along the way. There always will be. You are a leader and you are there to handle the more difficult problems. That's a big part of what you do (Ex. 18:22)! As a result of implementing The Jethro Model, you feel confident that your team is organized in a way that pleases God. People are being cared for *while* the mission is steadily progressing forward. *You* feel generally satisfied and your team is standing the strain. But you know things still could be better and you're not completely comfortable with everything. Perhaps you can't quite identify what the issues are but you've just got a feeling that things can improve.

> **The team leader needs to champion a Continuous Development Culture.**

Don't ignore those feelings. Your job isn't done yet, and in some ways it never will be. This is because everything is a work is progress. Every aspect of The Jethro Mandate will need ongoing monitoring and development. The team leader needs to champion a Continuous Development Culture. Great leaders always live with a certain level of *holy* dissatisfaction. It is a holy dissatisfaction because it isn't wrong to feel this way. The Holy Spirit is stirring it up! This holy discontent is a recognition that we haven't arrived yet. It conveys the sense that there's more that we could *be* and there is still more that we could *do*. This is a common experience for fully committed Christians when it comes to their personal, spiritual journey. We are not yet perfect are we? I know that I am not completely satisfied with the way that I love and follow Christ. Nor have I yet completed all the God-glorifying missions that he has for me to accomplish. But I want to. And, by Christ's grace and power I will! This is the kind of proactive response that holy dissatisfaction provokes. It doesn't cause us to give up, rather, it inspires us to press on; to stretch; to change; to grow; to embrace the Continuous Development Culture. This was the experience of the Apostle Paul. He never felt like he had 'arrived'. He never felt that he could just sit back and let it all slide. I wonder if you can sense the holy discontentment in Paul as he wrote these words:

> "Not that I have already obtained all this, or have already been made perfect, but I press on to take hold of that for which Christ Jesus took hold of me. Brothers, I do not consider myself yet to have taken hold of it. But one thing I do: Forgetting what is behind and straining toward what is ahead, I press on toward the goal to win the prize for which God has called me heavenward in Christ Jesus" (Phil. 3:12-14).

Nothing in this life will ever be perfect. This is true with regard to you, your team and your mission. The question is, how do you deal with that? Do you give up? Do you simply downgrade your goals and expectations? Do you say, 'Close enough is good enough'? Or do you press on, strain toward what is ahead and lead the Continuous Development Process? Your answers to these questions matter, because the way you respond to this holy dissatisfaction is another thing that distinguishes a great leader from a mediocre one. What happens, or *doesn't* happen, will have a big bearing on whether your team remains *good* or transitions to *great*. What you choose to do in response to the challenges in this chapter will dramatically affect the overall success of your God-given mission. In this chapter I'll dare you to do what few have the courage to do; that is, to *review everything*. I'll be challenging you to review everything and everyone, including yourself. Especially yourself! The evaluation process will be careful and considered. It's measured, it's meaningful and it will mostly be really positive. All the elements of the review will have already been articulated and agreed on as part of the Role Description process. There will be no surprises. Are you ready for this? I think you can be confident that you are! The Jethro Model has made you 'review-ready'.

> **I believe that constant reflection on the quality of your life's work is essential in the light of eternity.**

Some leaders and readers of this book may have reservations about the appropriateness of reviewing people as part of the Continuous Development Culture. You might be asking yourself questions like these:

a) Is the rigorous reviewing of everything spiritual?

b) Is it Biblical?

c) Isn't this an exercise that only belongs in the ruthless world of businesses and corporations?

d) Shouldn't we just focus of God?

I am convinced that the Continuous Development Culture is essentially spiritual, completely Biblical, will advance the mission *and* is totally honoring to God. I believe that constant reflection on the quality of your life's work is essential in the light of eternity. Rather than hoping for the best when we get to heaven, we should be constantly assessing the caliber of our contribution to the mission *now*. A Continuous Development Culture ought to cause more glory for God and bring you great eternal reward! For these motivating reasons, it is worth our constant care and attention. The Apostle Paul practiced great vigilance with regard to the continuing excellence of his service. He knew that God would ultimately review his life's work. He wrote:

> **In this chapter I'll dare you to do what too few have the courage to do; that is, to review everything.**

> "But each one should be careful how he builds. For no one can lay any foundation other than the one already laid, which is Jesus Christ. If any man builds on this foundation using gold, silver, costly stones, wood, hay or straw, his work will be shown for what it is, because the Day will bring it to light. It will be revealed with fire, and the fire will test the quality of each man's work. If what he has built survives, he will receive his reward. If it is burned up, he will suffer loss; he himself will be saved, but only as one escaping through the flames" (1 Cor. 3:10-15).

Paul understood that everything he'd done for God would be graded. There would be a divine quality assessment. Here, the Bible not only teaches that God *will* review our contribution to His overall mission, but it also provides a calibration tool. God's review will have some sort of grading system; from zero through to gold. Here are the review 'assessment levels' as set out in the Bible:

- Gold
- Silver
- Costly stones
- Wood
- Hay
- Straw
- Nothing

> **The quality of our good works for God will be rated in God's review.**

As Bible scholar F. W. Grosheide wrote, "The obvious explanation of the enumeration of these materials lies in the fact that it constitutes a list of decreasing values and increasing flammability. The subsequent words show that this is the point of view."[16] We will use these words in the Implementation Elevators section at the end of this chapter. It may be helpful if we *loosely* equate these calibrations to a grading system that we are more familiar with:

- Gold — High Distinction
- Silver — Distinction
- Costly stones — Credit
- Wood — Fail
- Hay — Fail
- Straw — Fail
- Nothing — Fail: no work submitted

So in view of God's rigorous review of our life's work, doesn't it become starkly apparent that we also need to be conducting careful reviews in relation to our contribution to the mission? Everything needs to be honestly evaluated. Please understand that this is *not* a salvation issue. The Bible says, "For it is by grace you have been saved, through faith – and this not from yourselves, it is the gift of God – not by works, so that no one can boast" (Eph. 2:8-9). We are saved when we put our faith in the Person of Jesus and his gracious Work for us on the cross. Nevertheless, having been made a new creation by so great a salvation, we have been created in Christ Jesus to do good works. God prepared these in advance for us to do (Eph. 2:10). The quality of our good works for God will be rated in God's review. Those who made a careless, 'straw-like' contribution, will be saved but still suffer a loss: "he himself will be saved, but only as one escaping through the flames" (1 Cor. 3:15). Some people will enter God's glory with nothing to show for their life spent on earth. Some people, however, will enter glory with gold-class honors!

Moses lived and led with a view to pleasing God and fulfilling his calling. He was going for gold! To this end, he made improvements along the way to make things better and to ensure the success of the mission. One of the most significant improvements that Moses made was in response to Jethro's review of his leadership. When Jethro reviewed Moses' single-handed attempt to lead God's people, he concluded that it was "not good" (Ex. 18:17). The Israelites had already come to the same conclusion (Deut. 1:14). Jethro then mandated that Moses implement the Jethro structure. And Moses resolved to do it. This development improved things greatly. Jethro gave Moses a Role Description. Once Moses knew exactly what he was to do, he was able to get on and fulfill his unique role excellently. Consequently, his contribution to the mission went from good to gold. The Biblical reviews of his life and ministry say as much. The Bible says, "God led his people like a flock by the hand of Moses" (Ps. 77:20). Further, as the Book of Deuteronomy closes, there is a rave review of Moses' unique contribution and lasting legacy:

> "Since then, no prophet has risen in Israel like Moses, whom the LORD knew face to face, who did all those miraculous signs and wonders the LORD sent him to do in Egypt... For no one has ever shown the mighty power or performed the awesome deeds that Moses did in the sight of Israel" (Deut. 34:10-12).

How would you like to be rated at the time of your review? Gold, I can safely guess. It takes a lot of care and attention to get to gold. You'll need to rigorously review everything in a positive and faith-filled way. So, in the light of The Jethro Model, let's look at how you can do this. All the elements are there, so there will be no surprises. Everything here will be important to the Continuous Development Culture. Team leaders will need to be attentive to everything listed below. We'll start with reviewing the Mission Resolution.

1 REVIEWING THE MISSION RESOLUTION

Getting the Mission Resolution right is necessary because everything flows out of knowing your mission. Have your Mission Resolution in front of you and ask yourself the following questions.

> Does it articulate the mission in a clear and compelling way?
> Are the actions it inspires the right sort of actions?
> Does it help you easily see what your next strategic steps should be?
> Are the stated aspirations the right sort of aspirations?

Give your Mission Resolution a rating, from zero through to gold. If you've captured the essence of what is to be accomplished, then proceed to the next review heading.

But, what if you still have some doubts about the precision of your Mission Resolution. What can you do about that? Firstly, I would suggest that you revisit the content of the chapters on mission and complete all of the Implementation Elevators again. Go through them slowly and prayerfully. As part of this process, perhaps you could invite your team and/or a wise outsider to accompany you in this quest for clarity. You want to be looking at the big picture and attending to the details at the same time. Resist the temptation to give up too quickly or radically change the course of the mission. The process is usually a refining one rather than a complete revision. Even small changes, like a word or a phrase, can be important in this refining process.

If you revisit the Implementation Elevators as I've recommended and uncertainty remains, my second piece of advice would be to stick to the mission as you know it. If you suspect that the Mission Resolution isn't exactly right but you believe that you are *on the right track*, press on in faith! Clarity will *progressively* come as you move forward on the mission as you know it.

Another happy possibility in the future is that you are now within reach of accomplishing your mission. In other words, you've almost achieved what you, under God, resolved to do. Fantastic! Your task then would be to *re*-vision the mission. You will need to discover what new goals are to be achieved and what new roles they will require. This is an exciting part of the Continuous Development Culture.

You need to review your Mission Resolution at least every year. If your conviction is that you've got it right, then you won't need to spend much time on this. If you are uncertain, bring that before the Lord. Ask your team for their perspective. Share your doubts with discerning people. Remember, it may take time to lock in on the mission with precision. You can't short-circuit the process. Be patient and don't get too discouraged.

2 REVIEWING THE PROGRESS OF THE MISSION

So, you've reviewed your Mission Resolution. Now it's time to look backwards and assess your progress with regard to accomplishing the mission. This is part of the Continuous Development Culture. As team leader, you need to gauge progress. Has there been any advancement? Are you moving noticeably towards your goals? Are you generally satisfied with the way things are evolving? Rate your overall progress from zero through to gold. Let your rating be an intuitive one. Just record your general impression. This is a very helpful exercise.

Once you've completed the above exercise, the next challenge is to try to specify the reasons behind your response. This should ideally be done when you have a fair bit of time because you're attempting an in-depth analysis of everything that has been going on.

Your aim is to identify each of the significant factors that informed your response to the above exercise. Use this as a starting point for a wide-ranging evaluation of all that's happened to this point. In this exercise, your task is *dissection*. You want to take it all apart

> **If you suspect that the Mission Resolution isn't exactly right but you believe that you are *on the right track*, press on in faith!**

and consider all the pieces. You want to scrutinize everything and everyone to determine whether it, or they, are taking the mission forward or holding it back. You're looking for all the contributing, maintaining and inhibiting factors. Once you have some *facts* in front of you, based on a rigorous assessment of everything, you can then best determine how to respond to each of them.

I've provided a tool [*below*] to help you with this process. It's designed to help you identify:

1) what or who needs to be commended and celebrated for providing momentum – these are the *accelerators*;

2) what or who is arresting further growth and developments and needs addressing – these are the *restrainers*.

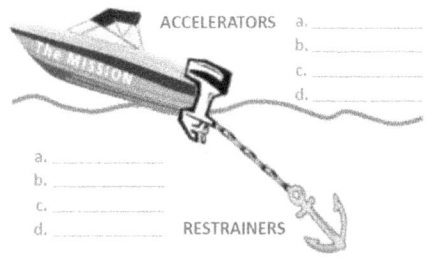

Accelerators are those people and things that have propelled the mission forward. They are like the huge engine on a powerboat. You need a lot of energy to overcome natural inertia and get a boat going. Accelerators provide that. They create momentum, which is such a precious commodity on a mission. Some examples of *accelerators* in the story of Moses and the mission to reach the Promised Land are:

    a) Aaron's genuine support for Moses that helped him get going in the first place;

    b) Jethro's mandate to Moses which released him to lead effectively;

    c) the encouragement of victories over enemies who tried to block their progress.

Restrainers are those people and things that have held the mission back. They arrest progress. They are like a dragging anchor. They diminish, and might even threaten to extinguish, momentum. Some examples of *restrainers* with regard to the Exodus and the gaining of the Promised Land are:

    a) Pharaoh's resistance to the Exodus;

    b) the constant grumbling and disobedience of the Israelites;

    c) unfaithful spies and their negative report.

Accelerators and restrainers are the identifiable dynamics that impact on the mission. Some propel the mission forward, and some inhibit progress toward fulfillment. As you review your mission it should become apparent that there are people to be commended and things to be celebrated because they contributed to the momentum of the mission. It will also become clear that sometimes there are people and problems that impede progress. When a restraining influence is identified it needs to be addressed for the sake of the team and the mission. In the Implementation Elevators section there is an exercise that encourages you to review the progress of the mission thoroughly.

Once you've completed the task in detail, determine how you are going to respond to each of the elements that you have itemized. Just reflecting on the dynamics in and around your mission isn't enough. These reflections should lead to right responses. Taking appropriate action is part of the Continuous Development Culture. In many cases, the appropriate response will be recognition and reward. In other instances, there might need to be improvements in a process, or even a complete overhaul to the way things are done. Sometimes, you will come to the uncomfortable, but unavoidable conclusion, that a person on your team is having a detrimental influence on the mission and its progress. Now, the way you respond to the restraining elements will be very important. If there is a team member that is holding things back, consider your course of action very carefully. Remember, accomplishing the mission isn't your only consideration. The *way* you get there matters as well. It's the way of love. Find ways to coach and encourage that team member to make a positive contribution. Use the 'Team Member Review' (#4 below) as the opportunity to talk openly about what's not working and what needs to improve. There will be occasions when you have to let a person go. This possibility will be minimized, however, if you recruit well in the first place.

> **Just reflecting on the dynamics in and around your mission isn't enough. These reflections should lead to right responses!**

3 REVIEWING YOUR OWN PERFORMANCE WITH REGARD TO YOUR ROLE

The team leader sets the tone. The team leader is primarily responsible for the progress of the mission and its ultimate success. So, *before* a team leader reviews anyone else in their team, they need to 'self-review'. We find a small sample of 'self-reviews' in the Bible. In Acts, Paul reviewed his teaching role to the Christians at Ephesus and said:

> "Therefore, I declare to you today that I am innocent of the blood of all men. For I have not hesitated to proclaim to you the whole will of God" (Acts 20:26-27).

Paul assesses his performance with regard to his mission to the Ephesians and concludes that he has fulfilled all that was required of him. Jesus was able to pray to the Father:

> "I have brought you glory on earth by completing the work you gave me to do" (Jn. 17:4).

And of course, Jesus completed his role as Sacrifice for our sins with:

"It is finished" (Jn. 19:30).

So, in the light of God's ultimate assessment of your life's work for Him, evaluate your own performance. Perhaps you could rate the quality of your performance using the following sample questions:

a) Are you fulfilling your commitments as per your Role Description?

b) Have you negotiated a Role Description with each member of your team?

c) Are you doing all you can to recruit your Dream Team?

d) Are you relating well with your team?

e) Are you communicating well and often?

f) Are you creating a sense of 'team'?

g) Are you standing the leadership strain?

h) Is serving on your team a rewarding experience for those involved?

i) Are the necessary resources flowing into the mission?

The Resolute Leader teaches the importance of each of these contributions and provides guidance as to how to perform each task well. Have a sober-minded yet faith-filled approach to this (Rom. 12:3). Make sure you don't become overwhelmed and demoralized. As I wrote at the top of this chapter, nothing will ever be perfect. It's good to have a holy dissatisfaction about things that could be better. We need to face these realities with the kind of faith and approach that doesn't cause us to give up. Your lead can and will improve as you stretch forward toward the prize!

 # 4 HAVING YOUR PERFORMANCE REVIEWED BY OTHERS

Senior leaders and team leaders need to lead by example and have their performance reviewed by others. While self-reviewing is an essential skill for a leader, we all have blind spots and a tendency to overlook those areas where we ourselves might be failing to perform. Trusted people need to form a review panel. They need to be able to speak into our lives and our lead. We may even need a rebuke from time to time. I marvel at the humility of David who wrote, "Let a righteous man strike me – it is a kindness; let him rebuke me – it is oil on my head. My head will not refuse it" (Ps. 141:5). So resolve to be reviewed. It will enhance your performance and bring great blessing to you and those around you.

 # 5 REVIEWING YOUR TEAM DESIGN

Teams change. People's circumstances change. People move on. Sometimes, teams *need* to change. The mission has expanded. The goals have been adjusted. While some changes are unforeseen and unwanted, a team leader needs to anticipate developments and make the required adjustments. Reviewing your current team design is often a precursor to the redesigning process. Often, the team that got you *here* won't be exactly the same as the one that will get you *there*. A team leader needs to be ahead of the curve and imagine a new Dream Team. Ask yourself, "Where are our fresh challenges and opportunities? What new roles are required and who could fill them?"

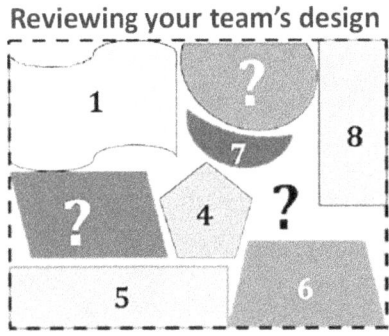

Reviewing your team's design

This reviewing and reimagining exercise helps when it comes to conducting reviews on individual team members. You can pre-think any adjustments that you would like to effect. Now you can go into the review process with a game plan. There may be a role adjustment that you would like a team member to make in order to fit with future goals. It may be that there's a brand new role that an existing team member could potentially and happily fulfill. If you've created a Role Description for that new role, you can present it to a promising leader. Review your team's design and redesign if necessary.

6 REVIEWING THE PERFORMANCE OF A TEAM MEMBER

As was established in the chapter on Role Descriptions, the only firm basis for the review of a team member will be the Role Description. As a reviewer, you need to ensure that you confine your discussion to the agreed tasks and culture. The Role Description functions as a kind of covenant. The team member will have put their name to this document. It's the point of reference for a Review.

The review should be done one-on-one within the time-frame negotiated. This will help ensure a timely, open conversation, and limit the possibility of embarrassment if there are difficult things to talk through. I would recommend that the review process simply follow the order of headings listed in the Role Description. Using the Role Description template provided in this book, let's consider some of the discussion and negotiation possibilities under each heading.

   a) **Name of the Mission.** This probably won't generate a lot of discussion, so we shall proceed.

   b) **Mission Resolution.** This *is* worth talking about. Everything follows from the mission so don't just skip over it. Ask the team member to reflect on the statement and how they feel about it. Is it clear and compelling to the team member? Take note of the responses. Keep these things in mind. They may be affirming or lead to helpful adjustments.

   c) **Name of the team member.** Since the Role Description functions as a formal agreement, remind the team member that they are committing to the negotiated tasks, cultural commitments and goals. They are putting their name to it.

d) **Leadership structure**. Ensure that the leadership structure is clear to the team member. Invite questions with regard to how it works. Perhaps take this opportunity to advocate for the advantages of the Jethro structure. This might also be the ideal opportunity to gauge if the team member has further leadership aspirations.

e) **Role title**. This probably won't generate a lot of discussion either.

f) **A detailed description of the specific role**. Don't assume that 'as it was, so it shall be'. People's roles can adjust according to their desires and also the demands of the mission. There should be room to negotiate. You want each member of your team to be energized and their efforts maximized! So listen carefully to their reflections and suggestions as you renegotiate the Role Description. A wise team leader, however, won't simply be reactive in this process. The role of a team leader is to constantly develop the team according the challenges and opportunities confronting the mission. An implication of this is that, *as you redesign the team*, you may need to *reassign some roles*. Come to an arrangement that best satisfies the team member and the mission's future.

g) **Culture-carrying commitments**. Were the values of the church and team upheld? What areas might need some attention and improvement? Encourage the team member who embodied the culture admirably. Coach the person who needs to improve.

h) **Goals**. Celebrate what has been accomplished. Determine why a goal was not reached. Were there mitigating circumstances beyond anyone's control? Were expectations unrealistic? Did someone let the team down? Critique things thoroughly. Let this goals-review be a context for the arrangement of fresh performance targets.

i) **Time commitment**. The demands on people's time can change. Be realistic about the time commitment required to fulfill the renegotiated role.

j) **Duration of the commitment to the role**. This ought to be renegotiated each time. I would go for as long a commitment as seems reasonable. It might be that the team member is tentative about making a longer commitment because they are uncertain about their future involvement. This would be a good time to acknowledge that uncertainty. This awareness will notify the team leader that the role could be vacated and a new recruit required.

k) **Role review time frame**. Normally, reviews will be conducted annually. In some circumstances, however, a shortened time-frame might be appropriate. This could be so in the case of a new recruit. You might arrange to meet a new team member after the first few months to see how things are going. Another circumstance in which a shorter time-span for a review might be advantageous is when there is concern about a team member's performance or influence within the team. Sometimes, if things aren't going well, a year can be too long!

l) **Support provided**. This is a great opportunity for honest feedback. Was the promised support forth-coming? Was the agreed support (e.g. training, reading and mentoring) actually helpful? This is a good time to discuss what the team member perceives as their need by way of support. If it's feasible, tailor the support to the needs of the individual. Remember, however, that a Role Description is a kind of covenant. Don't make a support-promise you can't keep!

So, there we have the eleven headings that can frame a review if you are using The Jethro Model template provided in this book. As you can see, there are no surprises. On a final note, I would recommend that you don't necessarily wait until the formal review to critique someone's performance. This is especially true if there are significant problems with the team member. Instead, quietly and as quickly as possible, let them know that they are not meeting expectations. Make sure you are specific and explain why you've come to your conclusion. Be encouraging, provide support and believe for the best! If the team member responds positively then you will be able to commend them during the next scheduled review. Scheduling in a more informal mid-year review would help ensure issues are dealt with in a timely manner. This would allow for on-the-go adjustments and ensure that everybody is right on target.

> **Scheduling in a more informal mid-year review would help ensure issues are dealt with in a timely manner.**

But what if a team member's review is unfavorable? While most Reviews will be positive and an opportunity for affirmation, sometimes it becomes apparent that a team member isn't working out. This is a problem that needs to be addressed. So how should a team leader respond? It isn't possible, of course, to address every scenario here. Nevertheless it might be helpful if I anticipate a number of likely situations and suggest some courses of action.

1) **Misconduct**. If a team member has been involved in the kind of misconduct that would compromise the integrity of your team and your mission then I would recommend that that person be suspended from ministry for a time. The length of time would need to be determined by the team leader (in consultation, I would suggest, with a more senior leader). Ideally, they will be restored to the team at an appropriate point in the future and redeployed on the mission. If it is fitting, create a pathway back onto the team for such a person. Repentance, reconciliation and restoration are the goals (Gal. 6:1).

2) **Not fulfilling role**. If someone is not fulfilling their role responsibilities, then there are a few options. They are as follows:

   a) renegotiate the Role Description so that it represents a more realistic contribution;

b) give the person reasonable time and opportunity to improve. Give them another chance to prove themselves. This requires patience and a supportive environment;

c) be open to the possibility of a mission mismatch and explore other possibilities for the team member.

The story of John Mark may well be instructive here.

John Mark's Story

John Mark was one of the first Christians. He served on a small but significant 'evangelism and relief' mission team alongside Barnabas and the Apostle Paul (Acts 12:12, 25). However, something went wrong and the team fragmented. In Acts 13:13 we read, "From Paphos, Paul and his companions sailed to Perga in Pamphylia, where John [Mark] left them to return to Jerusalem." While no reason is immediately given for this departure, the issue is raised later in the Book of Acts while Paul was recruiting for a second missionary journey. Paul was unwilling to include John Mark on the new mission team and gave an unfavorable review of John Mark's performance on the initial missionary journey, citing that he "deserted them in Pamphylia and had not continued with them in the work" (Acts 15:38). Paul obviously felt that everyone on his small mission team needed to be absolutely reliable. The Apostle had concluded that John Mark could not be trusted to finish what he started. So, he refused to include him on the team. Barnabas disagreed with Paul's assessment and a sharp disagreement ensued (Acts 15:39). In the end they parted ways. Paul recruited Silas for the missionary journey and departed on his God-given mission (Acts 15:41). Silas had helped Paul earlier and had proven leadership credentials (Acts 15:22). This partnership seems to have endured (Acts 16:19-40, 17:10-15, 18:5; 2 Cor. 1:19; 1 Thes. 1:1; 2 Thes. 1:1). Barnabas took John Mark on a mission to Cyprus (Acts 15:39). Later, John Mark and Paul apparently reconciled, Paul describing him as a co-worker (Col. 4:10-11; Phlm. 24) and "helpful to me in my ministry" (2 Tim. 4:11).

So when there is an unfavorable Review, here are some options and outcomes to consider:

1) The chemistry of a team should be taken seriously. Paul felt he couldn't trust John Mark and nothing Barnabas said dissuaded him from that view. As team leader, Paul made the best decision from his perspective. John Mark wouldn't be part of that mission team. That's a perfectly reasonable option. Sometimes, you will need to let someone go.

2) Failure does not have to be final. John Mark, with the support of Barnabas, was given the opportunity to prove himself.[17] A person may well deserve a second chance or another opportunity.

3) Two missions might be better than one. Barnabas and John Mark became a new team with a different mission focus to that of Paul and Silas. In God's wisdom, this divergence increased the reach of the Gospel.

4) Any broken relationships can (and should) be reconciled in time. John Mark learned to be a faithful leader and later rejoined Paul's team.

Clearly, there isn't just one way of dealing with a situation in which an individual isn't working well within a mission team.[18] Not every team member is going to work out. That's an unhappy but realistic expectation. If genuine attempts have been made to encourage the growth of someone in your team, and a subsequent Review highlights that there is a mission mismatch, you may decide to let that person go. In circumstances like these, do all that you can to help that person explore other avenues of service and ensure that your relationship remains as healthy as possible.

SOME HELPFUL TIPS FOR CONDUCTING A REVIEW

I want to finish this chapter with some tips for team leaders on how to conduct a good review. These things will help make it a mutually beneficial experience. At the top of the list (and I can't emphasize it enough) the Role Description frames the review. But here are some other helpful hints:

- **R** Role Description frames the review.
- **E** Ease into it. Don't rush headlong into the review. Make the relational connection first.
- **V** Venue is important. I would suggest a space that allows for robust conversation but is still a relaxed environment. Don't sit behind an intimidating desk. Ensure all chairs are comfortable and the same. If you are meeting in an office, simply have a coffee table between you and the interviewee. These arrangements encourage relational openness.
- **I** Invite genuine feedback. This is not just a verbal invitation. Make sure body language encourages openness. Take relevant notes readily for reflection and response.
- **E** Express the hard things in an optimistic way. Don't shy away from raising a concern. This is the appropriate opportunity to do that. A great leader can be relied on to ask the questions his team hopes he won't. Just don't crush them. Pursue rigorously, preserve dignity.
- **W** Win, win! Want the best. Don't settle for less. You want the best outcome for the team member and the best outcome for the mission, so strive to find a way to ensure success for all concerned.

CHAPTER SUMMARY

God will review our work at the end of time. The Apostle Paul revealed a kind of graduated scale by which success is measured – from zero to gold. In the light of this Great Review, we ought to be going for gold right now. This involves a commitment to a Continuous Development Process. Formal, thoughtful reviewing provides a framework for this. As a team leader you need to:

1) Review the Mission Resolution;

2) Review the progress of the mission;

3) Review your own performance with regard to your Role Description;

4) Have your performance reviewed by others;

5) Review your team's design;

6) Review the performance of each team member.

These reviews will usually be very affirming. But don't avoid the hard issues. Nothing will ever be perfect in this life or on this mission. You will always live with a level of holy dissatisfaction. Have faith! Press on, stretch out, change for good, grow bigger *and* better. Create and embrace the Continuous Development Culture!

Implementation Elevators

EXERCISE # 1: REVIEWING YOUR MISSION RESOLUTION

With your Mission Resolution in front of you, evaluate whether it captures, with precision, what God is calling you to do. Give your Mission Resolution an overall rating on the graduated scale below. Write down the reasons for your ratings.

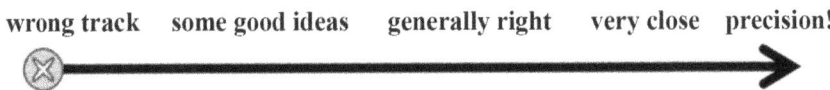

What do you think would help you move further towards precision? Take some appropriate action!

EXERCISE # 2: RE-VISIONING IF NECESSARY

In view of what has been achieved so far, does your Mission Resolution need to be re-cast because you have achieved (or are close to achieving) some of your stated goals? If so, begin the re-visioning process with the Implementation Elevators supplied in chapter 2.

EXERCISE # 3: REVIEW THE PROGRESS OF YOUR MISSION

Using the Tool below, identify your accelerators and restrainers.

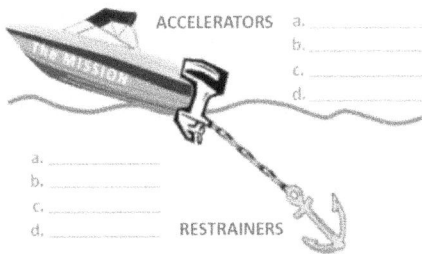

What needs to happen (commendation, a difficult conversation etc.) in response to the above assessment? Make a list and respond to each one in a disciplined manner.

EXERCISE # 4: REVIEW YOUR OWN PERFORMANCE

With your Role Description in front of you, rigorously assess your own performance as team leader. Ask questions like:

    a) Are you fulfilling your goals and commitments as per your Role Description?

b) Have you negotiated a Role Description with each member of your team?

c) Are you doing all you can to recruit your Dream Team?

d) Are you relating well with the people that you are leading?

e) Is serving on your team and on the mission a rewarding experience?

f) Is the mission being resourced appropriately?

g) Are you reviewing everything thoroughly?

h) Are you standing the strain?

Rate your performance on the chart below.

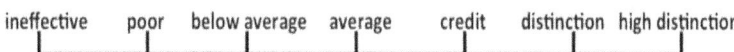

What could you do to improve?

EXERCISE # 5: BE REVIEWED

Submit to being reviewed annually. Assemble a suitable group of people who can speak into your life and lead. Arrange for an informal review half way through the year.

EXERCISE # 6: REVIEW YOUR ROLE DESCRIPTION

With your Role Description in front of you, consider the 'Satisfaction level'. Tick the corresponding box if you feel positive about the following:

- ❑ **S** kills and gifts used optimally
- ❑ **A** ffirmed by others
- ❑ **T** eam is integrated and motivated
- ❑ **I** nvigorated by the role
- ❑ **S** tanding the strain
- ❑ **F** uture looks fruitful
- ❑ **Y** ielding growth

Give an overall rating as to the suitability of your Role Description on the graduated scale below.

mismatch   some good ideas   generally right   very close   perfect match!

What do you think would help you move further towards your role being perfect for you?

EXERCISE # 7: REVIEW YOUR TEAM'S DESIGN

With the Role Descriptions of your team members all in front of you, consider the grand design of your team. Consider carefully the adequacy of the mix of roles.

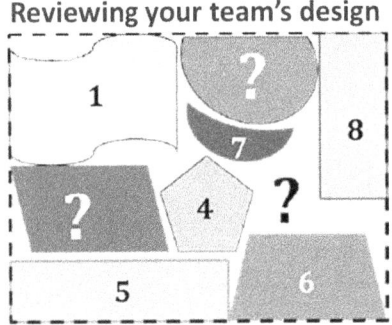

Reviewing your team's design

Given any developments with regard to your team and your mission, *and* anticipating future challenges and opportunities, are there any team design adjustments that will need to be made?

Is there a role adjustment that you would like a team member to make to fit with future goals? How would you approach that person concerning this proposed change?

EXERCISE # 8: PLAN FOR A GOOD REVIEW EXPERIENCE FOR YOUR TEAM MEMBERS

In the light of the tips for conducting a good review provided in this chapter carefully pre-plan your approach to leading this process. Consider the following:

R ole Description frames the review.

E ase into it. Make the relational connection!

V enue is important. Where would be the best place to meet?

I nvite genuine feedback.

E xpress the hard things in an optimistic way.

W in, win! How could everyone come out a winner?

EXERCISE # 9: REVIEWING THE PERFORMANCE OF A TEAM MEMBER

Team leaders must assess the performance of their leaders. Use the chart below. Invite each team member to assess their own performance. Create a constructive dialogue around this exercise.

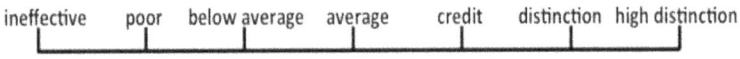

Agree (if possible) on a mutually beneficial way forward. Is there, however, a hard call that you need to make? Pray and think through how you will approach that difficult conversation.

EXERCISE # 10: REVIEWING A TEAM MEMBER'S ROLE DESCRIPTION

With the team member's Role Description in front of you, take the opportunity to discuss the appropriateness of their role in the light of the 'Satisfactor'. Tick the corresponding box if the team member feels positive about the following:

- ❏ **S** kills and gifts used optimally
- ❏ **A** ffirmed by others
- ❏ **T** eam member is integrated and motivated
- ❏ **I** nvigorated by the role
- ❏ **S** tanding the strain
- ❏ **F** uture looks fruitful
- ❏ **Y** ielding growth

Give an overall rating as to the suitability of the Role Description on the graduated scale below.

       mismatch some good ideas generally right very close perfect match!

What do you both think would help the team member move further towards the role being perfectly matched to them? If necessary, revise the role and redesign the team accordingly.

Chapter 10 IMPLEMENTATION–TEAM LEADER

Moses listened to his father-in-law and did everything he said

(Exodus 18:24)

Implementation	
Reviewing	7
Resourcing	6
Rewarding	5
Relationships	4
Recruiting	3
Roles	2
Resolution	1

> **This leadership teaching is based on Scripture and the central lesson in Jesus' story still applies: if something is well constructed on a solid foundation, it will endure the inevitable extreme conditions that will come against it. But, you've got to put it into practice. The advice needs to be implemented.**

We have now constructed the seven levels of The Jethro Model: Resolution > Roles > Recruiting > Relationships > Rewarding > Resourcing > Reviewing. You start by articulating your mission, then each level builds on the one before it. The preceding chapters have sought to explain the purpose and substance of each of the levels. Along the way, I've offered some practical advice to help you implement Jethro's leadership mandate in *your team*. Your challenge now, should you choose to accept it, is to action the principles taught in *The Resolute Leader*. Will you build your team on this solid foundation? What you build on really matters! You need to put these principles into practice. Jesus said:

> "I will show you what he is like who comes to me and hears my words and puts them into practice. He is like a man building a house, who dug down deep and laid the foundation on rock. When a flood came, the torrent struck that house but could not shake it, because it was well built. But the one who hears my words and does not put them into practice is like a man who built a house on the ground without a foundation. The moment the torrent struck that house, it collapsed and its destruction was complete" (Lk. 6:47-49).

Now, this teaching of Jesus was directly related to his own person and words. It wasn't given with reference to The Jethro Mandate. Nevertheless, this leadership teaching is based on Scripture and the central lesson in Jesus' story still applies: if something is well constructed on a solid foundation, it will endure the inevitable extreme conditions that will come against it. But, you've got to put it into practice. The advice needs to be implemented. Jethro said to Moses, "Listen now to me and I will give you some advice" (Ex. 18:19). Moses, having received the inspired mandate, had a choice – to implement or *not* to implement. The Bible reports that Moses, "listened to his father-in-law and did everything he said" (Ex. 18:24). You now face a similar choice. Instigating The Jethro Model

will give your leadership a lift and enable your mission to reach new heights. That's why I refer to it as 'Seven levels with a lift'. What could be stopping you making this ascent? What can you expect on the way up? I'll try to anticipate some of the questions that you might have at this point and endeavor to answer them. My hope is that I will convince you that implementation is not only possible, it's vital!

QUESTION # 1: What if no other team in my church is utilizing The Jethro Model? Can an isolated team still adopt the model fully?

The answer is definitely yes! The Jethro Model is very versatile. It can be implemented by a small church or mission team. In the final chapter of the book, I will encourage church-wide adoption of The Jethro Mandate. But even if your team alone applies the advice given here, the benefits will be huge! This book makes the case for team-based implementation.

QUESTION # 2: If my church doesn't implement The Jethro Model, what do I do with the 'hard case' problems when they come along? Who would I refer them 'up' too?

Every church has a senior leader or some senior leaders. You can probably identify them fairly easily. Develop a relationship with an appropriate senior leader who is willing to tackle those problems that are too difficult for you. Never attempt to deal alone with a problem, burden or dispute you know you cannot handle. Perhaps, in extreme circumstances, you will have to find wisdom beyond your experience level because there is no-one else who can deal with the issue. Ask God to give it to you. Otherwise, pass on to a senior leader those problems that are too difficult for you.

QUESTION # 3: Can I just use parts of The Jethro Model, rather than all seven levels?

No doubt, each part of the model has its own benefits. Rewarding your team members, for example, is always a positive thing to do. Some chapter ideas *could be* implemented without reference to the other levels. Nevertheless, some of the higher levels of The Jethro Model cannot be implemented confidently without strong support from the levels below. For example, it would be potentially disastrous to conduct a review of someone's performance without a Role Description as a point of reference. That would not be a very safe situation. What you are left with is invisible rules, unwritten expectations and half-remembered commitments. That won't be good enough. Further, it's hard to recruit when potential team members are not exactly sure what they are signing up for. The mission needs to be clearly stated to remove all confusion. It's no good vaguely saying, 'This mission leads to a Better Land'. The problem is that *you* are thinking about the Promised Land while *they* are thinking about Disneyland! That's a tour that will end in tears. The Jethro Model, is a seven level structure, and every level is dynamically related to the others. They are not intended to be treated in isolation from each other.

> **The Jethro Model, is a seven level structure, and every level is dynamically related to the others.**

QUESTION # 4: How long will implementation take?

In answering this question, I will assume that you have around you an existing team or the beginnings of one. Your implementation timeframe will depend on variables like these:

I   Influential team members – Do they see the benefits of it? Do they understand and support the changes? It may take time to overcome initial resistance or indifference. Put this book in their hands!

M   Mood for change – Are your team members dissatisfied with the current way of doing things and ready for a positive change? This could help things move along!

P   Persuaded? – Are you personally convinced that this is the way to go? Your passion will create momentum!

L   Leadership culture – Does The Jethro Mandate comply with the Constitution of your church? Do you need to seek approval to implement this? Ask a senior leader for advice.

E   Envision the Model and the Mission – If people can see how The Jethro Model enhances the ability to accomplish the Mission then they will be willing to implement quickly.

M   Map out the implementation process – Can you roughly see the steps you need to take to full implementation? When you can plot the way forward, step by step, you will get there in good time!

E   Energy levels – Have you got the kind of energy required to continuously teach it, promote it, defend it and apply it? If you do, you'll push through at good speed.

N   Nerve/Courage – Have you got the nerve to complete all the levels (including reviewing) in the face of persistent opposition? People don't usually like change. If you waiver, momentum is lost.

T   Timing is everything! – Wait for the right time. Too fast and you'll put people off. Too slow and you might miss the opportunity. Leaders are stewards of 'right-timing'.

Taking those variables into consideration, I think a team leader should anticipate that implementation of The Jethro Mandate would normally take around a year. As you can see, it will take a lot of resolve. It will be a test of character. It will require disciplined action. The following is a suggested time-line. Play around with it. Adjust it according to your context. Whatever you come up with, it will be helpful to have some implementation time-targets. Then you will have a better idea of how long it will take.

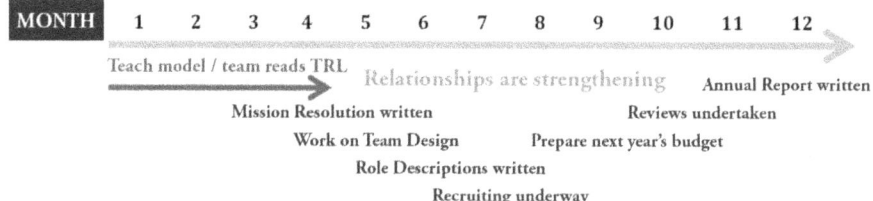

During the first quarter of the year, I would be teaching the model over and over again, fielding questions and receiving feedback. People will want to know *why* you are implementing this. Knowing The Jethro Model well enough to explain it is essential (Deut. 1: 18). If you have your team reading this book it will do a lot of the hard work for you. People will need to *know* what they will need to *do*. As this is happening, I'd make a start on articulating the Mission Resolution. Remember, everything flows from knowing what the mission is as clearly as possible. Roles will also need to be defined, so work on designing, refining and recruiting your team during this early stage as well. By the time you reach the six-month-mark, you will have probably constructed the first three levels. You will be well on your way. You may not have everything exactly the way you want it. There will be some trial and error. But you will get better at it as you go. Take the long view. Imagine how good it will be when The Jethro Model is widely understood, highly valued and deeply embedded in your team culture.

> **The exciting reality is that implementation of The Jethro Model will turn a good leader into a great leader. This is because the success of your God-glorifying mission will be based on a God-given, time-honored, road-tested, leader-mobilizing model.**

QUESTION # 5: What if I don't build The Jethro Model into my team?

If you are a very capable leader, then you will probably still build a good team and do some good things even if you don't implement The Jethro Model. You will do this largely on the strength of your personal gifting and charisma. Your role will resemble that of Moses in the early days. Everyone comes to you with their needs and concerns. This will work to a point, and you will have some *limited* success. If you're *not* an especially gifted person and you *don't* implement The Jethro Model then the prognosis isn't so bright. Chances are that the lack of a solid foundation and structure will stifle care and stall progress. There's a heightened probability that your team will fragment and your mission fail. One way or another, if you don't implement The Jethro Model you will find that:

1) you will struggle to cope;
2) you and your team will lose focus as to *what* precisely the mission is;
3) your team members won't find serving satisfying and rewarding;
4) your effectiveness will be diminished;
5) resources will dry up;
6) people will become increasingly dissatisfied as their needs go on unmet;
7) your mission will need to be down-graded or abandoned altogether.

So you have to ask yourself the question, 'Can I afford *not* to implement The Jethro Model?'

The exciting reality is that implementation of The Jethro Model will turn a *good leader* into a *great leader*, even if you're not an especially gifted or charismatic person. This is because the success of your God-glorifying mission will be based on a God-given, time-honored, road-tested, leader-mobilizing model. Often, the very best leaders don't have headline-grabbing personalities, or even the greatest gifting. What they *do* have is the resolve to apply proven principles in a disciplined, methodical way. If you are a good leader and you aspire to be a great leader, The Jethro Model will be of immeasurable help! And if you happen to be a person of great, God-given giftedness and capacity already, then implementing The Jethro Model will help take your leadership impact to new God-glorifying heights. Moses was an extraordinary person. He ranks in the top tier of all-time-great spiritual leaders, but his lack of leadership structure was holding things back. So God directed that he implement all that his father-in-law mandated.

I've attempted above to answer some anticipated questions. Hopefully, I've convinced you as to *why* you should implement The Jethro Model and provided some realistic expectations for when you do. As you can see, you will need to approach this task with strength of character and resolute actions. You will need to be a resolute leader.

IMPLEMENT THE JETHRO MODEL LEVEL BY LEVEL

Having resolved to proceed with implementation, it is now a matter of creating and developing your team by systematically applying what has been taught in the preceding chapters. Follow the chapter order because each new chapter builds on those before it. Make sure you complete the Implementation Elevators as best you can. Revisit the questions and refine your answers from time to time. This will help you become a more effective leader. Diligent application of The Jethro Model will help ensure you accomplish your God-glorifying mission.

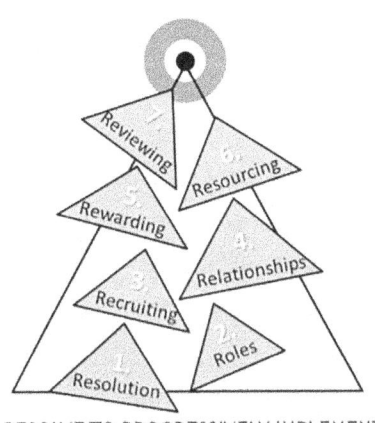

RESOLVE TO PROGRESSIVELY IMPLEMENT
THE SEVEN STEPS OF THE MODEL

Chapter 11 IMPLEMENTATION–CHURCH LEADER

*Moses listened to his father-in-law
and did everything he said*

(Exodus 18:24)

There are a number of high-level challenges that face Pastors and senior Christian leaders. People who have never led at a senior level almost invariably underestimate the complex demands associated with such a large sphere of influence. Leaders of a hundred, and certainly leaders of thousands, need to be highly capable. King David was such a leader. The Bible says that, "David shepherded them with integrity of heart; with skilful hands he led them" (Ps. 78:72). We need to exhibit both of those attributes– a heart of concern for those we lead *and* the skills to lead them where God wants us to go. The same sort of commendation was made with regard to Moses and Aaron (Ps. 77:20). These three leaders led a 'flock' consisting of millions of people. Moses and Aaron led them to the Promised Land, while David oversaw the crucial, final stages of occupation. Both missions were extraordinarily difficult and placed huge demands on the senior leaders. Nothing much has changed really. Sure, you probably don't lead millions of people. Nevertheless, Pastors and senior Christian leaders need to exercise careful, skilful oversight as they lead God's people forward on the mission. This is your mandate.

A GREAT CHURCH NEEDS MORE THAN A GREAT STRUCTURE

The Jethro Model provides a structural framework that will support your leaders and meet people's needs *as* you move your church forward. And it will help ensure that senior leaders can focus on those essential things that are part and parcel of leading and growing an effective church; things like great preaching and powerful praying. You know best the main things that God has called you to do for the extension of his Kingdom. The Jethro Mandate will release you to do those things well. Interestingly, there are some obvious parallels between the things that Moses was called to do and the ministry and mission of the New Testament Apostles. The table below demonstrates the similarities.

Exodus 18:19-22	**Acts 6:2-4**
Intercede for the people (v. 19)	Attention given to prayer (v. 4)
Teach God's Word (v. 20)	Ministry of the Word (vs. 2, 4)
Appoint leaders to meet practical needs (vs. 21-22)	Recommended appointment of leaders to meet practical needs (v. 3)

The structure was not an end in itself. It supported the other essential aspects of the life and mission of God's people. The apostles resolved, as did Moses, to fulfill their distinctive roles without neglecting the needs of the people *or* the mission of the church. Your church has a particular calling. You have a specialist role. The Jethro Model releases people to fulfill all that God has for them and the church. A great church needs more than a great structure. Nevertheless, a great structure supports a great church. Moses and the Apostles could testify to the truth of this time-honored principle.

I KNOW IT WORKS

I have already confessed that, as a rookie Pastor, I had little idea as to *how* to lead the church I was called to. I didn't have the required skills. In the Introduction, I mentioned the two major challenges that I was confronted with back then. The first challenge was to know precisely the mission I was called to lead. The second challenge concerned how to go about creating and developing a team to accomplish it. In this book, I've systematically set out what I have learned in response to those challenges. The Jethro Model, with its seven level structure, has provided me with a teachable, practical, systematic and implementable leadership framework for my church. This model will help you in your church as well. If you've been leading for a while, most of the principles taught here will be familiar to you. What The Jethro Model offers, however, is an integrated, graduated, leadership framework that will help you organize the *whole* church. It does this in such a way as to encourage *everyone* to be a part of the *overall* mission that God had given to the *whole* church. When you use The Jethro Model throughout your church, everyone can unite around a shared team creation and development process. You will share a common vision and a common leadership language. The benefits of this are obvious.

THE IMPLEMENTATION CHALLENGE

So, what is required on the part of a high-level leader in order that this seven level structure be implemented? What do you need to commit to? What do you need to do? Implementing The Jethro Mandate will help 'elevate' your church and its mission capacity from good to great. Ascent through each of the 'levels' will increase effectiveness, boost morale and greatly increase the possibility of extraordinary success! That's why I refer to The Jethro Model as having 'seven levels with an elevator'. In order to take this journey to the top, I believe that Pastors and high-level leaders need to commit to the following seven actions. They need to become part of the culture that they perpetuate. Senior leaders need to:

1) commit to a thorough implementation of The Jethro Model in their context;

2) articulate their church's overall Mission Resolution;

3) plan and execute the action steps required to achieve it;

4) align the whole church behind the mission;

5) arrange the whole church so that leaders are structurally connected;

6) recruit high-capacity leaders who will champion the mission and the structure;

7) get as many people as possible contributing to the accomplishing the mission.

Let's explore these seven challenges.

 # 1 COMMIT TO THE THOROUGH IMPLEMENTATION OF THE JETHRO MODEL IN YOUR CONTEXT

The Jethro Model is completely adaptable. It can be applied on a small scale, to any team in your church. It is also ideally suited to church-wide implementation. I've already demonstrated how the principles that I have extrapolated from Jethro's mandate can be of enormous benefit to leaders of a team. Nevertheless, I'll remind you again that this inspired counsel was originally given to help lead and care for around two million people! So whatever the size of your church, The Jethro Model will be applicable and will help you realize those goals that God has given you. What is needed on your part is a deep resolve to implement it. The Bible says that, "Moses listened to his father–in-law *and did everything he said*" (Ex. 18:24)[Emphasis added].

Perhaps, as you've been reading this book, you've seen the Biblical basis and the simple logic of The Jethro Model. By now, you're probably familiar with the framework of the seven level structure. You understand it conceptually. The thing is, the only way to enjoy the view from the top is to take the elevator – *level by level* – and implement The Jethro Model thoroughly throughout your church. This will take great determination. It will require great effort and will perhaps come at a considerable cost. I'm reminded of Jesus' words:

> "Suppose one of you wants to build a tower. Will he not first sit down and estimate the cost to see if he has enough money to complete it? For if he lays the foundation and is not able to finish it, everyone who sees it will ridicule him saying, 'This fellow began to build and was not able to finish'" (Lk. 14:28-30).

Of course, this teaching wasn't with reference to The Jethro Model. It was intended to alert would-be disciples of the costs associated with being a fully committed follower of Jesus. Jesus cautioned against launching into a long-term, multi-level project (a tower) without serious consideration as to the resources that would be required to complete it. That parabolic picture also helps illustrate the kind of resolve and rigor required to thoroughly implement The Jethro Model.

> **The only way to enjoy the view from the top is to take the elevator – *level by level* – and implement The Jethro Model thoroughly throughout your church.**

To re-apply an element of Jesus' story to our current theme, it would be easy to hurriedly and publicly launch The Jethro Mandate in your church. You know by now how beneficial it will be. Excitedly you lay the foundation of a compelling Mission Resolution and have it printed on posters and in every publication possible. But you soon discover that not everyone likes what you are resolving to do and a few vocal people are unwilling to align behind it. Then you discover that your attempt to organize teams structurally meets some resistance. After all, those teams and leaders have been happily going their own good way long before they'd ever heard of a 'Jethro Model'. To your great frustration, some long-standing ministries and leaders are reluctant to comply. This sort of resistance isn't uncommon. Sooner or later, the disheartening truth dawns on you: a thorough-going implementation of The Jethro Mandate in your church is going to take time. If you don't take the time and effort, you won't get the rewards. The unfortunate reality is that you can often observe in churches the ridiculous remains of unfinished, underestimated projects. These were hastily undertaken following attendance at a Christian conference or the reading of a book like this. The innovation might have been a towering success if only someone had sat down and realistically thought things through.

You need to count the cost. Obviously every church is different, so when you sit down to estimate the costs of implementing The Jethro Mandate you'll need to take into consideration all the dynamics of your context. Pastors and senior leaders should be able to anticipate most of these challenges. Here are some things to think about as you contemplate implementation.

- **I** Influential individuals – Who are they and how might they respond?
- **M** Mood for change – Is there a general dissatisfaction with the current way of doing things?
- **P** Persuaded – Are you personally persuaded as to the benefits of The Jethro Model?
- **L** Leadership culture – How would The Jethro Mandate fit with regard to the Constitution of your church and denomination?
- **E** Engagement on the part of other Senior Leaders – Are they mildly interested or passionately enthused?
- **M** Map out the process – Can you roughly draft the way to get to full implementation and imagine what it might look like when you get there?
- **E** Energy – Have you got the kind of energy required to continuously teach it, promote it, defend it and apply it?
- **N** Nerve/Courage – Have you got the nerve to keep building the structure in the face of some persistent opposition?
- **T** Tenure – Will you or other Senior Leaders be around long enough to see this whole thing through?

These considerations are part of calculating the cost. You need to be sure you can complete what you start. Only *you* know how to do this in a way, and at a speed, that is appropriate to your situation. Only *you* can count the cost of implementation. Of course, you've also got to count the cost of *not* implementing The Jethro Mandate. Obviously, Jesus wanted people to follow him. The warning recorded in Luke 14 was not given because the decision to be a disciple was ill-advised. Jesus clearly wanted people to follow him and be saved! He was, however, endeavoring to ensure that aspiring followers had realistic expectations. 'It will be demanding', he warned. That being said, the benefits will be far-reaching.

Jethro was well aware of the cost of *not* implementing his inspired structure. Something needed to change and quickly! The negative repercussions of non-implementation of The Jethro Model were four-fold:

1) an enormous, debilitating, unnecessary, personal strain on Moses;

2) general dissatisfaction on the part of the people of Israel who had genuine needs but little hope of them being met because the only avenue for that was a personal audience with one person;

3) a lot of untapped leadership potential because hundreds of them were seriously underutilized before Jethro came along;

4) the mission to reach the Promised Land was being jeopardized. This was because Moses was devoting too much attention and energy in an attempt to meet the day-to-day needs of individual people. Consequently, he couldn't adequately attend to the task of leading the whole nation forward.

Jethro, the seasoned priest and experienced leader, gave his leadership mandate in the nick of time!

2 ARTICULATE YOUR CHURCH'S MISSION RESOLUTION

Having decided to implement The Jethro Model right across your church or organization, you can now confidently commence construction – level by level. You will work with the same seven level structure as taught to team leaders, but you will develop it from a senior leader's perspective. That is, you'll be developing things on behalf of the *whole* church and its *overall* mission. Your Mission Resolution will probably be more general and more inclusive than that of a smaller mission team. Nevertheless, precision remains important and the words used ought to be carefully chosen and suitably weighted.

The Church that I lead has the following Mission Resolution: To grow Northreach to 1500 people, while planting 2 new, diverse Churches and sending 3 missionaries overseas. We are aiming to grow to 1500 strong within five years. Our church-starting and missionary-sending goals are 10 years targets. Our success or failure in reaching these goals in a timely manner will be obvious because the aims are clear and time-lined. These goals are so big and broad

In the next 5 years:
reach out and grow
our church to 1500 people.
In the next 10 years:
start 2 diverse churches in our city
and send out 3 cross-cultural missionaries.

that almost everyone can plan a part. Senior leaders ought to dream all-encompassing dreams like these. You need to formulate a church-wide Mission Resolution. Team leaders, for their part, should aim their Mission Resolutions towards the church's overall targets.

3 PLAN AND EXECUTE THE STRATEGIES TO ACHIEVE IT

Once senior leaders have discerned *what* God wants their church to achieve the next step is to plan *how* it can be done. It's time to strategize. Formulate incremental action steps. Invite as many people as practicable to participate in this process. You're seeking widespread and willing resolve to contribute towards accomplishment. That's why aligning the whole church behind the Mission Resolution is vital!

4 ALIGNING EVERYTHING BEHIND THE STATED MISSION

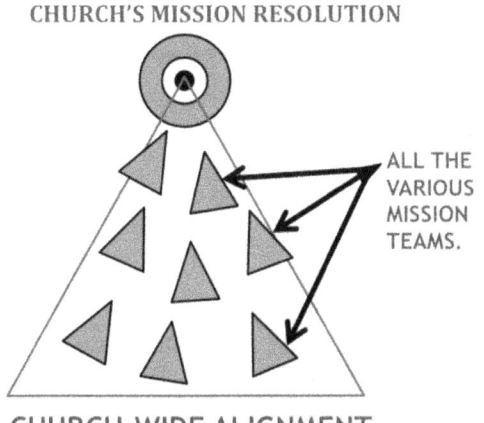

CHURCH-WIDE ALIGNMENT

We've already acknowledged that the role of a senior church leader is essentially different from that of a mission team leader. Many of the differences have to do with scale and perspective. A senior leader's Vision will necessarily be more oriented towards the *whole* church and the *overall* mission. A team leader will focus their attention on their precise mission and specific team. In Chapter 3, I made team leaders aware of the importance of ensuring that their mission is intentionally aligned with their church's overall mission. Most team leaders will be able to demonstrate their intentional contribution. That goodwill notwithstanding, in most churches there will usually be leaders and mission teams that are, at best, a little wayward of your goals or, at worst, at cross-purposes. Prior to the implementation of a Jethro-type structure, a church will typically have teams going in all sorts of directions [see illustration right].

Your mission is to align all the various mission teams with *at least some part* your church-wide Mission Resolution. This will necessarily involve convincing the leaders and teams of the importance of this. If your church has been unwieldy in this area then you will need to patiently help non-aligned missions correct their course. Persistent and persuasive teaching of The Jethro Model will be required. This book should

therefore be *required* reading! In extreme cases, 'rebel' leaders and missions will need to be cut out. That awkwardness is part of the cost of implementation. Senior leaders make these sorts of serious decisions. It goes with the territory. The benefits of that decision will, however, quickly become apparent.

The following is a list of some of the approaches I would take in an attempt to convince leaders and mission teams of the need to align behind the overall stated mission.

C ommunicate clearly and consistently.

O ne-on-one meetings with leaders.

N egatives into positives. Remind people of what's not working well.

V alue every leader and team and do your best to win them over. After all, they are willing volunteers!

I nspire them to participate (as opposed to a 'command and control' approach) with stories of what could be.

N ever give up! It will take time.

C ommend those who do align and get them to share why they did with others.

E ncourage everyone to read The Resolute Leader!

Senior leaders need to do these sorts of things well. Accomplishing the mission depends on widespread alignment and involvement. Below is a picture of what things could look like when all the leaders and all the teams get behind your church-wide Mission Resolution.

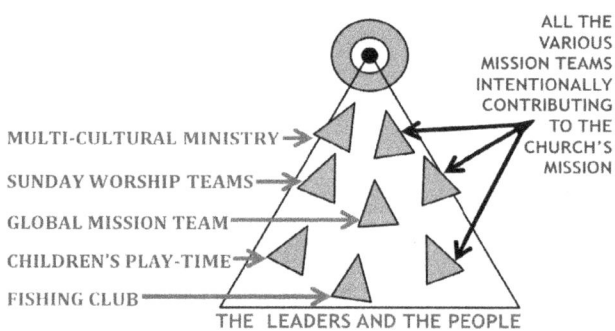

Great things are achieved through this sort of collective effort! We find examples of this in the Bible. When Deborah was a Judge of Israel, she oversaw a military mission, *the success of which* depended on the alignment of the forces of two different tribes of Israel. The

Bible provides a stirring account of the occasion when ten thousand people from the tribes of Zebulun and Naphtali *united as one* to achieve a collective victory. In response to the victory, and particularly *the way* in which it was won, Deborah sang, "When the princes in Israel take the lead, when the people willingly offer themselves – praise the LORD" (Judg. 5:1-2). These tribes united to ensure the overall success of the mission led by Deborah. So you will need to inspire church-wide engagement in order to accomplish your God-given goals. Every leader and team needs to be aligned behind the mission of the church.

To use my church as an example again, the senior leadership team of Northreach Baptist Church is tasked with the responsibility of ensuring that all of the different mission teams are intentionally engaged in the mission that God has given to the *whole* church. Each mission team should be helping accomplish an aspect or aspects of the overall Mission Resolution. This is a big part of our leadership role. This means that teams as diverse as the Children's Play-Time team, the Fishing Club team, the Multi-Cultural Ministry team, the Sunday Worship team and the Global Mission team should *all* have Mission Resolutions and strategies that articulate and anticipate their intended contributions to the stated mission of the whole church. This last point is worth reiterating. Each leader and mission team should have goals that intentionally contribute to the overall mission. The sum of the successes of each team should amount to the attaining of the overall mission of the church.

Aligning leaders and teams behind the mission is essential for synergy and success.

Next comes the need to support those leaders and teams well. This, in the spirit of Jethro's inspired Model, involves arranging every person, team and leader into a structure that offers organizational support.

 # 5 ARRANGE THE WHOLE CHURCH SO THAT LEADERS ARE STRUCTURALLY CONNECTED

Now, the Jethro structure is quite regimented. Its organizational structure has military parallels (Num. 31:14). There are tiers of leaders who are responsible for a certain number of people – "thousands, hundreds, fifties and tens" (Ex. 18:21). These leaders serve as 'judges' of the different sized divisions of the people (Ex. 18:21-22). This structural rigor can lead to two misconceptions:

    1) that it's all about 'command and control' and handing down verdicts from 'on high;'

    2) that it's restrictive.

In order to convince your church of the advantages of The Jethro Model, and to incorporate people willingly into the leadership structure, senior leaders will need to be able to counter these misconceptions. Here below is how I would respond.

To address the first misconception, we shouldn't think of their 'judging' in a legal sense. The role is more of a 'champion-leader', as in the Book of Judges. These champion-leaders are appointed to lead a certain number of people (based on their capacity to lead) and they are responsible for meeting the needs of those people as best they can. It isn't about 'command and control'. Rather its central concerns are *pastoral care* and *positive leadership*. As I stated before, people have a variety of problems, burdens and disputes (Deut. 1:12). These leaders have a mission to help the people they serve in times of trouble. They are deployed to do this on God's behalf. This is an onerous task!

To respond to the second misconception, the structure is designed to be liberating rather than unnecessarily restrictive. Given the onerous nature of the leadership task, it's easy to feel overwhelmed and under-supported sometimes. No one wants that! The structure is designed to support *empowered* leaders. The Jethro structure facilitates decision-making by releasing leaders to act decisively within their abilities. There are simple problems that are easily solved (Exodus. 18:22). Then there are more difficult cases (Ex. 18:22). Some problems will be "too hard" and require expert input (Deut. 1:17). Each challenge can be addressed at the appropriate leader-level. This is where clear, cohesive and communicative lines of leadership become important. No one gets stuck with a problem they can't handle. Problems don't get *pushed down*, but *referred up!* Dealing with on-going problems you can't handle, can be debilitating and can potentially derail the mission. When that issue gets handed on to someone with greater expertise in that area, it frees the leader to get on with their mission. Leaders responsible for 'ten' should know they have the support of someone who oversees 'fifty'. The 'ten' people would be a *sub-set* of the 'fifty'. In other words, the leader of 'fifty' may well be overseeing *five groups of 'ten'*. In such a case, the leader of the 'ten' would then be supported by, and accountable to, that leader of 'fifty'. When the relationship connection between the leader of 'ten' and the leader of 'fifty' is pin-pointed and positive, then the leadership burden can be shared. This is a great benefit of The Jethro Model.

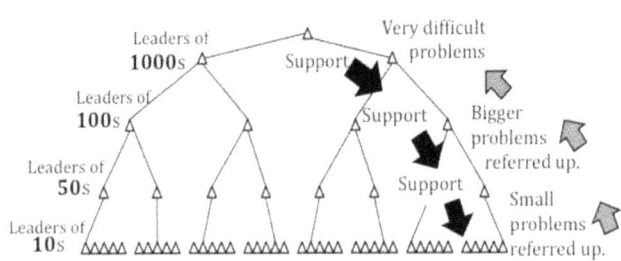

Having a *conceptual* framework alone for the Jethro structure isn't enough. You are going to need to know who is connected to whom. This will ensure that all the benefits of The Jethro Model are flowing through your church. You will need to create an organizational flow chart. Using the illustration above as a template, begin the process of organizing tiers of leaders according to the demands and opportunities of your context. Usually, the process is relatively straight-forward. The higher-capacity leaders (leaders of fifties, hundreds and thousands) will be apparent by virtue of the competent lead they are already providing. Nevertheless, this work takes disciplined effort and will require you to make judgments from time to time. In the process it might become apparent that there are leadership gaps that need to be filled. Or perhaps you will discover that some leadership connections need to be rearranged to maximize cohesiveness and effectiveness. Further, as your church grows, the number of teams and tiers will grow too. You will need to plan for this by developing leaders relentlessly. Again, having a structure isn't the goal. The goal isn't just to produce a nice, neat flow-chart. The purpose is to get the right leaders in the right places so as to reduce leader-stress, and to meet people's needs *while* fulfilling God's mission – that's what it's all about!

> **The purpose is to get the right leaders in the right places so as to reduce leader-stress, and to meet people's needs *while* fulfilling God's mission.**

6 RECRUIT HIGH-CAPACITY LEADERS WHO WILL CHAMPION THE MISSION RESOLUTION AND THE LEADERSHIP STRUCTURE

Once the structure is basically mapped out, senior leaders need to ensure that it is continually populated with appropriate leaders. Of greatest concern is identifying the leaders who will have the largest sphere of influence. These people will have a highly influential role, so you need to be certain that they can and will champion the mission and support the leadership structure. How can you identify the right sort of leaders? What kind of person is worthy of promotion to the rank of serving as an overseer? The Bible says that, "If anyone sets his heart on being an overseer, he desires a noble task" (1 Tim. 3:1). The holy aspiration to senior leadership is commendable. The Apostle Paul provided detailed lists of the character-traits and integrity-markers required of candidates for overseer roles (1 Tim. 3:2-13; Tit. 1:6-9). They are to be:

a) Monogamous (if married)
b) Even-tempered
c) Worthy of respect
d) Hospitable
e) Able to teach
f) Able to refute those who oppose sound doctrine
g) Light consumers of alcohol (if they drink alcohol at all)
h) Gentle
i) Not argumentative
j) Not in love with money
k) Financially above reproach
l) A good spouse and parent (if married and with children)
m) An experienced follower of Jesus

n) Well respected by people outside the church
o) Steadfastly committed to the truth of the faith
p) Blameless
q) Loving of what is good
r) Self-controlled
s) Holy
t) Disciplined

The Apostle Paul wrote that high-level leaders, "must first be tested; and then if there is nothing against them, let them serve" (1 Tim. 3:10). So, potential senior leaders need to demonstrate a proven track record in the areas of character, integrity, relationships and sound doctrine. These things are non-negotiable! Paul sought to fill the overseeing ranks of every local church with people who had these qualities (Tit. 1:5). Moses also chose leaders with a proven track record. He reported, "So I took the leading men of your tribes, wise and respected men, and appointed them to have authority over you – as commanders of thousands, of hundreds, of fifties and of tens" (Deut. 1:15). I would assume that the selection process for leaders of thousands of people would have been more rigorous than the appointment of someone to lead ten people. Much of what generally needs to be said about recruiting leaders has been covered in Chapter 5. Nevertheless, here are just six Bible-based traits to look for in a potential senior leader.

> I would assume that the selection process for leaders of thousands of people would have been more rigorous than the appointment of someone to lead ten people.

1) **Marital faithfulness**. Loyalty and covenant-keeping are vital to spiritual leadership. A demonstrably long and happy marriage is evidence of a resolve to stay faithful through thick and thin. This displays great character qualities. Senior leaders know how to love unconditionally and with firm determination.

2) **Emotional stability**. A self-controlled leader is a safe leader. Even-temperedness, gentleness, faithfulness and the like, are attributes that the Holy Spirit produces (Gal. 5:2-23). Look for long-term consistency in these areas. An out-of-control or argumentative senior leader can do untold damage. Further, hard-case problem solving and dispute resolution require a steady head and heart. Stable leaders make for competent mediators.

3) **Widely admired**. Paul says overseers should have earned respect both inside and outside the church. A wide range of people should be able to look up to them. This is not the same as just being popular. People can be popular for inappropriate reasons. This is about spiritual stature. Look for leaders of whom

it can be said that, "God has exalted them in the eyes of the people" (Josh. 4:14). These are the sorts of leaders that people will follow.

4) **Good at personal relationships**. We've already considered the importance of marital fidelity. In addition to that, leaders who are parents should demonstrate the ability to manage their *whole* family well. They need to have positive, nurturing relationships with their kids. Paul says that this is important because they are going to be leading the *whole* family of the church. They also need to be good at relationships generally. The success of the Jethro structure is premised on great leadership relationships. Senior leaders need to be expert at interpersonal dynamics.

5) **Deeply spiritual**. Senior leaders need not only to hold to the truth personally, they need to have the capacity to teach it, defend it and apply it in real-life situations. When Moses delegated the leadership responsibility of dealing with people's problems, burdens and disputes, the assumption was that these would be addressed in a manner consistent with God's Word. Dispensing conventional human wisdom was not enough. They were making judgments on God's behalf (Deut. 1:17). Therefore, their approach to decision-making needed to be influenced by love for God and fear of God. That's why it's critical that senior leaders demonstrate a long-held, deep knowledge of God and his Word. They must be experienced followers of Jesus.

6) **Disciplined in approach**. Leading a large group of people well requires a steady commitment to the right directions, values, actions and even structures. The people we lead are looking for consistency. Unwavering commitment to great goals inspires their allegiance. Steady commitment to taking the necessary action steps inspires confidence. Senior leaders need to do the right things, the right way, at the right time.

If you choose these sorts of leaders, you have the greatest opportunity to provide an overall lead that gains wide acceptance and galvanizes resolve. This is important, because your God-given mission will only be fulfilled when *as many people as possible* are actively contributing to the collective effort. To do something truly great, you're going to need to get a high level of participation. You will need to defy the 80/20 rule!

 # 7 GET AS MANY PEOPLE ACTIVELY INVOLVED AS POSSIBLE

I know what it's like to have just a few people carry the whole load. During the early days in my first church, we were verifying evidence for what's known as the '80/20 rule' or the 'Pareto principle'. This rule or principle states that, for many events, roughly 80% of the effects come from 20% of the causes. When

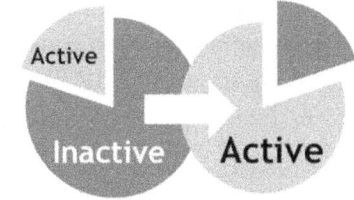

applied to the church this means that, usually, 80% of the mission is done by 20% of the people. That's just how it was when I started. Don't get me wrong, it was a normal, average church. There were a few great people doing some great things. No doubt about it. But, too few people were really involved. In many churches, most people aren't making a meaningful contribution to the church's God-given goals. This common dilemma is in line with Jesus' prediction that, the "harvest is plentiful but the workers are few" (Mat. 9:37). That's the bad news.

Here's the good news: things can improve! I had faith that they would. Jesus went on to say, "Ask the Lord of the harvest, therefore, to send out workers" (Mat. 9:38). I knew that I needed to pray for more willing leaders and workers who would be deployed on *their* God-given mission to meet needs. More and more people needed to be mobilized.

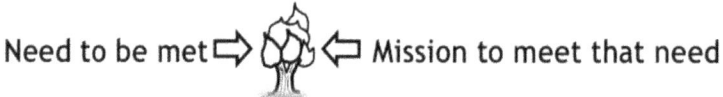

I also became convinced that I needed to organize the church that I led in order that the efforts of willing volunteers would be maximized. I hope you share this conviction! You need to create an environment within your church that is conducive to high levels of participation. I can guarantee that implementing The Jethro Mandate will prove to be a catalyst for higher participation rates in your church. The reasons for this are embedded within the seven level structure. I'll support this claim with reference to the seven 'levels' of The Jethro Model as taught in *The Resolute Leader*; Resolution, Role Descriptions, Recruiting, Relationships, Rewarding, Resourcing and Reviewing.

MISSION RESOLUTION

People want to know where a church is going. The clearer and more compelling your Church's Mission Resolution, the more it will capture people's attention, and catapult them into action. Time and time again, when people decide to join the church that I serve, the number-one reason given is that they like the mission; it inspires them. They want to be part of a church that is doing *what we're doing* and going *where we're going*. This enthusiastic alignment behind the stated mission predisposes them to active involvement.

Further, as the various mission teams within your church articulate their God-given missions, they will capture the imagination and participation of volunteers. Volunteers want to know what they are signing up for. Most importantly they want to know who the mission is aiming to reach and what the mission is aiming to do. Team Mission Resolutions will provide them with the required clarity and encourage them to join the mission that really resonates with them. Mission Resolutions encourage volunteerism.

ROLE DESCRIPTIONS

Role Descriptions are confidence inspiring documents. They establish healthy boundaries. Let's face it, there are two major impediments to people volunteering their services:

1) busy lifestyles and

2) negative past experiences in Christian service.

Many people feel overly busy. They have full diaries and feel time poor. We could argue about whether people's schedules reflect good and godly prioritization but the perception that most people have is that time is in short supply. Nevertheless, people can and will allocate time to something *if* they believe in it and *if* they are convinced that the role is manageable and the time-commitment is sustainable. Once people are assured of these things, they are much more likely to seriously commit to continuous service. Realistic expectations dramatically reduce drop-out rates.

There will also be people who join your church having served somewhere else before and it was a negative experience. Sadly, many churches and teams are disorganized and directionless. They throw recruits into roles that are ill-defined, unmanageable and have little regard for the gifts and passions of the volunteer. Sometimes, in organizations like these, there are unwritten expectations and invisible standards. To judge the performance of a volunteer by these is unfair. This creates a lot of uncertainty and insecurity. People who have survived this sort of experience are understandably reluctant to volunteer again. Their confidence is shattered. If a person feels they will just be 'used and abused' and then thrown on the scrap-heap they will, understandably, be unwilling to volunteer.

Role Descriptions are invaluable when it comes to addressing these two issues. The thorough implementation of Role Descriptions, for everyone at every level, creates clarity and certainty for people. Everyone knows exactly what is expected of them and the time commitment required. These things are negotiated with the appropriate leader as part of the process of creating their Role Description. The role will fit well in terms of gifts, passion and time. There are *no* unwritten rules or invisible standards. Any reviewing done will only be with reference to the Role Description. This is all very confidence-inspiring and encourages participation on a wide scale because it addresses the two major impediments to volunteering in the first place. The Jethro Model will increase volunteerism.

Further, excellent team design will be of great benefit here. The more your team leaders can create wide-ranging roles for well-rounded teams, the more 'room' they create for participation at many levels. Further, as Mission Resolutions are accomplished and bigger targets are set, more leaders will be required. Some leaders will be promoted from within to higher spheres of influence. This will create space for others to join the leadership ranks.

RECRUITING

The Jethro Model will make recruiting easier because the mission will be clear and compelling and the roles will be personalized and contained. Additionally, team leaders can be more proactive in recruiting rather than simply being reactive. Reactive recruiters wait for volunteers to come along and express interest. This is often how it happens and there's nothing wrong with this. Proactive leaders, however, can take more initiative. Because they have a clear idea of exactly who they are looking for, they can constantly be on the 'look out' for the right leaders for the right roles. I would say, anecdotally, that most volunteers are recruited in response to someone identifying them as potential team members and drafting them onto their teams. This drafting process is greatly assisted by an established integration process. This provides opportunity for all parties involved to test whether the person suits the mission and will fit into the team.

RELATIONSHIPS

Everything in The Jethro Mandate is intended to encourage supportive, cohesive relationships. Loving people is the mission. The relevant chapter teaches the importance of this. Relationships matter within teams and throughout the whole structure. Senior leaders need to manage and model this relationship priority. Senior leaders need to set the tone. When you meet with a leader who reports to you, that person should know that you care for them and not only the success of the mission. Your mission is to care for people while fulfilling your mission.

Appendix 4 is a template intended to help guide a meeting between a senior leader and the person who reports to them. It is designed for meaningful reflection in a relational environment with reference to The Jethro Model. It begins with questions about the personal well-being of the reporting leader. Those sorts of questions are not incidental to the structure. They are at the heart of everything. Feel free to adapt the template to suit your context.

REWARDING

Participation in a mission ought to be a rewarding experience. While we accept that there will be times of struggle and even a little drudgery, the experience of serving will normally be fulfilling. People are much more likely to become actively involved in your church when they see that the prevailing culture is full of encouragement, celebration and opportunity. When this is evident to all involved, you will begin to defy the 80/20 rule. The majority of people in your church will join a team and participate in the mission.

Senior leaders are responsible for the morale of the church. Your positive energy and your inspirational lead, will permeate everything. It will definitely encourage volunteerism. You need to be the champion-leader for *other* leaders. They ought to receive your praises in public and in private. You need to lead the Cheering Squad!

RESOURCING

Moses had great faith. Every senior leader should believe God for great things. Your church should see you as a person of faith-filled prayer. The people who follow you should know that you have great, God-glorifying expectations. People will follow leaders who exhibit these things. Remember that when God does something significant through you, it will elevate you in the eyes of the people. This isn't for your glory but it will help establish your lead.

As senior leaders, you are also entrusted with the tasks of the acquisition and distribution of resources. Therefore, team leaders will sometimes look to you to supply resources that will help them accomplish their God-given mission. It falls to you to make sure the process of applying for funding is as clear and transparent as possible. To this end:

    a) create a generic Funding Application Process for team leaders;

    b) consider the resource-boosting challenge as set out at the end of Chapter 7.

When mission teams are properly resourced, the efforts of volunteers are maximized. This kind of support is highly energizing and encourages people on the mission. People are more inclined to join teams that enjoy the resource-support of their church.

REVIEWING

The Reviewing process can be intimidating for some people. The challenge for senior leaders is to demonstrate the benefits of conducting Reviews and make the experience a (normally) positive one.

Listed below are many of the positive aspects of a healthy Review process:

    a) It is genuine dialogue. It provides an opportunity to talk about how things are going. This includes, of course, how the person being reviewed is feeling about their role and the effectiveness of the mission.

    b) There will be no surprises. The Role Description is the point of reference.

    c) It's an opportunity to say 'thanks'. By far and away most of the Reviews I've been a part of (as a Reviewer and a 'Reviewee') have been very affirming. This will be normal.

    d) It will help improve things. Perhaps performance does need to be improved in some area. Challenges like that are good for us. We all want our church to get better, don't we? When we see ourselves as an essential part of the whole endeavor then it shouldn't surprise us that we will be encouraged to grow and develop.

    e) It will bring great reward. God will rate our work for him in the world. Those of us who want a 'gold-level' reward won't fear a healthy challenge to improve.

Senior leaders need to submit themselves to a rigorous Review process. You need to lead by example. This begins with a thorough 'self-review' and culminates in a robust Review of your performance by your peers.

You also need to establish a culture of reviewing. You need to review everything and everyone in order to affirm, enhance and advance. This will be a difficult challenge for two reasons: people are reluctant to address potentially difficult issues and it is time consuming. You will need to exercise a patient determination in order to establish *and maintain* a culture of reviewing in your church. The benefits, nevertheless, will outweigh the cost. You will create a culture of constant improvement and this kind of environment is especially conducive to higher rates of volunteer participation. Why? Because people want to be part of a church that desires to glorify God and strives to be spiritually successful.

Christian's Story

A few years ago, Warren phoned me to see if I was interested in a position as a Youth Pastor at his church. I was searching for that sort of role. I really wanted the opportunity to create a leadership program that would provide a definite direction for ministry, clear Role Descriptions for everyone involved and opportunities to mentor leaders. Around that time, Warren introduced me to The Jethro Mandate. These concepts fitted perfectly with where my heart was at in regards to raising emerging leaders. I got the job, relocated the family and started working on a plan on the first day. My initial observations were that there was no definite strategy or structure in the youth ministry, the existing leaders I inherited were few and directionless and the Youth Group itself comprised only a handful of people.

Towards the end of the first term, I met with the leaders and cast a five year Vision for the ministry. The mission entailed reaching 300 youth and training 100 young adult leaders. I spoke to the team about hierarchies of leaders, Role Descriptions, a recruiting plan and using our existing relationships to build momentum. We resolved to implement the plan. Soon, things began to change for the better. A year later we had thirty youth and seven leaders. To this day, those leaders remain part of our core leadership team.

There are three things that we practice as leaders. Good communication, training and care. These are part of our culture. So each year, we start with 'boot camp' a week before Youth Group commences. This camp is tailored for leaders at different levels. In March, we run a full day training seminar with workshops. At the end of the year, I take the leaders on a team-building retreat to an island where we dream and work on our Mission Resolution for the next couple of years.

During a recent review of the mission, I noticed that we had a lot of tired leaders. I recognized that we needed to reinvigorate the leaders and make sure they felt appreciated. We decided that the best way to reward the team and to build relationships was to provide a free dinner before we started Youth Group on Friday nights. This is a full meal where the senior leaders host a table. The result is that we have achieved stronger community and deeper conversations about life and not just the mission. We have taken our meal to the next level and we have coffee and cake after Youth Group to help the leaders wind down and to thank them for their work. The feedback is that the whole experience is now much more rewarding for all involved.

In regards to recruitment, this is a yearly problem. We live in a city that is very transient and our young adults arrive to do a two to three year course then move back to larger cities. Every year we have to recruit around twenty new leaders. As we continue to grow, those numbers will escalate. Recruiting is, therefore, prioritized in the Role Description of every senior leader. It is also a major part of my role as Team Leader. Recruiting is my strength so I was happy to take on the larger load. At the end-of-year retreat on the island, we work out how many leaders we have lost and then we set a target quota. We encourage our leaders to recruit their friends so they may share in the journey.

We believe that we will soon have 200 youth attending Youth Group and between 50 and 60 leaders. We have therefore seen, at first hand, the success of The Jethro Model. Presently, on any given Friday night, there are over 150 people on the church property, mostly youth. On these nights I only have to interact directly with seven senior leaders. They, in turn, relate to the leaders who report to them. Following the Jethro structure through, each teenager is also cared for by their assigned leader. This frees me to be ready to handle any serious matters that might come up. As you can see, the principles taught in The Resolute Leader really work!

Postscript

At some point not long after the Exodus, Jethro resolved to reunite his daughter and grandchildren with Moses. What made him so firmly determined to do this? Perhaps his house was too small or the grandkids too noisy! We can't be sure. What we *do* know is that they travelled from Midian and met Moses in the desert near the mountain of God (Ex. 18:5). This family reunion afforded Jethro the opportunity to observe Moses' leadership first-hand. What he saw was not good. He knew that Moses needed a leadership overhaul. And so Jethro, the experienced leader, gave Moses, the emerging leader, some expert leadership advice. This book incorporates the content of Jethro's leadership master class. I've called it The Jethro Mandate.

My early leadership experience was not good. The murder on the steps of our church heightened my feelings of impotence and incompetence. God knew I needed a leadership overhaul and he sent Jethro to my rescue. Jethro's time-tested leadership advice helped to save my ministry. I not only survived but I've thrived under Jethro's tutelage and I'm so grateful to God for that. I believe implementing the principles taught in *The Resolute Leader* will help you thrive as well.

After Jethro had advised Moses, the Bible simply states that he returned to his home country (Ex. 18:27). The brevity of the report belies the pain of that parting. As far as we know they never saw each other again. Perhaps, back home in Midian, Jethro heard reports of progress from time to time. Rumors that filtered back to him from distant, desert places. There were amazing accounts of streams in the wilderness, victories over superior armies, of a mighty people on the move, and news of a man of faith called Moses. Moses, they said, who was leader of thousands of leaders. Moses, the rumor went, who had organized an entire nation such that it marched *as one* toward a Promised Land. Moses, they whispered, who talked with God and taught the people the way they should live.

I like to imagine old-man-Jethro sitting on his porch in Midian thinking about all those rumors and smiling at the way things turned out. In my mind he rocks on his chair as he remembers his son-in-law trying to do everything and failing. The situation was not good at all. But things were so much better now. Perhaps his thoughts ran something like this:

> *Leader of thousands of leaders, I hear them say. Well isn't that something! Last I saw that boy he was starting a massive recruitment drive. Yep, he had a lot to learn about connecting leaders back then. Now he has thousands of them! That's got to be good for everybody. And rumor has it, he's hearing from God all the time these days. Heard he spends hours in that Tent of Meeting. Don't remember him having much time for praying last I saw him. He was much too preoccupied for that. That boy couldn't see how important it was for him to be listening to God and teaching the people what he'd heard. He had no idea what his true role was then. Well,*

seems he's worked it out. I sure am grateful that God gave me those insights. And I'm glad to hear that son-in-law of mine was willing to act on my advice and see the whole thing through. [That's how I imagine it anyway.]

My invention notwithstanding, I wonder if Jethro ever realized just how crucial a role he played in the story of Moses' leadership success. I wonder if he could ever have dreamed that his inspired advice would be set out in the Bible and leave an indelible mark on the leadership consciousness of Israel. And could he possibly have imagined that 3500 years later, leaders would borrow from his leadership playbook – Christians who are called by God to create and develop teams that would accomplish *new*, God-glorifying missions. *The Resolute Leader* pays tribute to Jethro and his leadership legacy.

IMAGINE…

Now imagine your own leadership challenge. Think about how much better it will be when you resolutely know where God wants you to go. Imagine gaining kingdom-ground with a great team in which each leader knows exactly what to do. Your team is meeting a great need. Imagine working with and for each other so that everyone is standing the strain. Wouldn't that be a rewarding experience? And as God supplies what you need, you're reviewing everything as you go in order to be as effective as possible. In *The Resolute Leader* you have all the basic tools you need to stop imagining and start implementing. God bless you as you resolve to enact The Jethro Mandate.

APPENDIX 1

EXAMPLE OF A DIFFICULT LEADERSHIP ISSUE GOING TO MOSES

An example of an extremely difficult case 'going up' to Moses, is found in Numbers 27. The context is the people of Israel were preparing to enter the Promised Land in order to take possession of it, settle there, and farm the land for food. The Book of Numbers records the process by which Moses divides up the land according to God's protocols and directives. This leadership task involved the allocation of specific tracts of land to tribal groups and families. There was a lot at stake here! The survival of families, and even family names, depended on this. Understandably then, this distribution of land raised some seriously contentious issues. Numbers 27 records that the daughters of Zelophehad, approached Moses with a problem that needed his special attention.

> "The daughters of Zelophehad... approached the entrance to the Tent of Meeting and stood before Moses, Eleazar the priest, the leaders and the whole assembly, and said, "Our father died in the desert.... and left no sons. Why should our father's name disappear from his clan because he had no son? Give us property among our father's relatives"'" (Num. 27:1-4).

Under normal circumstances in ancient times, land ownership was associated with a patriarch, and possession was passed down to men along the family line. In this unusual instance, however, there was no male to inherit the land. This was a complex legal issue. There was no precedent. What was to be done? We might assume that other leaders had been consulted along the lines of the Jethro Structure but that this case proved too difficult for them, and so it went up to Moses.[19] The Bible says:

> "So Moses brought their case before the LORD and the LORD said to him, "What the daughters are saying is right. You must certainly give them property as an inheritance among their father's relatives and turn their father's inheritance over to them.
>
> "Say to the Israelites, 'If a man dies and leaves no son, turn his inheritance over to his daughter... This is to be a legal requirement for the Israelites as the LORD commanded Moses'" (Num. 27:5-11).

Working backwards through the above passage, we receive some significant insights with regard to why this problem went to Moses and the way he addressed it. The passage ends with a recognition that this directive was for the whole nation. That's senior leadership territory. This wasn't just a problem affecting one family or a one-off situation. Others would inevitably find themselves in the same situation. This decision would set a precedent, so it had to be right! Jethro had already recognized that part of Moses' leadership role was to represent the *whole* nation before God (Ex. 18:19). Moses needed to be involved in making the big decisions that had the most wide-ranging implications. He was to bring these difficult disputes and quandaries before God (Ex. 18:19, 22). This is just what he did. As to exactly *how* he received the answer to this problem we can't be certain. Yet we are assured that he *did* hear from God and that the gracious decision in favor of the daughters came with divine authority and enduring ramifications.

APPENDIX 2

THE CONTEMPORARY RELEVANCE OF THE JETHRO MODEL

You may be thinking to yourself, "OK, this was all good back then, but how useful will Jethro's structure really be for my team and in my church today?" There are four probing questions that test the contemporary relevance of The Jethro Mandate. They are:

1) Wasn't it just a provisional arrangement for forty or so years of the wilderness wanderings?

2) Wasn't it only a logistical tool designed to get God's people from A to B?

3) Wasn't Jethro's structure just an elaborate judicial system?

4) What about New Testament leadership 'models'?

Let's consider each question along with some relevant implications.

 # 1 Provisional arrangement or enduring template?

Was Jethro's leadership model only a temporary arrangement for the duration of the Exodus journey? In one sense, the answer is 'yes'; Jethro's structure was devised to meet an immediate need and it served God's people well through those wilderness years. Yet, in another sense, the answer is 'no'; it is apparent that its influence was enduring. It is believed that the structure was utilized beyond the events recorded in the Book of Exodus and "had important consequences for the future government of Israel".[20] That the structure was to have enduring implications makes sense when we remind ourselves that the trip from Egypt to Canaan wasn't supposed to last very long. [The forty year wandering was a consequence of a later disobedience.] It's hard to imagine that all the organizing required to set up the structure was just to cover a short trans-wilderness journey. No. While it's true that circumstances changed, the structure adapted accordingly to suit the situation. The important basic tenets remained.

> **The Jethro Model was designed to reach people and meet needs while the overall mission was being accomplished. These concurrent challenges confront the contemporary church.**

Jethro's mandate became a kind of leadership template for Israel long after they had entered the Promised Land. By template I mean that the basic principles and structure remained while accommodating new leadership scenarios. For example, in Joshua's day there were officers who led the people directly as Jethro advised (Josh. 1:10). Whether these same leaders judged disputes is uncertain.[21] Further, Glen S. Martin commented,

> **Jethro's model left an indelible mark on the leadership consciousness of Israel.**

"The wise counsel of Jethro gave impetus to Israel's budding governing structure that culminated in a triumvirate, of sorts, consisting of priesthood, monarchy and prophets. Alongside these would be elders... Such structure gave way to an even more elaborate organization under King David...".[22] So, the basic organizational principles continued to find application in changing circumstances. Undoubtedly, Jethro's model left an indelible mark on the leadership consciousness of Israel. Every time the Books of Exodus and Deuteronomy were read, the hearers were reminded of the qualifications and responsibilities of leaders to direct and care for the people entrusted to them.

The Jethro Model, as presented in this book, builds on the ancient and enduring principles established by Jethro and develops further ideas consistent with the original advice along with other leadership ideas found in the Bible. Just as the structure had important consequences for the future government of Israel, so it can find expression and application in the contemporary church today.

2 One trip logistics or are there ongoing implications

Was Jethro's structure primarily an aid for the administrative and logistical moving of Israel from Mt Sinai to the Promised Land? Or are there implications that find application today? Well, again, the answer is 'yes' and 'no'. Yes, the arrangement aided greatly in the practicalities of the journey. Their mission was to reach the Promised Land and the tiers of leaders no doubt dealt with many of the logistical challenges. But 'no', that wasn't the primary motivation behind Jethro's leadership formation. The 'end' outcome was described as satisfying the needs of the people (Ex. 18:23) and dealing with pastoral problems, burdens and disputes (Deut. 1:12-13). These problems were essentially spiritual in nature and they didn't end at Canaan's border. These are perpetual needs. The Jethro Model was designed to reach people and meet needs while the overall mission was being accomplished.

I believe that the church is always on mission. We are always on the move. We are heading toward what God has next. Your team and your church need to discover what the big mission is and, metaphorically, move from where you are now toward that Promised Land. There will be logistical implications. There will be administrative challenges. You will need some leaders who can handle those and more besides. Nevertheless, you will also need to reach out to people and care for their needs *as* you move forward on the overall mission. These concurrent challenges confront the contemporary church. Great leaders realize that both require energy and attention. Jethro organized the people so that *both* could be done *simultaneously*. That is the genius of The Jethro Mandate.

3 Just judges or did they have more general leadership roles?

Was Jethro's structure just an elaborate judicial system? Did the leaders that Moses appointed function exclusively as judges? Certainly, dispute resolution was an important part of their role. Nevertheless, the word 'judge' isn't used in a strictly legal sense. Rather, it has more of a *champion-leader* connotation as it does in the book of Judges.[23] Further, a diversity of leadership responsibilities is suggested in Deuteronomy 1:9-17. There, the leaders are reported to have exercised authority "of various kinds, military, judicial, *etc*".[24] Philip Johnston wrote, "Three different terms are used here (unlike Exodus 18): commanders, officials and judges. We don't know whether the terms were used interchangeably or whether the roles had become more distinct".[25] Johnston noted, nonetheless, that in Joshua's day there were officers who led the people directly (Josh. 1:10). His commentary suggests that the appointed leaders had a broad range of responsibilities. It is therefore probable that Jethro's structure was populated by leaders with a variety of leadership and people-helping roles, including judging disputes.

4 Superseded model or leadership classic?

Did the Jethro structure suit a particular point of history past and has it now been superseded by New Testament models of leadership organization? To answer this question we need to establish the nature of other New Testament leadership models. This quest proves difficult because there is no precise leadership structure elucidated there. Consequently, denominations have found Biblical validation for governance models ranging from rule by the bishop of Rome to congregationalism. We are sometimes provided with titles and roles but never with a clear enunciation of how roles related or leaders connected. It may well be that structures varied across the congregations and regions of the early church. It could even be that congregations turned to Exodus 18 for structural guidance. What we do know is that the original apostles and prophets set down what was to be believed and advanced the Gospel into new places. They led with apostolic authority. Itinerant evangelists spread the Word as well. Pastors and teachers were assigned to lead local congregations or perhaps clusters of churches. We also know that a plurality of leaders was to be appointed in each church (Tit. 1:5). These people were to 'shepherd the flock' (1 Pet. 5:2). Some congregations had tiers of leaders, some called 'elders' and others 'deacons' (1 Tim. 3). We can't be sure *how* all these leaders were organized. Nevertheless, there *must* have been leadership structures. This is a vital part of the church's life. Every group must determine how it will be led and who on earth has the God-given responsibility to set direction and settle controversies.[26] Otherwise leaders get hurt and people don't get helped.

So if we can't establish a clear New Testament leadership structure then it seems imprudent to carelessly discard The Jethro Model. The Jethro Model is in fact an enduring classic! I've sometimes heard it said that the Bible doesn't elucidate a particular leadership structure. I believe it does and that we have it here! As Philip Graham Ryken wrote, "Why is this passage included in the Bible if not partly to teach basic principles of spiritual leadership and authority?"[27] These time-honored principles are still applicable. The Jethro Mandate provides us with a Biblical, versatile leadership framework that connected a network of leaders who each know and fulfil their role in providing care and leadership to those entrusted to them. Jethro's structure is versatile enough to accommodate the leadership roles and responsibilities in your church. My hope is that *The Resolute Leader* will demonstrate that this structure and the associated leadership principles, far from being superseded, remain extremely helpful for the organization of your team and church.

APPENDIX 3

MOCK UP ROLE DESCRIPTION FOR A SMALL-GROUP TEACHER IN CHILDREN'S CHURCH

By way of example, here's a mock Role Description for a small-group teacher on a Children's Church team.

NAME OF THE MISSION TEAM – Children's Church

THE MISSION RESOLUTION – to support families in reaching their children and helping children to become fully devoted followers of Christ through Children's Church on Sunday mornings.

NAME OF TEAM MEMBER – Ellen Lovely

LEADERSHIP STRUCTURE – Senior Pastor < Children's Pastor < Unit Leader < Small Group Teacher

ROLE TITLE – Small Group Teacher

ROLE DESCRIPTION

a) to prepare weekly lessons using teaching materials provided

b) to build Christian love and trust with children in the small group

c) arrive early on Sunday, set up and pray with the whole team

d) assist in tidying up after Children's Church

e) attend team training meetings

f) phone follow-up with one child each week

GOALS

1) to create a data base to aid in the follow-up of Children in my Small Group

2) to pray for each child, each week

3) to streamline the set-up and pack-up process so that each takes 15 minutes

CULTURE – We want to ensure that children are safe at all times. We value each individual child as a person that God created and Jesus died for. We believe that Christian children have received the Holy Spirit and should be allowed to explore and use their gifts. We see our mission as supporting Christian parents in raising and discipling their children. Many children come from non-Christian homes. We want to share the Gospel with them and help them love their parents and influence their homes.

TIME COMMITMENT

2 hours to prepare lesson at home
½ hour to set up and pray prior to Children's Church
¾ hour actual lesson time
½ hour tidy up and debrief
? training from time to time

= around 4 hours/week during school terms.

DURATION OF COMMITMENT – one school year

REVIEW OF THE ROLE – every 12 months towards the end of the year with an informal 'catch-up' sometime over the mid-year break.

SUPPORT PROVIDED

a) the Unit Leader will be available to provide direct support

b) there will be training from time to time to help equip you

c) you will have all the teaching resources well in advance of the lessons

d) there will be substitute teachers available if you are unable to teach one Sunday every now and again

APPENDIX 4

SUGGESTED TEMPLATE FOR A MEETING BETWEEN THE SENIOR LEADER AND TEAM LEADER

The success of The Jethro Model largely depends on the quality of the connections between the leadership 'levels'. As a senior leader, your immediate responsibility is to care for those leaders who are assigned to you. You will need to be attentive to their personal needs, as well as help ensure that *their team* is functioning cohesively and fulfilling its mission effectively.

You will need to meet with the leader on at least a monthly basis and, perhaps, with the team from time to time. The meeting length would normally be for around one hour.

Prioritize time according to items of importance, leaving ample time for prayer with the Team Leader, i.e. allow 10-15 minutes each for points C, D and E (below), leaving 10 minutes for prayer at the end.

Take relevant notes that will help you reflect and respond, as well as prompt your prayers. Review the notes from the last meeting as a part of preparing for the next one.

Ensure that you have actioned any commitments made from the last meeting.

The following outline and questions can form a basis for discussion and provide opportunity for leadership mentoring.

A. **Senior Leader: Report back on any 'action' items from last meeting.**

B. **Team Leader: Report back on any 'action' items from last meeting.**

C. **Personal Questions asked of the Team Leader**

   1) How are you going generally? Encourage honest answers by using sensitive questions.

   2) How are you going with reference to your Role Description?

   3) Right now, would you describe leading your team on the mission as 'rewarding'?

   4) Do you feel like you're coping? Are you handling the strain of your role?

   5) Are there any problems or issues that are proving to be too difficult to handle? *If this is the case, it's the responsibility of the Senior Leader to help find a solution.*

   6) Are there any ways that I can help you personally?

D. **Questions regarding the Team and Mission**

   1) Does your Mission Resolution capture precisely what God is calling you to do?

2) Are you sensing that God wants to expand or adjust the mission?

3) What achievable goals have you set?

4) How are you progressing towards fulfilling each of those goals and, ultimately, the mission?

5) Does each team member have a clear Role Description?

6) What recruiting challenges and opportunities are you facing?

7) Is the team relating well? What would help improve these relationships?

8) How are you rewarding the people that you are serving with?

9) What are your resource challenges?

10) Are you reviewing your team members according to their Role Descriptions?

11) As you reflect on the dynamics of your mission, what are the accelerating and inhibiting factors at the moment (use tool below)?

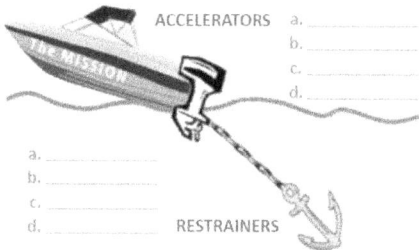

12) Are the people that your mission is intended to reach and serve generally feeling satisfied?

13) Are there any other things to talk about?

E. Actions

As a result of this meeting are there any actions that need to be performed before the next meeting on the part of:

a) the Senior Leader?

1)

2)

b) the Team Leader?

1)

2)

F. Pray together

END NOTES

1. "Calvin thought Moses acted by the Spirit of God, but Augustine was surely correct when he stressed that Moses had no legal right to do what he did. His own conscience likewise agreed, for he first "looked this way and that" (v. 12) and then buried the corpse in the sand."
Walter C. Kaiser Jr, (*Exodus, The Expositors Bible Commentary*, 1990) p. 311.

2. Alan Cole (*Exodus, Tyndale Old Testament Commentaries*, 1973) p. 61.
He had excellent spiritual credentials. 'Jethro' meant 'excellence', which may have been used more as an official and honorary title of respect. Jethro was also called Reuel. 'Reuel' meant 'friend of God'. Reuel was apparently his personal name and indicates a genuine friendship with God.

3. "Jethro completes his counsel to Moses not only with an assurance that the procedure he advises will bring much-needed relief to both Moses and the people, but also with the remarkable assertion that God charges (or "commands, orders"...) Moses to follow it."
J.I. Durham (*Exodus, Word Biblical Commentary*, 1987) p. 252.

4. Commenting on the parallel passage in Deuteronomy 1:9-18, Philip Johnston wrote, "Three different terms are used here (unlike Exodus 18): commanders, officials and judges. We don't know whether the terms were used interchangeably, or whether the roles had become more distinct."
Philip Johnston, (*Deuteronomy, The People's Bible Commentary*, The Bible Reading Fellowship, 2005) p. 24.

5. William Safire, ed. (*Lend Me Your Ears, Great Speeches in History*, W.W. Norton & Company, Inc., United States, 2004) p. 60–61.

6. *Lincoln's Gettysburg Address, 1863*, EyeWitness to History, www.eyewitnesstohistory.com (2005)

7. Keith Abraham (*Living Your Passion*, Passion Press, Australia, 2004) p. 32-33.

8. William Safire, ed. (*Lend Me Your Ears, Great Speeches in History*, W.W. Norton & Company, Inc., United States, 2004) p. 59.

9. *The American Heritage® Dictionary of the English Language*, Fourth Edition copyright ©2000 by Houghton Mifflin Company.

10. William Safire, ed. (*Lend Me Your Ears, Great Speeches in History*, W.W. Norton & Company, Inc., United States, 2004) p. 60.

11. "Jethro's solution... was to give Moses a portion of the work..."
Walter C. Kaiser Jr, (*Exodus, The Expositors Bible Commentary*, 1990) p. 311.

12. Alan Cole (*Exodus, Tyndale Old Testament Commentaries*, 1973) p. 141.

13. Philip Johnston (*Deuteronomy, The People's Bible Commentary*, The Bible Reading Fellowship, 2005) p. 24.

14. Quoted in *Celtic Daily Prayer* (HarperCollins, Great Britain, 2000) p. 73.

15. "God used the experiences Moses had along his spiritual journey to prepare him in a special way for a special work. By being faithful in small things, he was prepared for something big."
Philip Graham Ryken (*Exodus, Preaching the Word*, 2005) p. 72.

16. F. W. Grosheide (*The First Letter to the Corinthians, The New International Commentary on the New Testament*, Eerdmans, 1980) p. 85.

17. "Perhaps it was the family connection (Mark is called the cousin of Barnabas in Col. 4:10) but more likely it was the character of Barnabas to give those who failed a second chance."
    David G. Peterson (*The Acts of the Apostles, The Pillar New Testament Commentary*, William B. Eerdmans, Grand Rapids, Michigan, 2009) p. 447.

18. Marshall describes it as "a classic example of the perpetual problem of whether to place the interests of the individual or of the work as a whole first, and there is no rule of thumb for dealing with it".
    I. Howard Marshall (*Acts, Tyndale New Testament Commentaries*, Eerdmans, Grand Rapids, Michigan, 1980) p. 258.

19. J. I. Durham (*Exodus, Word Biblical Commentary*, 1987) p. 251.

20. J. Crichton (*Jethro, International Standard Bible Encyclopaedia*) p. 1055.

21. Philip Johnston (*Deuteronomy, The People's Bible Commentary*, The Bible Reading Fellowship, 2005) p. 24.

22. Glen S. Martin (*Exodus, Leviticus, Numbers, Holman Old Testament Commentary*, 2002) p. 79.

23. Alan Cole (*Exodus, Tyndale Old Testament Commentaries*, Inter-Varsity Press, 1973) p. 140.

24. J. A. Thompson (*Deuteronomy, Tyndale Old Testament Series*, Inter-Varsity Press, England, 1974) p. 86.

25. Philip Johnston (*Deuteronomy, The People's Bible Commentary*, The Bible Reading Fellowship, 2005) p. 24.

26. Mark Dever (*The Church*, B&H Academic, Nashville, Tennessee, 2012) p. 116.

27. Philip Graham Ryken (*Exodus, Preaching the Word*, 2005) p. 488.

About the Author

Warren Crank
B. Min. (ACT); Grad. Dip. Min. (QBCM); Dip. Theol. (QBCM)

Warren is a Queensland Baptist minister with around twenty years ministry experience. He has been the Lead Pastor of two churches: the Ipswich Baptist Church and Northreach Baptist Church in Townsville. When he began leading the Ipswich Baptist Church it was a small traditional church of 120 people, meeting in a small building. When he finished his call as Lead Pastor, the church had grown to a vibrant church of around 400 people and relocated to a renovated sports centre. Northreach church has grown to more than 1,000 people and has recently started two new churches. Warren is passionate about identifying, training and releasing leaders into their God-given mission. He is married to Ellen and has three sons.

CHI-Books proudly recommends …

The Point Brisbane … It's where people like you stay!

The Point offers a range of accommodation styles from studio rooms to junior suites, with state-of-the-art meeting facilities that feature spectacular panoramic views towards the CBD, Brisbane River and Story Bridge. It has all the features and services, including complimentary Wi-Fi internet access available throughout, everything you would expect from a 5-star hotel. The Point Brisbane also offers a range of state-of-the-art meeting facilities that feature spectacular panoramic views towards the Brisbane CBD, River and Story Bridge.

Relax and unwind in the Lambert Restaurant and Lounge. It offers a menu of modern Australian cuisine that incorporates high quality, locally sourced produce and only the freshest ingredients. Enjoy a full buffet breakfast, a la carte lunch and/or dinner while taking in the lovely pool views. Recreational facilities include a 19m outdoor heated lap pool and gymnasium.

Situated in picturesque Kangaroo Point close to the Brisbane River within easy access of the CBD, Fortitude Valley and South Bank.

A courtesy shuttle service operates weekday mornings and the hotel now offers a turn down service and valet parking.

Enjoy the comfort and convenience of Brisbane's leading independent hotel.

www.thepointbrisbane.com.au
Reservations: 1800 088 388
Reservations@thepointbrisbane.com.au
21 Lambert Street, Kangaroo Point, Brisbane, Queensland

www.ingramcontent.com/pod-product-compliance
Lightning Source LLC
Chambersburg PA
CBHW080503110426
42742CB00017B/2983